Facsimile from a manuscript letter by Thomas Wolfe

[Continued on back cover lining]

Lot 15ᵗ

BOOKS BY THOMAS WOLFE

Look Homeward, Angel
Of Time and the River
From Death to Morning
The Story of a Novel
The Face of a Nation
The Web and the Rock
You Can't Go Home Again
The Hills Beyond

THOMAS WOLFE'S
LETTERS TO HIS MOTHER

THOMAS WOLFE'S MOTHER

Julia Elizabeth Wolfe

From a painting by Constant van de Wall

Thomas Wolfe's
LETTERS TO HIS MOTHER
Julia Elizabeth Wolfe

———

EDITED WITH AN INTRODUCTION

BY

JOHN SKALLY TERRY

Department of English
Washington Square College
New York University

NEW YORK

CHARLES SCRIBNER'S SONS

1943

Introduction.

BY JOHN SKALLY TERRY

The first time I ever saw Thomas Wolfe and his mother together was early in January, 1934. Tom had for some time secluded himself in Brooklyn and spent his days and nights writing and rewriting OF TIME AND THE RIVER. When he invited me by phone, he was quite excited and enthusiastic. As always, if he was under the influence of his feelings, he stuttered and stammered.

His mother was here, he told me, and they wanted me to come to the dinner which she was preparing in his apartment. His voice expressed much pleasure over the promised feast and the presence of his mother. To this situation as to all others, he responded simply and fully, like a child.

When I arrived at 5 Montague Terrace, I rang Tom's bell, the door-latch clicked, and Tom yelled down for me to take my time climbing the stairs. His apartment was high up on the fourth floor of an old brownstone building. It was the one which he occupied until it was described and its address given in an interview published in the *Herald Tribune;* as a result Tom had to move to a hotel to escape a line of his readers which formed at his door the day the interview was published.

I entered the big living room and was introduced by Tom to his mother. The introduction was interesting in its revelation of Mrs. Wolfe's attitude toward those whom she was just meeting, for she has developed a method. She was standing in the center of the room, with her great hands calmly clasped in front of her, waiting. Tom gave me a Southern handshake, put his arm around my shoulders and led me to Mrs. Wolfe. Warmth and cordiality to his friends was as natural to him as breathing. He was always concerned about the comfort and well-being of those with him, and would sometimes embarrass friends by his solicitude.

"John," he said, "this is Mama!" and then, "Mama, this is my old friend, John Terry!"

Mrs. Wolfe took my hand into both of hers, and smiling slowly and cordially, welcomed me. I have noticed since that in all her meetings with people, she speaks slowly, easily, while getting the new person into her consciousness. Even at crowded receptions, she always takes time to get to know each individual she meets. One might as well try to hasten the Rock of Gibraltar.

Immediately after greeting me, she proceeded, in thoroughly Southern fashion, to tell me what she knew of my home town, and that one of her favorite boarders for years had come from there. She then began to tie me into her knowledge by asking numerous questions about me and my family. There followed on her part a brief flood of personal reminiscence which Tom finally stemmed by asking, "When do we eat?"

The main dish which Tom had bought for our dinner was an eight-pound, very thick porterhouse steak, one of Tom's favorite foods. He liked rare steak, hot, juicy, and red—none of your thin-sliced anemic steaks for him! This magnificent item must be eaten immediately after cooking and is never put on the fire until the guest has arrived. As a result of this custom, I was privileged to hear a short debate which revealed a fact which I would remember about the mother and son,—that Mrs. Wolfe carried her saving habits to the n-th degree, while Tom was lavish in everything he did.

Mrs. Wolfe wanted to cook only about two pounds of the steak—the whole thing was enough for a week, she said.

"No, Mama," argued Tom, "let's cook it all and enjoy it right now." Quite a little banter and persuasion was necessary to get Mrs. Wolfe to cook the whole great hunk of beef.

The apartment in which we were undergoing these experiences consisted of a large living room, poorly furnished, and a fair-sized bedroom, equally devoid of care. The chief piece of furniture was an old table, work-worn and ancient, but still sturdy. It was marked by many cigarette burns, and its surface was dented like a shield after a hard battle. There were three severe straight chairs; a worn-out couch which had one arm off and resembled the Alps in its hills and valleys; one good arm chair and another with a broken arm. Along the wall which one faced as one entered the room, at the sides of a great black marble fireplace, were full bookcases built of plain box lumber, unstained and not very steady. At the right, as one entered, and opposite the windows, was one alcove containing a gas range and another with an electric refrigerator which bumped and hummed as refrigerators did then. Tom claimed that this sound stimulated him by its rhythm. On the old table and on this refrigerator he did most of his writing. The three front windows were large, but revealed nothing except a great apartment house which stood between Tom's home and the New York Harbor. He bragged, however, that he had a view of the East River, and to prove his contention he demonstrated how, by leaning out, one could get a glimpse of it, and hints of the Brooklyn and Manhattan Bridges. The adjoining bedroom contained a cot, an old battered bureau, and a straight chair. The cot looked uncomfortable, but was long. For the latter quality Tom was grateful, since it was difficult for him to find a sleeping place long enough to accommodate his great six feet, seven inches.

All over the place were scattered books, papers, and other debris of a reader's pursuits. The mantelpiece bore the telephone and piles of old letters. The most important thing in the room was a great drygoods box on the bare floor. It held large bundles of pencilled and typed manuscripts, ledgers, and other accretions of the years of Tom's writing. No one except Tom ever touched this material. It sounds unbelievable, but he could reach his hands down into this great mass and after a while, in an uncanny way, find the desired bundle.

Tom was not one of your carefree, sophisticated bachelors who surround themselves with fine *objets d'art*, expensive dishes, and silver, and paintings and prints. His walls were bare except for a Corn Exchange Bank calendar. His pots and pans were heterogeneous in every way, but they served. Many of his equally varied dishes were nicked or cracked. They also served.

All that Tom Wolfe was really interested in, as far as his living quarters were concerned, was pencil and paper—these were the only essentials to.him.

Mrs. Wolfe busied herself completing the supper, and finally laid the table; then she urged Tom to get himself some dishes and knives and forks, but he lightly shooed away any such suggestions.

The meal proved delicious. Mrs. Wolfe is a skillful cook who knows how to make food taste good. But no time was spent in merely eating, though that was taken care of with gusto. Talk flowed, and Mrs. Wolfe proved that she could talk more volubly than could her son. We were all gay and hungry. We ate with relish the steak, big red sliced tomatoes, green beans, cabbage, potatoes, and hot biscuits, and drank steaming cups of coffee. The floodgates of Mrs. Wolfe's memories were opened. She told us story after story of Asheville and herself. Already I knew about many of the matters she related, as Tom had made use of them in his writing.

As I observed these two who so thoroughly enjoyed each other, but who were equally egocentric and self-assured, many of their individual traits came out in sharp perspective.

I had noticed, for example, as Mrs. Wolfe had moved calmly around the room while preparing the meal, how self-reliant she was. She absolutely refused any help; no one could really help a woman who had so much self-reliance. Her shrewd, falcon eyes, bright and piercing behind her spectacles, took in absolutely everything. Tom's eyes were lively, dark, and piercing, but they were very large. Both gave in their eyes a sense of judging and weighing external evidence; they did not just look at things; they observed them. Mrs. Wolfe was more objective in her glances; Tom's eyes revealed a highly introspective mind, sensitive, absorbing, putting all he saw into his vivid consciousness. Mrs. Wolfe often smiled or pursed her lips in a knowing manner; her mouth was small and always tight, full of will power, self-control, determination. In fact, her mouth revealed more of her feelings than did her eyes.

As Tom talked, his small but full-lipped mouth was very mobile, and sometimes the upper lip was lost as he extruded his prominent lower lip. He talked and ate with amazing gusto. His laughter was robust and loud, as he emitted great *wha, wha's,* and finally when he could no longer express his vast amusement thus, he would round his lips and emit great squeals and screeching *whee's,* blotting out all other sounds. He would slap his thighs and actually howl with merriment. Mrs. Wolfe was equally as merry; she laughed often too, but her laughter was quieter, made up mostly of long-continued *heh, heh's.* Both, after laughing heartily, nearly always found it necessary to wipe the tears from their eyes.

The energy of each was so abounding that an explosive climax from either seemed imminent any moment. They were both earthy, fun-loving people who valued themselves supremely and viewed life as a thing to be savored to the full. Theirs was a grand egotism.

The heads of mother and son showed little physical resemblance. Mrs. Wolfe had a delicate-boned face, and fair, thin skin which was as delicate as ivory. Her nose was small with a strong, but not prominent bridge, and was rounded at the end. Her small cheekbones just broke the flatness of her wide, round face. Tom's olive-complexioned face was large and unusually pale; his brow was massive, his nose long and not well formed, for it too had a smaller bridge than one would have expected. His black hair was always unruly, and since he seldom took time to get it cut, his great head often resembled, in its titanic nobility and volume, the Bourdelle bust of Beethoven. His large brown eyes dominated all his other features, and often in moments of deep thought he would close them, almost as if to cut off the outside world, and to hide what he was undergoing.

Mrs. Wolfe revealed in her conversation that she thought of time in terms of the seasons. She thought of time as might a person of primitive Colonial America—in terms of the birds and flowers of the field, of the moon and the sun and the stars.

Tom knew already that he was the butt of time's great joke; he had none of his mother's power of waiting. His plans and dreams were actually those of a superman. As he said over and over again, he always felt that time slipped away under him like a great river. For his mother, time flowed gently on; she used it for her purposes, and she resigned herself to it. Time was hers.

During years of association with Tom I found that there was hardly a moment when he was not fearful that time was escaping him. He could not keep pace with it; for nearly every appointment, business or personal, he was late. He worked against time, never with it.

That tremendous coffee pot on his alcove stove was filled and drained to the grounds, night after night, to stimulate him to more gigantic endeavor.

But then, again, mother and son were much alike. They were both ready to leap into action at once. They were absolutely convinced that they could accomplish whatever they attempted. Mrs. Wolfe knew her superiority; there was simply no question about that; no one took precedence over her or her people. She would have sat down to chat as comfortably with Queen Victoria or the Pope as she would with a mountaineer. She often reminded Tom, her eyes twinkling, that three great Americans were born in February: Abraham Lincoln on the 12th, Julia E. Wolfe on the 16th, and George Washington on the 22nd. She judged great or small with equal conviction.

But mother and son differed in their sense of values. Mrs. Wolfe was deeply impressed by wealth and social power. Tom evaluated people more for their intrinsic spiritual value. He always satirized great fortunes and magnates. Mrs. Wolfe made no bones about her respect for power and money. She was extremely opportunistic in her outlook. She planned to get rich herself, and she positively threw nothing away; she was of the string-saving type.

Tom did not care for money at all. He spent it lavishly as long as any remained in his pocketbook, and then would look blank as he gazed into his empty purse.

The powerful natures of these two were expressed in their hands. Mrs. Wolfe's hands were very masculine, in gesture and in size; but they have remained supple and pliant, strong in sinew, with visible tendons and big veins. In conversation she often made large, sweeping, oratorical gestures; however, her hands could be very gentle in nursing the sick, or in performing other delicate feminine tasks.

The son's hands were enormous, with long graceful, tapering

fingers. They were seldom in repose, and were as expressive as his words; strong, artistic, powerful. To control them he often rested them, when he was standing, on the small of his back, or he kept them in his pockets. One favorite repose for his right hand was around a great stein of beer.

Many have wondered that a physically delicate, middle-sized woman could be the mother of such a giant. He towered six feet, seven inches, but his whole physique was well-proportioned except for the fact that he had rather long arms, even for his height.

There was not a lazy bone in either mother or son. Mrs. Wolfe has continued into her eighties to run a tourist home (the O.K.H.—or Old Kentucky Home, so often mentioned in Tom's letters to her). Tom, when busy at his studies or writing, became so active that he actually forgot to eat, to bathe, to sleep regularly. He would continue to work until absolute physical exhaustion stopped him.

Both mother and son worked hard and persevered greatly, but the mother still carries on. She never pressed a point unless to do so was unavoidable, but, like the proverbial water dripping on stone, she finally had her way. Tom had some of this quality of sustained effort, but he often worked spasmodically, and was more demanding of quick results. He had little patience.

Both of these persons liked attention; they liked to be valued at what they considered their own worth. Mrs. Wolfe enjoyed the limelight, as did Tom. It was only after he had tasted the bitter side of fame and realized the cheapness and petty selfishness of those who haunt the famous that he decided fame is deceitful and brings a poor reward.

There was never any doubt in the mind of either Tom or Mrs. Wolfe as to the value of their lives. Mrs. Wolfe is convinced that through her teaching school as a young woman, and through giving Tom to the world, she has contributed to civilization. Tom was also sure of his worth. He excoriated humanity for giving such small recognition to the artist; especially did he berate America for its lack of appreciation of its creative spirits. He was impatient with what he considered the pretense of modern education; he was disgusted with its self-righteous assumptions, with empty scholarship which he said paraded knowledge without wisdom. Teaching, he felt, should be carried on to develop originality. When he found any sign of creative talent in anyone, student or friend, he loved and fostered it. He welcomed and nurtured any kind of originality in people, no matter in what field, but especially in the arts. Man's progress, he believed, has been due mainly to the artist, and he was sure that man's most important work is that of the artist. He shouted with pride that he was an artist, and that the world should some day know it.

The spiritual convictions of Wolfe and his mother rested on a mystical basis. Mrs. Wolfe evolved a very personal religion, a strange, beautiful mixture of presbyterianism and spiritualism—though she would refuse either name.

The son's religion, too, was a highly individualized philosophy, mainly based on a strong desire to see humanity better itself, with the artist as the greatest force in working out man's destiny.

All these fundamental characteristics were of course not entirely revealed to me on the first night that we talked together. For we did talk all night. When Tom and his mother got together, they found so many fountains of interest were loosed that they could not stop the flow of memories until both were worn down by the need of sleep. However, it did become evident to me that night that Tom and his mother were fundamentally alike, and later association revealed this truth to me even more clearly.

When, a few days after our dinner, Mrs. Wolfe decided to leave New York, she chose to leave on a midnight bus to take the B&O to Washington, from Jersey City. Tom never tried to get his mother to change her plans. He knew better than to try. On the night Mrs. Wolfe left Brooklyn, the three of us walked from 5 Montague Terrace to the bus station which was then on Joralemon Street. Tom decided to rush on ahead to make sure that the bus did not leave without his mother. His seven-league legs took him quickly out of ear-range, and Mrs. Wolfe confided in me.

"I believe I could have been a writer myself," she said, "if I'd had a little more training. Tom thinks he knows a lot about people's characters. Humph! He's as easy to fool as anybody else! But they can't fool me!"

We soon reached the bus station. Mrs. Wolfe, then in her seventies, kissed us goodbye, boarded the bus, and waved a cheerful farewell, as the bus pulled out into the night.

Mrs. Wolfe visited Tom several years later at 865 First Avenue, New York, just after he had delivered an address to the Boulder Writers' Group in Colorado. One day, just before noon, Mrs. Wolfe, Tom, and I were in Tom's apartment. Tom had been invited by a lady of great means, but one whom Mrs. Wolfe held in great disdain as beneath her and Tom, to come to a luncheon. Ten other prominent guests, writers, artists, and dramatists, were to be there. Tom was to be the guest of honor. As time slipped by that morning, Tom kept remarking that he did not know what to do. Mrs. Wolfe told him not to worry; just to send a telegram. Tom had already sent one, and had received a refusal to excuse him from his engagement. Finally, after Mrs. Wolfe kept urging him to go and phone, and after I had refused to take any part in advising him, he went down to the corner cigar store to explain over the phone that he could not come. In about a half hour he came back redfaced and laughing. He yelled, "Well, I'm ruined—just plain ruined—that's all! She's never going to speak to me again!"

"You're lucky!" remarked Mrs. Wolfe with much satisfaction.

"But," explained Tom, "whether she ever speaks to me again or not, she certainly did speak enough this time. Why, I could not get her to shut up. I got so tired of her screaming that I told her she needn't take my damn ear off, and then I hung up!"

Tom then told us how the lady said she had had twelve chickens slaughtered for lunch. Then he threw a big paper bag which he had brought back with him, onto the table, and laughed uproariously.

"There," he said to his mother, "there's our lunch!"

In the bag was a bunch of carrots; nothing else. But Mrs. Wolfe cooked these and other things she had in the apartment, Tom went down and got a quart of French wine, and we had a gay luncheon.

That afternoon we rode by automobile up to a well-known Chinese restaurant just above One Hundred and Twenty-fifth Street, on Broadway. Mrs. Wolfe talked the whole way up, swapping comments mostly with Tom. As we left the apartment, Tom picked up and jammed into his overcoat pocket a good-sized bunch of typed manuscript—that of the speech he had delivered at Boulder. He explained that his agent had sent by mistake only one-third of the manuscript to the *Atlantic Monthly*. It had been immediately accepted for a stated price. Then, when Tom discovered the error, he wrote the editor that there was three times as much material as the editor first examined, but that the magazine could have the whole thing for the same price as first offered for one-third of it. Whereupon the editor replied that the article was too long for an *Atlantic* article, and that it should not be serialized. Tom then told us that the *Saturday Review of*

Literature had bought the article and planned to serialize it in three issues.

The only copy he had, he said, was the one in his pocket. We all went into the restaurant and sat down and ordered and began talking. Suddenly Tom decided to show us something in the manuscript. He got up and went to his overcoat, to get it. But his pocket was empty. He rushed out on Broadway, and in a moment came back waving the retrieved papers. They were somewhat dishevelled and many sheets had wet muddy margins from their bath in the gutter. But they were all there. This manuscript later appeared in book form as *The Story of a Novel*.[1]

It was on this trip through the city to the restaurant that I found that what I'd learned to be true of Tom, as to power of observation, was also true of his mother. She could, while riding, keep up a constant flow of reminiscence. I thought she had noticed nothing. But I found that she had observed almost everything we had passed on the way uptown, and I realized that at some later date she would be able to go into detail about what she had seen on the trip.

The habit that Mrs. Wolfe and Tom had of never throwing anything away, whether from their memories or from their actual possessions, is responsible for our possessing some very fine treasures. First of all, Tom's books are fictionized versions of what happened to him; they all mushroomed out of his gargantuan memory and were reshaped according to the artist's desire. He was a "chiel among us takin' notes." Just as precious as his novels, I believe, will be these letters which Tom wrote to his mother. Her saving habits, as well as her devotion to Tom, caused her to guard carefully almost every letter Tom ever wrote her. She believes that only those were lost which she turned over to other members of the family to read.

[1] Charles Scribner's Sons, New York, 1936.

When, two weeks after Tom's death, I was with Mrs. Wolfe in New York, I suggested to her that she should collect all his letters to the family, for I was sure they should be published. Some months later she came to New York and brought three large suitcases full of letters. One batch she had found under the back porch of her boarding house. Many pages were faded, some partly rotted away, and others torn. But most of them were well preserved.

These letters were written on every conceivable kind of paper —yellow second sheets, an extraordinary collection of all sizes and shapes of writing and scratch sheets, on hotel, club and steamer stationery. Obviously Tom picked up whatever he found handiest when he began to write. Tom had a habit of not numbering his pages, and many letters had to be patiently reassembled.

Observing that these precious letters seem to have been recorded so carelessly reminds one of the fact that once while Tom was a student at Chapel Hill in Edwin Greenlaw's composition class, he rose one day and read an excellent article which he had written on toilet paper.

Almost all these letters, except those written in the last three or four years of his life, were dashed off in seemingly great haste, many of them in scrawling pencil script, others in equally scrawled ink. Tom developed a kind of shorthand; for instance, his *ing* and *ed* endings to words were indicated by a mere wriggle of his pen. The wonder is that so many of these obviously hastily written letters read so magnificently, in prose that is often as eloquent as the best in his novels. The only doubt as to whether they were hasty or not rests upon the fact that, in his letters, after his death, I found literally dozens of letters which he had written and never mailed; he had copied them perhaps and kept the ones found in his files. Another indication of care is that in some few instances there are two or three versions of an unfinished letter.

It was quite an interesting but arduous task to get these letters properly arranged and typed. They were among Mrs. Wolfe's most precious possessions, and she loathed the necessity of letting them out of her sight to those who struggled to type them, Mrs. Julia Gilliam Gurganus, Miss Gertrude Breitbart, and Mr. Frank Plasmati. There were so many words that remained doubtful to the typists even after the most careful scrutiny, that many had to be studied and weighed for a long time before a final choice of meaning could be made. I do believe, however, that the letters as finally printed are as correct as anyone could possibly make them. Mrs. Wolfe has many favorites among the letters, and these she would read countless numbers of times, lovingly and with explanations of their background. Needless to say, as soon as the typing was completed, she took the letters back to Asheville and has them safely stored in a huge fire-proof safe.

In order to get as full a record as possible of what Mrs. Wolfe remembered of her famous son, we used a dictaphone. She and I had talked together so long and often that I was familiar with the more important episodes, having heard them dozens of times. She proved an excellent dictator. She would sit with the receiver at her mouth, and talk away, while rubbing her right hand on her knee. Occasionally I would have to ask a question, but so firmly did she have most of the material in mind that much of it flowed without any important breaks. The experience of having an eighty-year-old mother record her vivid, clear memories of an illustrious deceased son is indeed unique. Those who have never heard Mrs. Wolfe talk cannot imagine how detailed and clear is her memory. She remembers things that happened forty or even sixty years ago better than most people can remember what happened to them last week.

Quoted below are excerpts from these recordings. The reader will recognize that she is a good story-teller, as Tom always knew. From her he obtained much material which he used in *Look Homeward, Angel* and in his short stories and other novels. It is obvious that he caught her style and mannerisms, and relied almost verbatim on her account in *The Web of Earth*,[1] one of his best short pieces. Her son literally took her sagas and wove them into great epics. Of course most of the material which Mrs. Wolfe dictated cannot be reproduced here because of lack of space. The majority of it will appear in the biography of Thomas Wolfe which I am now preparing, and for which I shall welcome material.

Mrs. Wolfe wrote Tom long, newsy letters, in which she too attained a simple eloquence. Tom often showed me letters from his mother, and would ask, "Don't you think that shows a wonderful woman?" The post card which she wrote to her son on October 30, 1932, is a good example of her writing. As a matter of fact, she could write almost as much on a post card as most people do in letters. This message will also reveal to those who know Tom's writings, why October held such a spell for him.

The post card reads as follows:
"Dear Tom—

"You may have forgotten that I am your mother, but, this month; days scattered from the 3rd to 27th have recalled joys and sorrows of the past 47 years. Leslie's birth, 18th. 47 years ago. Grover & Ben, 40 yrs, ago, 27th. & yours on 3rd., 32 years ago—Then Ben's death 20th., 14 years. Yes, I have lived through this month, all the full years, all over again. The human heart, mind & body, is a wonderful construction—it still endures all the changes of pain, joy & sorrow, for they all stay with us till our time in the flesh-life ends. Mabel came 22nd for 2 days, & Fred

---

[1] Contained in *From Death to Morning*, Charles Scribner's Sons, 1935.

is home—gave up job with one Co. and will get connected with another Co. I hope you have completed the book and Scribners will soon have it at the press—Then you can take a rest. I still have some fine sweet grapes looking for you. It is very mild to-day & I hope will be till after Roosevelt is elected. Let me have a line. Lots of love."

"Mother"

MRS. WOLFE TELLS OF TOM'S BABYHOOD

"When Tom was a baby, he was a very beautiful baby, and had such bright eyes and a high forehead. He looked like he had more head than body—had such a fine head and face. He could talk when he was twelve months old and he being the baby I kept him a baby. I think he has written it up himself that he slept with me until he was a great big boy. He wasn't weaned until he was three and a half years old.

"When a prominent Doctor—he wasn't my doctor at the time, but he was Mr. Wolfe's after—he and another doctor were arguing about healthy children and babies. Dr. Glenn said to this other Doctor, says, 'There's a child whose mother didn't wean him until he was three and a half years old.' Said, 'You know the old argument that children should be weaned before they're a year old?' Said, 'It hurts the child and it hurts the mother.' 'Now,' he said, 'there's an example of a fine looking child, healthy, and nothing wrong with the mother, either.' Said, 'What're you going to do about that?'

"I think we just weaned Tom off by the other children laughing at him and talking to him about being just a baby. He still nursed. But it was a habit with him, that was all: he didn't really need it. Oh, when he was about a year old, he could toddle around, he'd come up and pull to me, and I think Mr. Wolfe told him at first, says, 'Ask her now, right nicely, Please Ma'm,' says, 'maybe she'll take you up and nurse you.'

"Well, he learned to say 'please ma'm.' He thought that was the name of what he wanted—it was 'please ma'm.' So every time, especially if I had company, he'd come and say, 'Please ma'm, please ma'm.' And, oh, I'd say, 'You don't want anything; you've had your dinner. You don't want to nurse.' And they said, 'Oh yes, you must take him up. Any child that can ask so nice that way must be taken up.'. . . .

"Tom explained in *Look Homeward, Angel* how he lost his curls. Well, he had beautiful curls, beautiful brown hair, and a heavy head of hair. I kept it curled every day. It struck him around his shoulders. He often said they called him a girl because he had curls and wanted his hair cut off. I told him, 'Oh no, I want to keep it long, you know.' Said, 'Ben and Fred had kept theirs long until they were eight years old and I wanted to let him have his.' So I kept putting him off until it had to be cut off. One of the neighbor boys that he played with had what the old fashioned people called lice in their heads, and Tom caught them. So there was nothing to do but to clip his curls.

"I just said that I had to give up my baby. I fixed his hair and tried to curl it over, you know, while it was short but he never wanted long curls any more. Though his hair was beautiful, even short, it would kind of curl up at the ends—it still looked like a baby's. He was proud that he was a boy.

"They had called him a girl because he had long curls and he thought, 'Well, I'm growing up to be a man; I haven't my curls.' But the sad part to me—my baby was gone—he was getting away from me."

MRS. WOLFE TALKS ABOUT TOM'S CHILDHOOD

"Tom liked to look at pictures, or picture books of the other children which they had outgrown and for which they had no other use. But they were delighted to scatter the books around him when he was sitting in the baby carriage, or on a comfort on the floor with pillows around him. They would read the little stories printed under the pictures and before he was two years he could read anything they read to him. He would say, 'Read about that picture.'

"Tom could talk when he was year old and the whole family, since he was our baby, gave lots of attention to him. They all got tired of their old books and stories Tom wanted them to read, so any little new book of stories they found on a counter they would buy and bring home to him. Mr. Wolfe did the same. He took such a delight in getting new books for him and would talk—take him on his lap to read him the new story.

"I sometimes laughed at him. He would say, 'You know an old fool is the biggest of all.'

"And I was the same. But I tried to be more reserved and would say, 'I guess we loved the others just as much.'

"When Tom was at or near the age of five, Max Israel, a neighbor boy, was six and ready to start to school. So Tom said, 'Dress me, I'm going with Max.'

"I let him go, thinking the teacher would know he was too young, but after a short time he came running almost out of breath with a little paper in his fingers, saying, 'Give me the money to buy the books.'

"I tried to persuade and tell him he was too young, but no—the teacher had given him the paper to get his books. I thought he would soon get tired of school and if he wanted the books or whatever she had written, his papa would buy them. So I sent

him to the office and Mr. Wolfe made him happy: sent him home
with his school supplies.

"Every morning, 'Hurry Mama, I don't want to be tardy.' He'd
heard the others say the same. He never was tardy, and he
thought the school was the greatest institution and kept that idea
all through the years after. Always a student with highest grade
marks.

"He attended the City graded school till he was eleven, then
a private boys' school four years. Tom had a remarkable memory
and did not have to put in all his time in preparing lessons
assigned to him. So out of school he read 'most all the books in
the Public Library. Miss Jones, the Librarian, told me that she
was sure he had read more books than any boy in North Carolina,
and that he rarely read boys' books but advanced ones. . . ."

"While we were on a holiday at St. Petersburg, I took him over
to the school and the teacher was very anxious for him to enter
but they found his books were all different and cost considerable.
Tom asked me, he says, 'We don't know what might happen. We
might not stay here very long and that's just extra expense, buying all those books I won't have any use for when I get back home
for they're different from ours. And I have my books with me,'
says, 'suppose I study and you be the teacher.'

"I asked him, says, 'Will you do that?'

"Says, 'Yes,—'

"Well, we had our lessons every morning. He often laughed.
He says, 'Mama, don't you know you're giving long lessons?'

"I says, 'Why you can study those lessons.' Says, 'They're not
too long.'

"He did study them. There weren't any too long for him. He
said they were so much longer than the teacher in Asheville gave
him. And we got back home and he entered in the same class.
I noticed one day, I said, 'Tom, don't you bring any books home?'

"He said, 'Don't have to.' Says, 'It'll be a month before they catch up to where we studied when we were in St. Petersburg.'

"Tom had grown to be a very tall boy. He plead for long trousers, wanted to be a grown-up boy. Still, I wanted to keep him a boy as long as I could. At Christmas time, 1914, I bought him a nice suit, with long trousers. He was going over to his sister's to spend Christmas Day. The day before he left, Ben fixed him up that evening to see how his new suit fitted him. He certainly looked fine in that suit. It was a nice suit, and it fitted him to perfection. Well, he was so proud. He looked fine. I told him to wear his short pants down there and dress up Christmas day with his new suit, and keep it kind of for a dress-up suit, for he had another suit practically new. He'd only had it about a month. But we couldn't get Tom back into a short suit anymore. He'd wear the coat but he wanted long pants. I had to go and buy him extra pants.

"That was two years before he entered Chapel Hill."

HOW TOM CAME TO GO TO THE UNIVERSITY
OF NORTH CAROLINA AND TO HARVARD

"Mr. Roberts had been principal of the Orange Street [in Asheville] and he resigned. Said he wanted to organize a boys' school and he picked out the boys that he thought could make the grade. And Tom was one of them and he wanted Tom to be in his school. Tom went to Mr. Roberts for four years. At a cost— I think the tuition was just a hundred dollars a year.

"It was English literature that Mrs. Roberts taught Tom. She seemed to be very good too, in that line. And he finished there in the spring of 1915.

"During the summer after he finished the private school of Mr. Roberts, Tom wanted to go to Virginia, to the University of

Virginia. Mr. Wolfe said, 'No,' he says, 'You belong to North Carolina and you must go to Chapel Hill. And that's a good school.'

"And I says, 'Tom,' I says, 'go down to Chapel Hill; papa wants you to go there, and he might decide not to send you anywhere if you don't go where he wants you to go. You go down there for the first year and it will be very easy if you decide after the first year to go over to the University of Virginia.'

"Well, he made up his mind that he'd go and he never said anything about changing, after he went the first year. He was so enthusiastic about the North Carolina school, Chapel Hill, he didn't think of any other place. . . .

"Mr. Wolfe advised him to go to Chapel Hill, and he would pay for it, so he did. He furnished the money for the four years at Chapel Hill."

"Tom returned from Chapel Hill [after four years there]. He graduated in June 1920 and that summer Mr. Wolfe wanted him to take up law, be a lawyer—study law. Tom didn't seem to have a tendency that way, so he went up to talk to one of our leading lawyers, Heywood Parker, who was also considered a literary man, too.

"Mr. Parker told him that there was always room at the top for a better lawyer, says, 'Though if you have a talent and want to be a journalist, I'd advise you to take up journalism. There's more future to that than there is to law. Everybody seems to be wanting to study law and the profession is over-crowded now.'

"Tom decided then that he wanted to go to Harvard for further education and Mr. Wolfe said, 'No, I'm finished with you now.' He says, 'If you don't take up law,' says, 'take up something else or go to work. Not many young men, even at Asheville, have finished at the University of North Carolina or any other University,' he says. 'I'm through with you.'

"Tom came to me and says, 'I'm going to Harvard. If you don't pay for it, I'll have to borrow the money.' I told him, 'Well, to go on.' That I would pay the bills.

"At that time, Colonel Bingham had written to the University —wanted a teacher of English and they recommended Tom to do it. So the Colonel sent over for Tom. Tom went over and had a talk with him. He told him that he wanted to go to Harvard, that he was afraid that if he stopped for a year that he'd never get to go, and he knew too that his father was very sick and that he was hesitating just at that time and so he called our physician, and asked him, says, 'Do you think Papa's going to pass out this year?' Says, 'If so, I'll stay and teach. But I want to go to Harvard; I'm afraid if I stop for a year I can't begin again.' Dr. Glenn said, 'Why, Boy, go on to Harvard,' says, 'We can't tell; I can't tell anything about how long your papa's going to live,' said, 'he may outlast you or me. He's been sick so long.' Says, 'He's a sick man.'"

MRS. WOLFE RELATES THE RECEPTION OF
"LOOK HOMEWARD, ANGEL" IN ASHEVILLE

"Tom sent me an autographed copy on the 15th of October, [1929], of Look Homeward, Angel. I think the book was released on the 18th, but when I got it some time during the day I sat down and I read—I don't think I slept. I suppose I stopped to eat my dinner, but I read till three o'clock in the morning— almost finished the book. I couldn't quite grasp the meaning of it all.

"He pictured some of the places in Asheville that I recognized. And of course there were no names. He built around some characters.

"Sometimes I'd laugh, but again I'd cry. It was ridiculous

in some ways, but I didn't look upon it as being anything serious.

"The day I received my book, my daughter Mabel Wheaton called me up and she said, 'I understand that someone has said that Tom has written up the family and the people and—has given them terrible names, and all.'

"I laughed and said, 'Why that's all right, even if he calls me old Caroline Peavine.' I says, 'Why if he makes a success of it,' why I says, 'I'll stand by and it'll be all right.'

"Well, this old woman was a character of years back, you know, a character that everybody knew on the street, a comical looking old woman.

"She was a tall angular looking woman, carried a cane, not so old but, oh, a mountaineer, and I think people thought she was a disreputable character but she kind of begged her way . . .

"She was a comical-looking old figure; I'd hate for anybody to compare me to her but I said if Tom had written me up looking like that old woman why it wouldn't make a bit of difference to me as long as he made a success. It would be all right with me.

"People in Asheville seemed to imagine that Tom had written up the people, and picked his characters out of Asheville. While no one spoke to me about it—they would look at me when I passed them in the street. I'm almost a mind reader, could almost tell what they were thinking about. But they didn't speak out; well, they were either afraid to speak to me or didn't have the nerve to say anything about the book.

"Some of his friends would call me up and call me Eliza. I laughed.

"I answered as if I thought they ought to be glad to be acquainted with Eliza. . . .

"It tickled me, you know, to think—I'd heard about some of them picking themselves out of the book, but I didn't recognize them myself when I read it, so I said, 'Have you read the book? You ought to get it and read it.' And—that I was proud of Tom.

"One member of my family was so upset about the book when he bought it and read it, he said he'd thrown away $2.50 and he said he just burnt the book up because he didn't like it. And now today he thinks it's—of course his mind is entirely different —that Tom was a great writer.

"The newspapers have quoted me that I said, 'Cæsar had his Brutus; Jesus had his Judas; and we have Tom,' but that was all false. Asheville papers at the time of the publication of *Look Homeward, Angel* reported that some member of our family had made this remark, much to the anger of the person accused. This bitterness continued and was so great that Tom didn't know whether he should come back home or not. He knew he had many friends there, but he didn't want to meet these people that gossiped around and were bitter towards him.

"Not long before he made a visit back home in 1937, Mabel, Mrs. Wheaton, my daughter, said she was visiting her aunt, speaking about Tom—that he might come back again, and that he was famous now, recognized as a genius everywhere. Her aunt says, 'Well,' she says, 'one woman says that he ought to be lynched when he comes back.'

"Mabel says, 'Well, he won't be lynched; he'll be coming back,' she says, 'they'll meet him with a band.' My daughter Mabel said that.

"Just the same, when he did come back home, all those people that expressed themselves as being bitter towards him were anxious to give him the glad hand and gathered around him as much as if they'd been his dearest friends. For a couple of months he could have no rest. All these people flocked around him that didn't mean anything to him—just took all his strength. He didn't get much sleep—worked down—not much rest—

"He didn't care to come back.

"In Asheville at that time—I believe the newspapers really considered Look Homeward, Angel—as a kind of history of the town, and didn't look upon it as being imaginative literature, but I think now they see it in its right light."

MRS. WOLFE TELLS ABOUT TOM'S LAST VISIT TO ASHEVILLE

"Tom's last visit to Asheville was in 1937. He came on May 6th for a visit, I think, about ten or twelve days, and he had a lovely visit. He seemed to be so happy and contented. During his visit, he decided he'd like to have a cabin back in the mountains.

"He found a very nice cabin in the woods about fifty miles out from Asheville, between the river and the Oteen Hospital, Government hospital, back in the woods, very quiet place back there. He ought to have been able to live out there in a quiet way. But it was too close to Asheville. So many people found that he was out there. He couldn't keep it a secret, so he had no rest. The young people seemed to worship Tom. People that, of course, he never knew but they'd admired him and they just didn't understand that he needed rest and they didn't give him any rest day or night. Some who visited him were: Frances Reynolds, Marjorie Pearson, Max Whitson, Lillian Weaver, Taylor Bledsoe, Robert Bunn, Charlie Westall and his wife Brownie, and others.

"He rented this cabin for July and August, and lived in it. He meant to do quite a lot of work, writing, and get some rest. But he didn't get very much work done and no rest at all. Tom didn't keep the cabin locked up, but he had a refrigerator, and he kept a supply of groceries, beer, in that refrigerator. He'd come into town at night and have dinner, go back out there about one o'clock and he'd find the cabin filled with young people having their—ah—dancing to—they had a victrola out there. They'd dance to this—to music and they'd stay there all night long, drink up all his beer, he said, or anything else, and said, 'Oh, we're going to stay and cook breakfast for you.'

"Tom rented a cabin for July and August and had paid the rent for both months, but the last week he wasn't at the cabin at all. . . . He went to the Battery Park Hotel and didn't let anybody know where he was. He went up there to get a rest before he went back the first of September to New York, and he left on the second day of September.

"He went through—down through Virginia,—Tennessee and Virginia, on his way back. He brought or had shipped about the time he arrived in July a large wooden box of manuscript, came by express, was insured. . . . The express on that—I paid it for him—was $11.28 and I thought that was his safe, and I asked him if he meant to use it.

"But he never opened that box and on the 19th of Sept. he wired, called me, said send that box back to New York to his address. He was giving up his apartment at 865 First Avenue. And I sent it the same day and wrote him a card."

In his novel *Of Time and the River* Thomas Wolfe said that he tried to portray a man's search for his spiritual father, the adventure of a young man seeking an anchor for his faith.

His mother he did not have to seek. She was always with him; he had her constantly in mind. In letters, he wrote her a detailed record of his life, and, in reply, her letters to him were as voluminous as his to her.

Mrs. Wolfe exercised great influence over Tom. He wanted her to believe in him, to sympathize with his ambition as an artist. She responded fully and stood by him in his greatest needs, financially and spiritually. She gave him strength. He said that she was like a force of nature, heroic in character.

In this comparison he was right. Mrs. Wolfe has always been dauntless; she has triumphed over disasters that would destroy the weak. Her life flame has burned steady and whole. Attentive to the material side of life as well as to the spiritual, she has forged ahead, sure of her power. At the age of eighty-two she, with her daughter, invested in a large house and lot in Washington, D. C. As proof of the wisdom of her act she quoted me a passage from PROVERBS:

> "She considereth a field, and buyeth it;
> With the fruit of her hands she planteth a vineyard. . . .
> She looketh well to the ways of her household,
> And eateth not the bread of idleness.
> Her children rise up, and call her blessed. . . ."

Then she added her conviction that she had made a good investment. Her initiative and courage have matched those of the pioneers who came early to America, conquered its vastness, and made of it a home.

Her son Tom, earthy, sensuous, welcoming life on any terms so long as he could feed his appetite for beauty, feared only those enemies,—disease, madness, death,—which might prevent him from achieving his great goal.

When disease struck him down in Seattle in the summer of 1938, it took the combined efforts of Tom and the rest of the family to prevent his seventy-eight-year-old mother from going alone across the continent to him. Finally, informed that Tom had been ordered to Johns Hopkins Hospital, she refused to sit idly by any longer, but traveled from Asheville to Chicago and met the train which had brought Tom, his Sister Mabel, and the nurse, cast. As the party continued on this, Tom's last journey, Mrs. Wolfe fed him fruit which she had grown at the Old Kentucky Home in Asheville.

At the hospital she refused to give up hope; she stayed with Tom every possible moment. When, after a few days, tuberculosis brought death to her son, she was grieved that she had not been permitted to hold his hand at the end.

"The nurse didn't call me until he passed on," she said. "I had always been with the others, with all the other members of the family—the children when they took their last breath; in fact, I held their hands until the very last."

At first deeply despondent over Tom's death, she later cultivated his old friends and took renewed interest in affairs. Her life has since been made rich and very worth living by the world's constantly growing recognition of the genius of her baby, Tom, so tragically cut off at mid-journey.

On February 16, 1940, Mrs. Wolfe came into her kingdom. Her eightieth birthday was celebrated in grand style by friends of Tom's who had now become her friends. Flowers overflowed the beautiful apartment of Sue Flanagan and Georgia Sprague at One University Place, where the birthday was celebrated. Writers, artists, educators paid their tribute to her son. Messages came from Governors, college presidents, and other prominent citizens. Chancellor Harry W. Chase of New York University told of Tom's days in Chapel Hill at the University of North Carolina; Mrs. Maxwell E. Perkins spoke of Tom's happy association with her husband, editor in Scribners, who was unable to attend; Edward C. Aswell, editor in Harpers, told of his task of culling three books: *The Web and the Rock, You Can't Go Home Again,* and *The Hills Beyond,* from a mass of manuscript eight feet high; Younghill Kang, author of *The Grass Roof* and *East Goes West,** interpreted Tom as an artist and teacher. In the group were Clayton Hoagland, editorial writer of the New York *Sun,* Constant van de Wall, the artist who had painted a portrait of Mrs. Wolfe, and many others who had known Tom

---

* Charles Scribner's Sons, New York, 1931 and 1937 respectively.

well. As chairman, I wove the various speeches together with anecdotes, since I had known Tom during his career from a lanky college youth to world-famous author.

Mrs. Wolfe made the last talk of the evening. She wore a black silk gown with a white scarf around her shoulders. As she stood before us, she clasped her hands, like a great singer, under a corsage of orchids. In a clear, well-modulated voice she spoke of how much at home she felt in New York. This city, she said, had become *home* to her now, for here Tom had found those who recognized his worth and fed his spirit.

She told of how strange it seemed to her that most of those present were either unborn or were babies when she was forty, and that none of them was alive when she had married. She traced the decades of her life.

Her bearing was noble. As she stood, smiling and calm, taking these people into her heart, she told of a dream she had had when a girl. She dreamed, she said, that a sister who had recently died, took her to heaven for a visit. When Julia asked to see a younger brother who had died many years before, the sister said, "Oh, he's not here; he is on a higher, happier plane."

"Aren't you happy?" exclaimed Julia.

"Oh, yes," replied the sister, "we're as happy as we know how to be!"

Mrs. Wolfe's cup was full. She stood like a queen who has at last come into full recognition in her kingdom.

In Asheville, N. C., on February 16, 1943, over one hundred persons braved sub-zero weather to attend a reception at the Old Kentucky Home in honor of her eighty-third birthday. She wrote me: "They all said I did not look a day over sixty. I was dressed in a princess dress. The girls all said I beat them all in figure. . . . Next time I'll have my eighty-fourth (birthday party) in Washington or New York, so you can be there and do the honors!"

Thomas Wolfe's Letters to His Mother

DEAR MAMA,—

I was promoted to the 4th A grade from the 3 B grade.

Fred [1] was promoted also.

We went to the park Thursday night and it rained and we got soaking wet.

When I took my examinations I was so good on my studies during the year that I only had to take one examination.

We had our sunday school picnic up at Overlook Park this year and I ate so much that I could hardly eat any supper.

It rained all afternoon and so we couldn't have any fun. I would rather we would have our picnic at Sulphur Springs much better.

Mama you left home at the wrong time. The summer crowd has begun to come in and you had better come home soon.

Good by

Your Son

TOM

[1] Tom's older brother, portrayed as Luke Gant in *Look Homeward Angel*.

[*Card*]

WINSTON SALEM, N. C.

Sept 1917

Take care of yourself and don't work too hard. Will write upon arrival at the Hill. Have had pleasant visit. Love to all.

TOM

Oct. 31, 1917.

MY DEAR MOTHER:

Those things we would like to do must often be deferred to the last. This will account for my tardiness in writing.

This military drill takes up about 15 hours of my time every week. It not only keeps me busy but the night finds me tired. We are now digging a complete set of trenches ½ mile from town. Compared to this, hoeing weeds in the garden was paradise.

I know you must have had a delightful time in Dayton and Chicago and I want you to tell me all about it Christmas. I'll pay you a visit then and, to tell you the truth, I wouldn't go home 'til then even if I had the chance. For we'll be so much the gladder to see each other. Thanksgiving is only three weeks from tomorrow and Xmas a short month beyond.

I want you to write me and tell me all about that wonderful dream you had about me. Do you believe in dreams? I suppose I'm a greater surprise to myself than to anyone under the sun. I am changing so rapidly that I find myself an evergrowing source of interest. Sounds egotistical, doesn't it? College life does more things for one than I would have ever dreamed.

Your check was returned yesterday because Pass Book was not at bank or something of the sort. I knew it was an oversight on your part so I wrote Papa [1] to attend to it.

---

[1] William Oliver Wolfe, portrayed as William Oliver Gant in *Look Homeward Angel* and in *Of Time and the River*.

Expenses are much higher. There's so much a fellow has to subscribe to and that you are morally bound to get. I try to ˈpay up" every check I get and then, naturally go broke. Sometimes I wish I were a plutocrat and had money to burn. There are so many things you would like to do and can't. However, I'm as economical as possible. When Xmas comes I'm going to try to borrow or steal a bank account in order to spare myself the embarrassment of writing home. The majority of the boys settle their accounts this way and, on the whole, it works the best because a boy, feeling more responsible, is more careful.

My work is progressing very well. I am also entered into some outside activities for it will never do to make the text book your god. Altogether, this is a most busy period for me.

I received Mabel's letter and I will answer it very soon. I trust Ralph[1] is enjoying a prosperous business. Give my love to all.

Your aff. son,

Thos Wolfe.

ATLANTIC HOTEL
NORFOLK, VIRGINIA
July 6, 1918

DEAR MOTHER:

I am writing you a few lines to let you know what I have been doing and how Fred is. I have been working as time checker at Langley Field until the 4th. By that time I was consumed by mosquitos and bed bugs so, upon the persuasion of several of my school mates who are working here I decided to find more lucrative employment. Arriving in Norfolk day before yesterday

[1] Thomas Wolfe's sister, Mabel, married Ralph H. Wheaton, who was long affiliated with the National Cash Register Company. He is portrayed as Randy Shepperton in *You Can't Go Home Again*.

I went around to the Government Employment Agency. A young North Carolinian working there told me to go to work as a first class carpenter[1] and told me if I would he would get me the job. So I start to work Monday at Porter Bros. who are building a big Quartermaster Terminal here. Will make about $7.00 a day if I can put my bluff across. Believe I can. Don't worry about me. I can always make a good living up here. Whether I save it or not is a very great problem as everybody up here seems to have entered a conspiracy to see how much they can get out of you without making you squeal. It is rather hard to write home after ten hours labor but I will try to write one of the family once a week. I am sunburned to a tan from my sojourn at Langley Field. My stay there was a valuable experience and I made many friends who seemed genuinely sorry to see me go. My boss out there told me I could have a job any time I came back.

Tell Mabel that I have not as yet seen fit to look up Clara Paul altho I have been over to Portsmouth once or twice. Take good care of yourself and don't work too hard. I am thinking more and more strongly of joining the Navy but of course I shall let you all know before doing anything of this nature. Fred is in barber shop getting shaved. He is well but *somewhat* nervous. So am I altho mine is more suppressed and I exhibit it by working jaw muscle rather than by talking. I find that three or four hours association with a nervous person puts me in this state.

Mr. Martin[2] seems well and has shown a very great interest in me for the family's sake which I, of course, appreciate. He will be totally blind in a few more months, the doctors say. It is a

---

[1] This episode appears in Look Homeward Angel. Tom had never driven a nail in a board in his life up to this time.
[2] Dinwiddie Martin, a lawyer in Norfolk, Va.

very great pity. He becomes very morose sometimes and broods to me over his troubles. It is all rather pitiful. Now please don't work too hard and give my love to everyone with the assurance I will soon write.

Much Love

Tom.

This paper is camouflage. Am staying at Y.M.C.A.

CHAPEL HILL, N. C.
Monday (Dec. 16, 1919)

P.S. Much Love to all of you and please don't *blame me* for not writing

Dear Mother:

A few lines written between breaths, as it were. I have never been so horribly busy. Have not a moment to call my own. Exams are here and I am divided between studying for them and getting out a feature edition of the Tar Heel[1] of which I am now Editor in Chief—highest honor in college, I believe. Everyone runs to me with this and that and I am busy not part of the time but all of it—sleeping five hours is essential but I can't spare any more. I have my last examination to-morrow but will be forced to stay around when all the rest are gone getting out Tar Heel to send to students all over the State. It's hard, I know, but you must pay dearly for college honors.

I get lots of praise: faculty say Tar Heel's editorials which I write have been steadying influences on campus this unsettled year, but you get tired of praise when you're too tired to think, almost.

This is literally my first opportunity of writing any of you.

[1] A weekly newspaper published by undergraduates in the University of North Carolina.

Do you want me home? If so, let me know immediately. I shall need money—a considerable sum. Your last check—$25—did not cover my debts as my room and board were $30 alone and I also had books equipment etc. So there is debt of approx. $15 on last month together with $30 for this month. I have signed up for a room on campus with another boy after Xmas—He deposited $10 for me and I'm to pay him. Of course this is counted in on my room rent next term. I'll need $70. Sorry bill is this large. If you think best I stay here deduct expense home and send rest. Pardon my lack of enthusiasm but I'm all in and must go to an English conference with my professor

Tom

[The first page of this letter was lost]

Sept., 1920

Now, foolish or headstrong, as you will, I must make or ruin myself from this time on, by my own pattern. You may think me very foolish, very unwise, if I do not accept the Bingham [1] offer and come home—to teach. But let me paint you a picture of the probable future. "You can write and teach, too," you will say. Yes, yes, how fine, how hopeful that all is. In ten, fifteen years, I will be a sour, dyspeptic, small-town pedant, the powers of my youth forgotten or regressed—bitter, morose, blaming everybody but myself for what might have been. The awful thing about most people is their caution—the crawling, abject bird-in-a-hand theory.

The security of the present job—with its safe wage—is ever so

---

[1] Tom, just before his graduation at the University of North Carolina, was invited by Col. Robert Bingham to teach at the Bingham School, a military academy in Asheville, N. C.

much better than the uncertain promise of future glory! What matter if you kill your soul—your fire—your talent—you can play the game safe and manage to live. Live! Two or three months ago, I think, I was still a boy. Life has a certain golden colour. It was desirable and glorious. In a certain sense that has changed. I will tell you what has happened, and I do not tell you this to appeal to your emotions or your sympathies. I am past that. On the train coming up I developed a heavy cold, which hung on most persistently after I got here. The thing got down into my chest and a week or two ago, I began to cough—at first a dry cough—then a rattling, tearing, sort of cough, full of phlegm. I became worried. My right lung was sore. Of course I had to be out in all kinds of weather, and this didn't help. One night I started coughing here, in my room, and I put my handkerchief to my mouth. When I drew it away there was a tiny spot of blood on it. I was half sick with horror and I tried not to think of it. Thereafter when I coughed I kept my mouth closed and coughed in my throat. I swallowed pneumonia salve at night in huge balls, and rubbed my chest with the stuff. I ate cough drops. The cold got better, the cough subsided, it has gone now—and the soreness has disappeared from my lung. But that is not the important thing; when this thing happened—which, I think, meant little—I thought the most, and saw the slow but certain advance of the old skeleton with the Scythe—I saw the sure destruction—the erasure and blotting out of my dreams and my poetry—and myself—and I couldn't face it. And then, almost in a miraculous fashion, I steadied, my mind cleared, and the old fear left me. I kept thinking of the words of Socrates just before they put him to death "For I hoped that I should be guilty of nothing common or mean in the hour of danger"—and these words gave me courage, and a measure of hope. And now, I feel,

I can go on with a firmer step, and a more resolute heart. There is a new fatalism in my beliefs and I feel ready for whatever may come, but, whatever it be, I mean to express myself to the last ounce, meanwhile. I feel strong—I believe I look healthy—I have a good appetite—and since the work ended I have slept long. I weighed yesterday and with my overcoat my weight was over 200 pounds. So if there is a sore or corrupt place in me I feel that the rest of me—which is strong and healthy—should be able to put it down. And if that is true of my life—why not there as well. If there is a sore or a corrupt place in my life—why should not the rest of me—that part of me which has fed on poetry, and the eternal tragedy and beauty—wipe out old stains and ragged scars. I shall not call on you for more help; I doubt if anyone but myself can help me now. Be assured that I have you all ever in my mind but I have chosen—or God has chosen—a lonely road for my travel—a road, at least, that is pretty far removed from the highway and even the best of you—those who love me and, I believe there are a few—may have sympathy but little understanding. For all that you have done, I am ever mindful. How can you doubt that I ever forgot it—but don't remind me of it too much at this time.

The world has come heavily upon me and Life has had me on the rack and has all but broken me—I need all my strength and it will yet be well. Good-bye for the present, and may God bless and prosper you all and bring you fortune and health. All of which I thought myself an indistinguishable part grows dim and faint upon the shores of a receding world—I am alone on a perilous sea—and yet, God knows, I do not cease to love and think of you all one whit the less.

For the present you may forward my mail to this address and as soon as I have another I will write and let you know. Please take care of your health, and keep warm, and eat food that is sufficient to sustain you. My love to Mabel and Fred,[1] and tell them I will write as soon as possible.

Faithfully your son—TOM

[*A post card written on September 29, 1920, from Cambridge, Mass.*]

DEAR MAMA:

I had about lost all touch with the world I knew about when I wrote this card. I am well located with a North Carolina professor doing graduate work here, at 48 Buckingham St. I am writing you tonight. This is a great place with a lot of freaks a lot of snobs and a lot of good fellows. Over 6,000 enrolled. No one knows you and you don't care.

TOM.

CAMBRIDGE, MASS.
2 Oct., '20.

DEAR MAMA:

I take this opportunity of writing you, after some delay. I am well settled, established as to room and board and have my course arranged.

Uncle Henry and Aunt Laura[2] have been more than kind to me. Last Sunday (I got here Sat.) after 2 days in New York, I went out to see them at their home in Medford, really a suburb of Boston. Stayed to supper. Uncle Henry gave me some useful advice regarding Harvard and the next morning I went down to his office at 60 State St. and at his advice, got a $400 bond from a surety company. It cost me $5.00 but everyone here has one, as

---

[1] Tom's sister and brother, born September 25, 1890, and July 15, 1894, respectively. Mabel is portrayed as Helen Gant in "Look Homeward Angel."

[2] Mr. and Mrs. Henry A. Westall, of Boston. Henry Westall is Mrs. Wolfe's oldest brother.

it is the most convenient and businesslike arrangement. They would not take the $200 tuition in advance—only $50 for the first quarter year. My trip up, including fare and pullman, which was a little over $40.00 cost me about $65.00, and I now have about $130 left after paying tuition, buying books, paying fees to several university ass'n clubs, pressing, laundry, etc. I have bought some shirts and a couple of neckties. I shall take the remainder of my money and pay for my room here the first half-year and for my board at Memorial Hall, if possible, for a couple of months. I am rooming at 48 Buckingham St. with Professor N. A. Walker, of Chapel Hill, who is here with his wife and children for a year of graduate work. Next to me is William Polk, a good friend of mine at Chapel Hill and in the front room Albert Coates and Skinner Mitchell both of Chapel Hill. In addition there are about a dozen Carolina men taking work here as well as a half-dozen Trinity men, all of whom I know. It makes it very congenial. As to my course the faculty here have been splendid in giving me the work I want. My experience in writing plays under Mr. Koch [1] at Chapel Hill has helped me considerably. George Pierce Baker is the great dramatic teacher up here. Koch is a former student of his. When I tried to register up for his English 47 known all over the country as "The 47 Workshop" I was told I could not by any means get in since the course is restricted to 12 people and mature writers all over the country submit plays a year ahead of time (one of his requirements) to get in. I went around and saw Mr. Baker who just got home from England where he went to gather material for the pageant he is writing for the coming Pilgrim Tercentenary. He thawed out immediately when I told him I was under Koch at Chapel Hill for two years and he commented

[1] Frederick H. Koch, founder and director of the Carolina Playmakers of the University of North Carolina.

enthusiastically on the work Koch was doing saying he was one of his "pets." He asked me if Koch had produced any of my plays and I told him two. He then asked their names and altho he had not read them he was familiar with their titles, as he has kept up with their work. So he's letting me into the sacred circle of the "47 Workshop" and even suggested that we might put on a couple of the Chapel Hill plays, one of mine included, "To show these people here what you're doing down there."

Nearly every year a play is taken by Baker from his class and put on Broadway, some of the most famous successes of recent years having been written here. "Stop Thief," "The Nigger," and many others. Of course I do not hope for any success like this in competition with seasoned and mature writers, but he told me, "When you come into my course it is with the intention of eventually being a playwright. If you have the ability I'll make one out of you." It is a great prospect for me, but I know I must work. In addition I am taking a comprehensive course in American Literature from the beginning, a course in Shakespeare under the world authority Kittredge, a course in the Romantic Poets under Lowes, and a course in French, all of them implements and resources for the writer's trade. There is no doubt of the greatness of Harvard. Her size is appalling but one can get here just what he wants under the biggest men in America. You see all kinds of queer freaks in the student-body, hundreds of boys go to classes dressed in golf tweeds and stockings, use the broad A, and so on. It is a peculiar sensation to see a student drive to class in his Packard or Stutz roadster, yet this happens. Altho you see many of these rich young fellows, sons of the great moneyed families of America, you see thousands of others here for what they can get, and practicing strict economy. It is a heterogeneous mass of humanity and if there is anywhere in America where you can get a national outlook, it is here. Or, if you choose, you can become a first-class jack-ass in knee-britches, as some of the fellows I have told you of. Harvard is much maligned because of this type, but in a place with over 6,000 students you are bound to find them. The old democratic atmosphere of Chapel Hill is unknown here, not because these men are snobs but because it is every man for himself and everyone 'tends strictly to his own affairs. You get used to it and don't mind it, and gradually you pick up an acquaintanceship of 50 to 100 men. Harvard is no place for a man to start college. A small place like Chapel Hill is infinitely better. This place is for men who begin to "find themselves," who know what they want and are here to get it. If I had to start all over again, it would be Chapel Hill first, Harvard later. I recognize the greatness of Harvard but more and more every day I have borne to me the greatness of Chapel Hill. Each contributes to you much that the other cannot give. And of course my love and affection will always be first with the University, with its unpaved streets which become pools of mud when it rains, and its brown dirty old buildings. The *spirit* of Carolina is just as great as that of Harvard. I am boarding at Memorial Hall, the best and cheapest, $32.00 a month and the food is first-class in every way. I am going to get a menu and send you. I am feeling fine, and am in good spirits with a determination to make the most of my chances.

Bite of autumn in the air today for the first time. Been very warm up to now. Don't know if Papa and Fred are home but am writing Papa note now before rushing to dinner. Read him this letter. Tell Fred and Mabel I'll write tonight. Love to all.

TOM

48 Buckingham St.
Cambridge, Mass.

CAMBRIDGE, MASS.

(1920 or 1921)

Dear Mamma:

I got your letter the other day, and am hastening to answer it. I have drawn checks for $25.00 each on Wachovia checks for my last tuition fee of $50.00, and lesser checks for other expenses. I had to pay $15.00 to have my 25,000 word thesis typewritten and ten dollars for a pair of shoes.

I have wanted you to see a sample of the kind of work I am doing, and I am sending you a duplicate copy of my play 'The Mountaineers' which was given a performance here this Fall. It will be put on the regular programme for next year, I think. For a one-act play it is somewhat long, and will stand condensation and polishing but it is the real thing and deals with a great tragedy, the tragedy of a fine young man who returns to his mountains with fine dreams and ideals of serving his people. It is not a feud play, although the feud is used. The tragedy of the play is the tragedy of this fine young man fighting against conditions that overcome him and destroy him in the end. When you read this play, I hope you will be aware of this tragedy, and the tragedy of the lot of those poor oppressed mountain people, old and worn-out at middle age by their terrific hopeless battle with the mountain.

The hopelessness of their lot is summed up in the last speech by May the mountain woman. I daresay you have seen May a thousand times, skinny, sallow, ugly, toil-worn, and with a dead, dull, sullen look on her face, chewing a snuff-stick, and with her hair pulled back in a tight, painful knot. The point of this play, Mamma, grows out of my indignation at the idea most people have of mountain life, growing out of the romantic stories of mountain life by such writers as John Fox, Jr. and others.

You and I know this is not the truth. When the girl in this play speaks of "the romance of mountain life" and the boy asks her "how many beautiful mountain girls have you seen" he is saying for me the things I want to say,—the truth, that the life is not a romantic affair, with beautiful golden-haired girls, and dashing outlaws, but a terrible sordid story. And always in the background of this story is the picture of those monsters, the Mountains, racing like hounds across the horizon, shutting these people eternally away from the world, hemming them in, guarding them, and finally killing them. I not only believe this is the truth but I know it and by God I'll write a great play, a long play on this someday that people will see and be thrilled by because they know it's Life, it's Truth! It's the best play that's been written here this year simply because I have burned with eagerness and desire to have the truth out. I couldn't have written it in North Carolina, crude as it may be in spots, because I am looking clearly across a 1000 miles and get the sense of perspective that is absolutely necessary.

I want you to read it and judge it not because I'm your son but on it's own merits and see if you think I have it in me to be a dramatist some day. I'm not speaking boastfully, I'm asking you earnestly to do this for me. All the critics in the world may *say* it's good but a man's own mother will *know*.

I'm writing a long play now that has gripped me heart and soul. I worked for months for an idea but none would come. Then suddenly about two weeks ago I awoke and the minute I got out of bed the *Idea* came into my head. In three hours the whole play had worked itself out detail by detail, clearly, and interestingly. I think it's a great idea. I hope I'll be big enough to write a great play for the stuff is there. I'll tell you all about it. I heard papa tell one time about a family of aristocrats in W. N.

Carolina who owned a vast quantity of Mountain land. Major
Love, I think he said was the man's name. They owned 500,000
acres and sold it for 20¢ an acre to lumber people simply because
they were impoverished by the War. They died in want. I am
using this as a basis for my story. The scene starts at the home
of Colonel Tasher Weldon 15 months after the Civil War.
Colonel Weldon is a typical Southern aristocrat. He fought
bravely for the South in the War and now he had retired to his
estate not being able to see that the old order is gone, that it is
gone, thank God, forever. He lives in the memory of his past
greatness when Oakmont was rich and flourishing, when he
owned a hundred Negroes. Now he is impoverished, owning
a vast estate of 500,000 acres of arable land but without capital.

We may look out the windows of his great living room and
see stretched out below by the side of a stream hundreds of acres
of fine loamy bottom land, wonderful for farming, but overgrown
and choked with weeds. In the distance on the other side of the
stream stretches his great forest. The Colonel has two sons,
Ralph and Eugene. Ralph is a replica of his father, a true aristocrat, handsome, lovable, dreaming, but a waster, a hard drinker,
no more. Eugene, the younger, is filled with bitterness and
broods in his heart because his father and brother will not wake
up and realize that they are making no efforts to avert ruin. He
points at the bottom-land choked with weeds and tells them they
are all choked with weeds, that they are living in the past, that
the South is bleeding to death from her wounds, and that they
the quality folks who fought so bravely in the war are making
no effort to fight the greater battle of peace, that they are letting
the country be given over to thieves, carpetbaggers, Negroes,
while they live in idleness. Do you begin to see the idea? The

Weldons are not merely one family. They stand for the whole of Southern aristocracy.

The Colonel and Ralph laugh at Eugene's idea that a Weldon is not too good to till his own land. And so the fight goes on in this boys heart, a mighty epic struggle—He the thinker, the Seer, realizing that the old order has gone, that it is man's highest duty to produce, to create—they the lovable but worthless aristocrats hating the idea, and tragically failing to realize that new times have come. Well, I'll give just the barest details now. Against Eugene's and his mother's protest that to sell their land at next to nothing is criminal, the Colonel hard-pressed for money, and unwilling to work or have his boys work, sells his 500,000 acres for 25 cents an acre to a New Eng. lumber firm.

Four years elapse. The money has been squandered living at the pace they set. The Colonel is an old broken man realizing for the first time how useless his life has been. Ralph, the gay, reckless young ne'er-do-well is killed in a gambling house in New Orleans. The Colonel dies. This is not supposed to be tragedy, but merely an event in the play. For the Colonel doesn't fear death, he knows that death is not tragedy, that his tragedy lies in his mis-spent and wasted life. Eugene the dreamer, the idealist is left the heir to a vanished kingdom and a decaying mansion. Eugene the boy who would have done great things has been conquered by the canker-worm of waste that has ruined his family and he is left sitting in his decayed mansion looking at the estate that once was his, from which already comes the sound of falling trees and buzzing saws. There is a very pretty little love story I haven't dealt with.

Christine Roably, the girl on the neighboring estate, daughter of Major Roably, is another aristocrat who can't realize the time of her father's glory is past. Maj. Roably sold his land when Col.

Weldon sold his, has squandered the money, died, and now Christine and 'Gene are in much the same boat. Deep in his heart 'Gene has always loved this girl but she was such a gay, teasing person, and he had lost all his gayety and his sense of humor by his brooding, that they'd never gotten along. He thinks she was in love with Ralph, the elder brother who was killed. The girl comes in and sees 'Gene sitting in the ruins of his estate. She is touched with sympathy and asks him what he is going to do. With sudden rage he tells her he's going to get away from it all, get away from the bitter reminder of terrible tragic waste that has ruined his family, that he's going into the world and try to play the part of a man for once in his life. "But, my dear," she says, "You don't know what you're saying. You're out of your head with grief. 'Gene, don't you realize you're Master of Oakmont now?"

Eugene bursts into insane laughter "Master of Oakmont. Master of a ruined kingdom, and a rotting Mansion—What a farce! Lord of Misrule. Master of Oakmont." Wild with grief he flings out of the house and leaves the girl weeping behind him.

The Last Act. Ten years have elapsed. The scene is the same, the great living room of the old house. But what a change. The door hangs open from one rusty hinge; two pieces of plank are nailed crosswise before it. The room is dilapidated and in the last stages of decay. Think of the terrible sadness that associates itself with a room that one has once seen so full of light, life and gayety. There is the sound of voices from a distance. Two men enter. They knock the boards from the door and come in. From their talk we learn that they are master carpenters, that the lumber company has acquired the house and is tearing it down for its own headquarters. Do you see what this house stands for? It is the symbol of the old South, the old aristocracy being torn down, to make place for the new, productive order. From the men's talk, we learn that the last of the Weldons, Eugene, went away ten years before and has never been heard from. A man enters. He is roughly dressed and his face is covered by a thick black beard. It is Eugene. Life has been tragic to him also, he thinks he too is a waster, he never found the pot of gold at the end of the rainbow. The men do not recognize him. He explains that he is a stranger and that he has been given employment by the lumber company and that the foreman has sent him up here to help them. The carpenters explain that the house is being torn down and they give him a hammer and a chisel and tell him to take the mantel down. Like a man in a daze 'Gene obeys but when he sets his chisel against the wall and starts to strike the blow he staggers back with a cry of agony. He can't do it. To strike the house that has sheltered him, warmed him, under which his father and that dear, gay brother moved, to strike the mantel on which his mother's hands have rested is like striking a blow against his naked heart. The men recognize him and respectfully go off to other parts of the house to leave him alone for a while to brood over his lost estate. Christine comes in. She is now the school teacher in the village. Sadness and the tragedy of waste has touched her life. She now knows what Eugene was embittered over.

She doesn't recognize 'Gene under his beard and he lowers his cap and pretends to be very busy with his work hoping to keep his identity undisclosed.

With a sigh she tells him she came to take a last look at the old house, what fine people once lived here, how sad it is now that they are all gone. Judson, Colonel Weldon's old negro butler comes in and begins polishing up the furniture. It is pathetic to see this old negro himself a reminder of the past who daily, in memory of his dead master, polishes the old tarnished finery. To those dim old eyes the place is as splendid as it ever was, he doesn't know that time has passed him in its swift flight also. "Jest you wait 'till Marse 'Gene gits back," he tells the workman—"He'll put a stop to dese goins on." Eugene is so overcome with emotion when he sees the old Negro that he can't resist saying a word to him. The old man instantly recognizes him and falling on his knees kisses his hand. Eugene tries to escape but Christine stops him. There follows a scene in which he blurts out his love for her, and tries to get away but she stops him and tells him she has waited. He can't believe she is in earnest, he thinks she is teasing as she used to, and he starts to go. When they go, they go together facing a new life, purged and strengthened by the life they have been taught by. On a little plot of ground with their lost kingdoms ever before them to remind them and strengthen them in their desire to produce, these two people, glorious forerunners of the New South, will settle down. Arm in arm they go out the door. At the door the sound of a plank being ripped away upstairs brings 'Gene back with a groan. "Take one last look at this room, 'Gene," she tells him, "and realize that this is past, that this was a fine life but a useless one. We are not living in the Memory of past greatness, but Now and Here. Are you ready to meet it?" Thus, they go out together, these two fine people, and as they go down the path one may hear the sound of hammering in other parts of the house. A castle is being torn from it's foundation, a mansion of the past is falling before the inexorable call of Tomorrow. From the distance comes the deadly whirring buzz of the New and the Curtain Falls!

Well, I have the stuff for a fine play here. I'm sorry I was so lengthy but I gave only the details, at that. I hope you'll be able to read it. I'm so fired up by it that I'm rushing doing at a tremendous clip. If you are able to get the one-act play to Mrs. Roberts [1] after reading it, you would oblige me.

Write me soon. Take care of your health. Love to Papa and Mabel. I'm writing soon.

—Love,

Том.

January 25, 1921

DEAR MAMA:

I am writing you late at night after returning from a trial performance of my one-act play which was put on tonight at the "47 Workshop" before a private audience of Workshop people. It is a strong play, I am told. And it will be produced I understand in the Agas Theatre at Radcliffe in March and from there it may be taken with two or three other one acts to Cleveland, Buffalo and New York. Don't say anything about it until I can give you more details. It is at least an encouraging beginning for me in a class of older and more mature men and I hope I can realize the promise I have shown in my future work. Examinations are upon me and I am working like a beaver. With my play and other work piling down on me I rarely get to bed before one or two o'clock these days, but I am going to take a rest after exams. which start next week. My term bill must be paid on Feb. 10th. It includes my tuition for the third quarter and my board for three and one-half mos. (I ate at the new cafeteria during the holidays, having my food charged) the amount of the bill will be approximately $200, I think, when certain items

[1] Mr. and Mrs. J. M. Roberts founded the North State Finishing School in Asheville, N. C., where Tom was a pupil from 1911–1915. Mrs. Roberts taught him English. She and her husband both recognized his great talents, and she certainly had a great deal to do with their early development.

are added. I got your letter and was happy to know you had done so well on the lot; also your last card with the news of the bank account. I appreciate your generosity. I am enclosing a note to Papa. If he is feeling bad I understand that he cannot write very well. It is all right. I hope his health continues good and pray he will stop worrying. I hope you will excuse the shortness of my note now. I am so dog-tired I can hardly write more, but I have to finish a thesis tonight which has already run up to 16,000 words. After a period of mild weather it has gone below zero. Bitter cold.

Love

Tom

48 BUCKINGHAM
CAMBRIDGE, MASS.
Monday Feb 21 1921

My Dear Mother: I am writing you as quickly as possible after examinations. I have not heard from any of them yet but I am sure I performed creditably and made high grades. One of my professors called me up and praised me highly for a thesis I wrote which, of course, made me feel greatly elated. I told you of my play being given a private performance and now I am confident of a production here and a road trip if my revision justifies it.

I have not paid my term bill and tuition (my board) yet ($200) or my room-rent for the next term (about $70) because I couldn't understand from your last letter how my account stood. I would need for this with a small margin about $300.

From now on I will practice strict economy I have not been extravagant but I know I have wasted some money, which has worried me considerably, and which I will try to profit by. The rest of the family hold it against me, I know, that I have been to school so much and spent so much, and there is much truth in what they are saying about me. But when I leave here this year it will be to make my prodigal journey of experience, which all must make, into the world, and I will try to return home some day justified in the eyes of all. If all you know should set them selves against me I want you to believe in me and hope for my success. And if the sound of my face hitting the ground is heard let it be known that it was the fall after an unsuccessful leap for a star.

Fred has written me from Atlanta. Send me his address as he didn't send one, I think.

I will try to get a job in Boston next summer, taking a course I want, perhaps, at the Harvard summer school at the same time.

Will you let me know about the bank acc'ts at once since my bill was due Feb 10. I will write Papa separately. I am sending this Special Delivery.

Affectionately your son

Tom

I will submit my report to you at once when the grades are in.

April 19, 1921, from Harvard

DEAR MAMA:

I sent you a telegram this morning in answer to yours which I got late last night and I hope it reached you early. I am sorry you should have felt any alarm on my account since I have never been seriously ill but was incapacitated for a few days. It was the first time in years that I have been completely knocked off my feet and I have something to tell my grandchildren about now regarding my first New England cold. They are terrible. They thought at first at the infirmary that I might have measles on account of my fever, but this proved to be only the aftermath of my cold which was breaking up when I entered the infirmary. I had one bad night with a high fever but after that I recovered quickly. At present I am nearly well but I have lost my sense of smell pro tem completely and most of my taste. This will come back gradually. Nothing is so deceptive as 'spring' weather up here. Three weeks ago we started to have warm lovely days and everything began to bud and then quicker than light the weather changed, dropping 50 degrees in one day and becoming cold, raw, damp. It was this barometric contortion that gave me my cold, and in all this winter up here has been one of the mildest the natives can remember and it was indeed a contrast to what I expected. I understand it has been very mild at home also. The springs are very late here and the weather is now wet and raw. This is a week of spring recess here but I am working hard in order to be even with the field when work starts on the last lap next week. I haven't seen Aunt Laura, Uncle Henry, or Elaine in some time but I think I shall visit them next Sunday. I have never seen Hilda.[1] Papa's letter cheered me up greatly because he seemed cheerful and happy in it, and I believe he is destined to be with us for many years yet. I got a nice letter from Mrs. Roberts a few weeks ago which stirred me considerably. They have had a hard time and have been forced to sell their last home in Chunns Cove to which they were attached. Mr. Roberts has been very sick with stomach trouble, you know, and the one strong thing about Mrs. Roberts since I have known her has been her invincible spirit, that is as brave and true as any I have known. They have been two dear, wonderful friends to me and

[1] Elaine and Hilda were daughters of Mr. and Mrs. Henry A. Westall, of Boston, and Tom's first cousins.

when I get a letter from her I flush at her praises for I know I am not big enough yet for them. It was through her that I first developed a taste for good literature which opened up a shining Eldorado for me. If you see her I wish you would give her my kindest regards. I got a letter from Frank [1] the other day and I shall answer him soon. Dietzie, a bright student, he says. We are all bright in this family. We may not amount to three whoops but it is not from a lack of intelligence. If Ben [2] had lived and could have been inspired with ambition I believe he would have been a great success. My confidence grows daily that within five years I shall write a good play. I have got to rub up against people, to experience things for myself, but I shall do it.

I suppose you have a garden growing. How's the fruit? I heard indirectly through Chapel Hill, that frost had injured the prospects. I hope the real estate business is flourishing. And, finally, I hope you are keeping your health good and that you don't expose yourself to the weather as I did. You needn't worry a minute about my health as my troubles are now over, except for a few trifles that will pass off in a few days.

With much love

Your aff' son

Tom

Wednesday (May 16, 1921)

Dear Mama: I received your letter the day before yesterday. I'm sorry to hear you've had trouble with my hand-writing but know

---

[1] Frank C. Wolfe is Tom's oldest brother, born November 25, 1888. Dietzie is his son.

[2] Ben, who figures so prominently in *Look Homeward Angel* and whose death was a most important and decisive episode in the book, was one of the twins, Benjamin Harrison and Grover Cleveland, born October 27, 1892.

it's bad. I'll try to write more legibly. It is true I did not send you a list of the courses I am studying this semester but it was not because I thought you would not understand their nature. I am continuing with the Eng. 47 (the playwriting course on which I am putting most of my time) and with Eng. 14 a course in the Elizabethan drama. In addition I am studying French and German, to meet the tests, and am reading heavily in the drama.

I have put in an application for a teaching position with the request that if I can't be located here I will be sent to New York or some large centre where I can keep in touch with the theatre. There is a playwriting competition here June 1; Professor Baker has but recently made a new contract with a New York producer who agrees to select one of the plays here every year and try it out in New York. I am trying to get two long plays in readiness for this contest. The winner who will be notified about July is paid $500 in cash and has the satisfaction of knowing his play will be given a chance. The competition of course is keen and I do not elevate my hopes. I only pray that "my muse" will not desert me in this, my supreme hour of need.

Professor Baker read the prolog of my play The Mountains— which I have expanded to a long play—to the class a week ago. To my great joy he pronounced it the best prolog ever written here. The class, harshly critical as they usually are, were unanimous in praising it. This circumstance bewilders as well as pleases me. I am absolutely no judge of my work. At times the work over which I expend the most labor and care will fail to impress while other work, which I have written swiftly, almost without revision, will score. Such was the case with my prolog; a thing of the utmost simplicity. Professor Baker is especially anxious for me to finish my other play the first act of which he had last year, and liked. This is the play of the decayed Southern aristocracy; it has never been adequately dealt with. I believe I told you the idea once: The action occurs immediately after the Civil War. The sons and their father—'quality folks'—are home from the wars. They are impoverished, all they have is their big farm, their mansion house,—and a vast quantity of timber land, 100,000 acres. Their's is the crime of indifference and sloth. Rather than make strenuous efforts to save their inheritance, they sell the vast estate for a pittance to lumber companies, in order to meet the needs of the lumber company. (*sic:* "of the family.") The story is the pitiful story of the decay and disintegration of a family, a family who represent a fine and beautiful life, but who also represent an unproductive order of society, and must therefore give way to the new industrialism. Throughout the action of the play the lumber company creeps nearer, like a great octopus, drawing in their land, bit by bit, until finally only the house remains to them. In the last act the house goes, too. It is acquired by the lumber company who decide to tear it down and build the headquarters of their offices on the site. As the curtain falls the sounds of hammers may be heard in all parts of the house; this house, symbolic of the romance and chivalry of the past, is being ripped from its foundations. Such, very briefly, is the plot on which I propose to erect my play. I have also the idea for another play, but I fear time will not suffice to finish it this Spring.

Winter is breaking here; already we have had some warm days. Outside of a cold some time ago, my health has been good.

I need no clothes but will be forced to buy shoes soon. I will exercise strict economy. I am in a difficult position but I will face it in my own way. If you think I am unmindful of Papa's condition, you do not know that it hangs over me like a Damocles sword.

I want above all things, to come home and see him, and see

you all. But if I come it is on a visit. I will not stay and stagnate. I've put a heavy burden on myself; the burden of vindicating your generosity. If I fail you need never expect me home. You'll never hear from me again. If I succeed, and it is on that I love to think, I will be able to return and afford you, I hope, a certain measure of satisfaction and pride. Meanwhile, whatever taunts may be thrown at me, if any, of selfishness, pride, conceit, snobbishness, or what not, strike against as tough a hide as a sensitive fellow can call to his defense.

I tell you if success depends on desperate determination I will not fail. I think if the realization ever came to me that I was doomed to eternal failure, that "my bright sun" would always be just out of reach—I think I would kill myself. Don't let this alarm you. The frame of my mind is perfectly normal these days; but I am terribly in earnest. I repeat: I am in a delicate, trying position before you and the family and I am trying to meet and solve the problem as honestly and courageously as I can. Of one thing I earnestly entreat you never to doubt: That is the sense of gratitude and loyalty I feel to you and Papa. That is stronger now in me than it ever was, stronger than, when as a little boy, we occupied the same room, stronger than when you took me on your trips to Florida and elsewhere. When I retire at night, when I wake in the morning I am conscious of the weight of my gratitude; it is the spur that drives me on.

Let me state this painful situation as plainly as I can. It is a subject so painful to me, who have been a taker and not a giver, that it is with difficulty I write these words. But let us consider every possibility. I will come home and stay for a short time. Then, in accordance with my fixed purpose, I will go away to my work, wherever it may be. While I am absent Papa may die. I foresee these consequences. Do you think they have not been gouged in my very soul? But I deliver myself up for judgment.

It is an either-or situation; there are no grounds for compromise. It is a question of Tom present or Tom absent. Tom present may feel better about it, and get more peace of mind (tho I doubt that) but Tom absent trying to justify the expense he has put you both to is a more manly figure.

I do not say there are not opportunities at home for young fellows or that the town has not many better and more capable young men than myself. It has, I know. But we must look and decide on our particular capabilities and the particular opportunities for those capabilities. And for mine, (if I have any) Asheville is not the proper seed-ground.

I wish that some divine agency could permit you to look into my heart, or into my head, as I write this. You would no longer doubt my utter sincerity, neither would you ever doubt the motives that determine me. If you accept this letter as a sincere, a painfully sincere statement of my point of view, I think you will come to see it is no longer merely a case of selfish personal ambition with me. I don't cut a very pretty figure, I suppose; I am open to the attack but, like old Martin Luther, I can't do otherwise: I have been guilty of repetition time and again in this letter because I'm so desperately anxious for you not to misunderstand me.

I am writing Papa under a separate cover. Also I'm getting off that long delayed letter to Mabel who, I trust, is in good health.

Uncle Henry sends love.

Your affectionate Son
Tom.

My grades midyear were Eng. 14: A—; Comparative Literature 7, B+; English 47 will not go in until end of year.

May 21 1921

DEAR MAMA: I am writing you this from Uncle Henry's office on State St. I finished my exam yesterday—which was in French. It was rather difficult but I am sure I passed with a creditable grade. I have never felt so let-down after an exam. I have worked constantly and been keyed up to a high nervous pitch for a week and I intend to spend the next two days sleeping.

Today, tomorrow & Thursday is Commencement at Harvard—a gay and colorful occasion. I'm going to see it. They are decorating the campus or the "Yard" as they call it with Japanese lanterns and it makes a very brilliant scene. The seniors have a number of queer customs here. Today Class day exercises are being held and tonight at Midnight after the day's festivities are at an end the entire campus will be cleared of every one but seniors. They (the seniors) will sneak out in nature's garb and bathe in two great pools that have been erected recently.

The ablutions in these pools represent the bathing in the fountain of Youth or the fountain of truth—probably the latter.

I am forced to move out this afternoon from my lodgings since the new tenants have let me remain several days until my exam is over. I don't know where I'm going yet. I have drawn exclusively on the Wachovia for several days as follows:

48.00   Room Rent (to N W Walker)
20.00 ⎫ These last have been indorsed by
20.00 ⎬ Uncle Henry and have been ex-
15.00 ⎭ pended as follows: $21.00 Redeeming

that am't of Central checks. $12.00 fee for taking Fr. exam yesterday, receipt of which I enclose—$3.50 half-soles—heels—patches on shoes—$1.00—two pairs of socks. This leaves $17.50 of the above amount which, with two or three small checks has

served to feed me and attend to my wants since Mem. Hall closed
12 days ago. I am afflicted with a big appetite, as you know, and
practice as I may I can't get out under an average of 75¢ a meal
at a cafeteria. Breakfast is less but supper runs it up. I am now
asking Uncle Henry to endorse another check for $15.00 as my
money is gone save for $1.25. With this money I shall do as
follows: $5.00 for the renovation of my suit which was worn
through in the trousers. I had to use my vest to patch the trousers
but the man has agreed to give me a good two piece suit pressed
cleaned and patched which will save me the purchase of a new
one. I am going to rest two days and then try to find a job. This
summer I'm going to rewrite & complete my long play which I
believe will someday see the footlights.

I have heard from two courses—one Am Lit (Eng 33) on
which I was fortunate enough to make the *ne plus ultra*—a grade
of A. On Eng 47—Mr. Baker's course in playwriting I have made
a grade for the whole year of B+ which the sec'y of the grad,
school told me was extraordinary.

In summing up my year's work I have done the following
things: completed 3 full courses for the degree of Master of Arts
—4 courses being required. Passed, (I hope & am confident) in
addition, elementary Fr. which is a requirement for Grad students who would get the M. A. Taken the Eng 47 which is a
course that demands the full attention of most students, in addition. Those getting the M. A. must make a grade of B or above.
My grade for the 3 courses is A, A—, B+ which puts me well
above the mark. It will be seen that I now need but one course
to complete my M. A. I cannot help feeling what I think is a
justifiable pride in my performance. I feel I have grown, developed, matured during the year and attained a point of view
which, win or lose, will never do anything but help me.

During the last two mos. I have gone at such a clip that I think you may pardon my lack of correspondence somewhat. I don't believe in the policy of "You write me a letter and I'll write you one"—it's so childish & foolish, but, I confess that now I'm left alone up here—my friends having departed—I would like to hear from you a little more often. I'm absolutely helpless, at present to repay you for what you've done for me with anything but my gratitude but I am capable of that to a pronounced degree. I know you're busy, never more so than at this time of the year, but I think a letter here lately from some one of the family would have cheered me up considerably.

I have mentioned all my debts to you I think with one exception I owe a Dr (sic) Dailing here $11.00 for services he gave me during my illness at the infirmary. In a previous letter I spoke to you of the term bill which is not due until July 20th.

I hope Papa got my letter & that he is stronger and more cheerful. I will write him more often now. Give my best love to him & tell him I did well on my work. Also give my kindest regards to Fred & Mabel & Frank—each of whom I shall write as soon as I get settled.

I hope this letter finds one of your own on the way.

Affectionately your son

TOM.

I will make some sort of arrangement with the Buckingham people for the forwarding of my mail.

P. S. Tom suggests this line in my handwriting to remind you that I am not only living but (as I think) very much alive. Therefore favor me with more than a line. H. A. W.[1]

---

[1] Henry A. Westall wrote this postscript.

42 KIRKLAND ST.

CAMBRIDGE, MASS.

(Envelope dated 7/15/21)

DEAR MAMA: I got your letter and Fred's last week and was overjoyed to hear from you. Of course the day before you wrote I registered at the Harvard Summer School and am now at work on my summer's course. I am also working on my long play which I hope to complete by the end of the session. My efforts to find a job were fruitless. At one time I thought I almost had a job as iceman for one of the Cambridge ice concerns. When the summer session closes Aug. 13 I will try again.

I am glad you like my report but disgusted that they should have sent in the report 'abs. on exam' for one course. I did perhaps my best work of the year in that course,—so good was my thesis, in fact, that the professor told me it was one in a 1000 and that I ought to lose no time in completing my training for teaching. I had no intention of teaching but his praise pleased me nevertheless. The thesis was the whole thing, the examination was merely nominal. The exam came in the morning. I thought it came in the afternoon and missed it. The professor at once went to the college office and tried to give me a special exam but they forbade it until the proper time. I will have to wait for my exam but when I do take it I am confident of an A on the course. That is my grade on the thesis.

My fee for registration at Summer School was $25.00 I am now staying at 42 Kirkland St, have a nice room with linen and bedclothes furnished which costs $4.00 a week. I am taking a complete course in English history this summer and when you consider that I have only five weeks in which to cover the whole field of Eng. history it will be seen that this keeps me busy. There is a reading list of twenty-four text books for the five weeks course—five books a week.

I think I wrote you in my last letter that my term bill for the last term falls due on July 20. This term bill amounts to $191. I am going around tomorrow to try to get an extension to Aug. or Sept. on it.

The heat up here is terrific. We have nothing at home to compare with it. The temp. itself is not so high; it doesn't go above 93° but the humidity is at times 20° to 30° above normal which causes great suffering and prostration among the poor people in the crowded districts. Today has been one of the worst.

The work I am doing this summer places me within a half course of my masters degree and leaves the way open to undivided work on my playwriting next year if I can arrange to return.

It seems, indeed, as you say, a long time since I was home but I can assure you that the passing months don't take me further from home in my thoughts but bring me closer to it.

I am troubled at your acc't of your sickness and hope by now you have found relief. Even the heat in Boston and Camb. is nothing when compared to the heat you endure in your kitchen but I hope you are not staying there so much this summer.

Dr. Greenlaw,[1] one of my best friends, from Chapel Hill, is teaching here this summer and has invited me out to lunch with him. Camb, as a whole, however, is now a lonely and deserted place.

I shall look forward to an early letter from you.

With much love

Your son

Tom

---

[1] Dr. Edwin Greenlaw, Chairman of the Department of English at the University of North Carolina while Tom was there, was praised by Tom as one of his two greatest teachers; the other was Horace Williams, who headed the Department of Philosophy at the University.

Aug., 1921

DEAR MAMA: If you're trying to hold out until I write you again you have the victory and I wish you joy of it! I have been under the weather here lately, several misfortunes conspiring to attack me at once so that I was simultaneously attacked by a cold, an upset stomach, a strained ankle and a boil on my heel that made walking unbearable; it seemed that all the afflictions of Job descended in a cloud upon me and I fear I bore them with nothing like his patience.

However I have recovered in part at least from my ailments.

As September advances I find myself puzzled as to my course. Since the Summer School closed in the middle of August I have done nothing. I must soon leave my present quarters at 42 Kirkland St as these rooms are all leased for next year.

It distresses me to know that I have been idle since summer school closed but I assure you I have for once in my life practiced a rigid economy since then. I have literally spent no money except for food & room,—not even for laundry,—I have gone nowhere and seen no one, with . . . [*The following page is lost.*] of my life to push me a little further toward the dim goal I seek.

If my beautiful dreams were to come true I would return home like a hero having justified myself but if, please God, they do not come true, I believe you would still want . . . [*The fragment ends here. Ed.*]

CAMBRIDGE, MASS

Sept 19 1921

DEAR MAMA: I have waited from day to day for some answer to my special delivery letter. Your last letter is five weeks old. In three and a half months I have heard twice from you. I wrote repeatedly at the beginning of the summer before I could get an answer. You are the only one who ever writes me from home now and you have about deserted me. I am deeply sensible to my obligation to you and to your generosity but how am I to interpret your failure to write me?

If I should get sick now it would hurt me more to hear from you than not to hear from you because I'm no believer in that kind of affection which remembers itself only in time of sickness or death.

Two weeks from today I will be twenty one years old—legally the beginning of manhood. If the time has come for me to go out on my own, so be it, but please try not to treat me with the indifference while I am alone and far away that has characterized your correspondence, or lack of it, for the last year. You would not be intentionally guilty of cruelty to me but unintentionally you have been. Uncle Henry says it is a family trait to forget once out of sight—but how in God's name can I believe you would forget me in a year's time.

You didn't want me at home, you said nothing about my returning and I shall see that your desires and those of the family are satisfied. You spoke in your letter of coming up here in September. Since then you haven't seen fit to inform me if you were coming, the date of your arrival, or any of your plans. I am being put out of my room here Thursday—it is leased for next year. I have nowhere to go. I have heard nothing from you. You are the only one with whom I can discuss my plans and you have denied me even that connection. I cannot, I will not write more. I am too deeply stirred, too grieved and disillusioned to add anything to what I have written.

I am no gold-digger, no parasite. I have had more than the others but I won't deprive them of a single penny. I never took sides in our family. I never took part in that wretched factionalism, the pairing off into. . . . [*The fragment ends here.* Ed.]

CAMBRIDGE, MASS.

Dec 1921

MY DEAR MOTHER: For ten days or more I have had hardly a minute I could call my own. My work has been heavy this fall and in addition I have lately been freed to attend the rehearsals of a play Mr. Baker is giving which will be over tonight. The Xmas holidays start Wed. afternoon and I'll be going at a clip up to that time. I'm going to work steadily through the holidays but I hope to get a couple of days off to rest. I am enclosing a couple of checks returned to me by the Harvard Cooperative Society which the Wachovia Bank had turned down, saying the account was a savings account, not a checking account. I paid the Society the $15.00 out of your last check, having already paid $50.00 for tuition to the University. This left $35.00, ten of which was spent in typing a one act play I have written for Mr. Baker, which is the best work I've ever done. He told the class it had done in one act what he had seen three act plays fail to do and he told me afterwards he was proud of it. He is the greatest authority on drama in America and in the last six years he has developed in this class some of the best dramatists in the country, several of whom have plays on Broadway now. I was in the depths of despair at the time but his talk has lifted me up again. He told me two days ago to revise the play Xmas and said he would put it into rehearsal here in the Spring. Don't spread this news but it has made me very happy. I believe I'll be able to do real work to be talked about when I'm twenty five years old. I have suffered a lot by myself on account of my youth in a class of mature men but I've got something to say in my plays. I believe that most of them haven't. At least one of them told me that and it made me walk on air. I'm sending you the two checks —I don't know how my account stands—I've drawn in all about $60 from the Central—but on the Wachovia only 35 or 40 I think. I don't know if the rest of those are coming back or not. Will you find out how it stands. I'm afraid to write any checks. I haven't seen Aunt Laura since Thanksgiving but I have an invitation to go to their house on Christmas Day. She has been good to me but she gives me so many learned lectures on the Westalls and family characteristics, and so on, that I'm a little fed up on her fare. I'm going to get over to Boston Monday and send all of you a few little trinkets for Christmas. I'll feel better over it. And now, my dear mother, let me wish you all a happy and a prosperous Christmas, free from the cares that have beset us. You needn't worry about me for work is an antidote for lonesomeness, I find, and I hope the future results of what I am doing will prove commensurate to your kindness and generosity to me.

I have a long letter to Fred written and am preparing one for Mabel. I enclose a note for Papa.

Affectionately Your Son,

THOS WOLFE

P.S. I am well, altho a little bilious lately. Let me beg you again not to make a draft horse out of yourself and to take good care of your health.

TOM

P.S. At the P. O. I find I have forgotten to enclose (or bring along) the checks. Will send later.

CAMBRIDGE, MASS.

Friday Dec 1 1922

DEAR MAMA: I hoped to get the letter off in time to reach you for Thanksgiving but it was not finished in time so I am writing you once again today. I hope you all had a nice day together. I spent the day at Professor Baker's and fared extremely well on turkey, cranberry sauce, and all the rest. Thanksgiving is first of all a New England holiday, you know. We went to the theatre in the evening. The only thing to interfere with my complete enjoyment was a heavy chest cold from which I am just recovering.

I was very glad to hear of your success with the Bryan Knoll lots.[1] It is, perhaps, better that you didn't sell them all, since the market may be better in the spring. It's too bad, of course, about Murray, but you seem to be fully secured. Did the Jews ever buy the Murdock avenue lot?

I am glad to hear of your proposed trip to Florida but am sorry it takes you in the opposite direction. Perhaps you could stand it here for a short time, tho the climate here can be about as disagreeable as any I know of.

We had our first snow of the year the other day, followed by some cold weather. Result, an epidemic of colds like my own.

I have finished the prolog and first act of my play and he liked them very much. I am now at work on the second act and intend to finish the whole three by Christmas.

I hope you are keeping the house warm, or that part in which you live, and that your clothes are warm, and that you get enough to eat. The O.K.H.[2] is not an ideal place for a winter

---

[1] Bryan Knoll lots was the name Mrs. Wolfe gave to real estate she purchased that spring from William Jennings Bryan.

[2] The Old Kentucky Home, Mrs. Wolfe's boarding house at 48 Spruce Street, in Asheville, N. C.

resort. I think you are right in holding on to it. It should be worth much more some day.

I have looked for my books and even chased around to all the freight depots here and in Boston but they haven't appeared yet.

Uncle Henry and Aunt Laura continue to get along like two cooing doves. They send their love. I see them ever so often. The last time I was out Harold[1] appeared. He is the enormous fat son, unmarried, who works in the post office. God save us! if all the peculiarities of Elmer,[2] Bacchus,[3] and Uncle Henry, were rolled into one they would fail to produce such an effect.

He was a guest to dinner, and brought his own bread, which he had purchased at a baker's shop. Where do they get their strange notions about food? Uncle Henry has it too. At any rate, they've been good to me. Remember that about them.

Don't give Effie Wolfe[4] the Harvard Classics book. I didn't steal it from her; I stole it from a friend,—at Chapel Hill. If I'm not mistaken it is a volume of chronicles—Froissart, Malory, Holinshed. The owner was John Aycock,[5]—son of our former governor. What I did with hers, if I ever had it, and I suppose I did have it, I do not know. Tell her I will return it as soon as she returns the DeMaupassant she got from Mabel. At any rate, if it's not her book it will not help her if she has the whole set.

I'm glad you're buying the Classics. They're beautiful books, and well selected. Last night (Thanksgiving) Prof. Baker took me down to see The Beggar's Opera—the first musical comedy—written in 1728 by Mr. John Gay, of London. We went back

[1] Harold Westall, Tom's cousin, son of Mr. and Mrs. H. A. Westall.
[2] Elmer Capan Westall, Mrs. Wolfe's brother, a lumber dealer in Asheville, N. C.
[3] Bacchus Westall, Mrs. Wolfe's paternal uncle.
[4] Effie Wolfe, the wife of W. O. Wolfe, Jr., a son of Wesley Wolfe, Tom's father's brother.
[5] A student at the University of North Carolina.

after the show and met the company—rosy faced English girls all the way from London. They were very nice and pleasant, and the show is amusing and tuneful, far more so than our modern musical shows.

Please write and let me know the state of things, and of your health. Love and best wishes to you all.

Your son,

Tom

CAMBRIDGE

Thursday, Jan. 4, 1923

DEAR MAMA: I got your letter this morning and am very much worried about your cold. Please avoid any recurrence of such trouble as you had a few weeks ago. Keep warm, and eat enough good food. I hope you are escaping most of the weather we are getting here now. It started to snow yesterday afternoon and this morning over a foot has fallen. I bought a pair of rubbers during the holidays (for 95 cents) and I'm wearing them. I've been trying to find a big pair of arctic overshoes which I bought last year and I can't find them among my belongings. Will you look around and see if I left them home. They are big heavy overshoes with iron buckles and completely cover your shoes. If you find them send them right along to me. The snow is very beautiful today but I know it will be terrible when it melts. We had another foot of snow during the holidays but this is deeper.

Thanks for the clipping. I saw Mr Koch when he was here and we sat up and talked until two o'clock in the morning.

I wrote Frank and Dietzie thanking them for the socks and I'm going to write Effie [1] right away.

[1] Effie, Tom's sister, now Mrs. Fred Wardlaw Gambrell, of Anderson, S. C.

Mabel's candy came somewhat crumbled up but very good. I finished another scene of the play during the holiday but read most of the time. I'm going to finish at least three this year and pray each night that out of that number one will find its way in New York. If I could only have a moderate success now— a three or four month run—it would make a man of me. It's the greatest art in the world—above painting, sculpture and novel writing—because it's so heartbreaking.

Professor Baker's secretary, Miss Munroe, made me a present of a Corona typewriter this morning. She refused either to rent or sell it but gave it to me outright and I'm going to do my typing from now on and try to save on typing. I'll have to learn sometime and its better now.

I went down town Sunday night and saw the crowds usher the New Year in. Everyone seemed happy, there was much noise and shouting, but, homehow, the coming of the New Year always brings sadness to me:—I don't know why. Man is such a mortal, perishable creature, and it seems a little like flaunting the news in his face that he has one less year before he too is dust, with tree roots twined among his bones.

There is something sad and terrifying about big families—I think often of my childhood lately: of those warm hours in bed of winter mornings; of the first ringing of the Orange St. bell; of Papa's big voice shouting from the foot of the stair "Get up, boy," then of the rush down stairs like a cold rabbit with all my clothes and underwear in my arms. As I go through the cold dining room I can hear the cheerful roar of the big fire he always had kindled in the sitting room. And we dressed by the warmth of that fire. Then breakfast—oatmeal, and sausages, eggs, hot coffee, and you putting away a couple of thick meat sandwiches in a paper bag. Then the final rush for school with Ben or

Fred, and the long run up the Central Avenue hill with one of them pulling or pushing me along.

There is great sadness in knowing you can never recall the scene except the memory; even if all were here you could not bring it back.

Sometimes Ben and Papa seem so far away, one wonders if it were a dream. Again, they come back as vividly as if I had seen them yesterday. Each tone of their voice, each peculiarity of their expression is engraved upon my mind—yet it seems strange that it all could have happened to me, that I was a part of it. Some day I expect to wake up and find my whole life has been a dream. I think we all feel this:

"We are such stuff as dreams are made on and our little life
    Is rounded with a sleep"

We soak our bread in tears and swallow it in bitterness. It seems incredible to think that flesh that once I touched, that held me on its knees, that gave me gifts and spoke to me in tones different from those of anyone else, is now unrecognizably corrupted in the earth.

These things may happen to others and we believe them; they happen to us and we believe them—never!

Yet somehow, in spite of all the stern persuadings of my reason, in spite of the inexorable and undeniable spectacle of universal death, I will fear no evil. Almost, I am tempted to say, I will believe in God, yes, in spite of the church and the ministers.

Please let me hear from you at once and take all kinds of care of yourself. I am well and working steadily on my play.

Your son

TOM

CAMBRIDGE, MASS.

Jan. 14, 1923

DEAR MAMA: I got your card from Miami and was very much surprised at your sudden departure from home, but very much pleased to know you had done the most sensible thing. At least you can now be free from colds and damps; the trouble with a severe cold such as you had early in the winter is that it hangs on doggedly from month to month, and with the variable temperatures at Asheville, this makes recovery difficult.

This is the most severe winter we have yet known. I read the other day that New England has thus far had twenty-four snows this winter. We have had two falls recently of more than a foot each. At one time with eighteen inches on the ground a hard rain began and continued long enough to convert this fall to a wet mush; it then grew cold, froze, and was in turn covered by another foot of snow.

It is a pretty, blue-skyed day, on which I write this, but I doubt very much if we see our Mother Earth before spring.

Mabel's card came this morning; she says she will return Feb., but I earnestly hope you will see the winter through, that is, until March 15th. The gain to your health and to your general well-being will be infinite. The difficulty people who work hard have to overcome is that of learning how to rest; unimagined and nameless fears that things aren't going right oppress them; they hurry home and find, of course, that affairs are exactly as they left them. I am sure you will find Asheville, the lots in Grove Park, and the O. K. H. in exactly the same places whether you return now, or wait until mid-March. Neither do I feel your presence at home will boost the price of Asheville real estate; surely it will be more pleasant to wait and return to find your property doubled in value.

I got the books; the express was $6.08 but I know it was the only available way of sending them. I am very glad to have them; it gives me a great feeling of security and comfort to have them. I love books, I believe, even more than I love girls. For I grow tired of girls; I leave them one by one never to return; but I never leave my books, they are the genii and magicians ready to be called forth to do my bidding at any time. I haven't visited a girl by the way since New Years, and a month before that.

I read or write steadily: I will read my complete play to class Wed (day after to-morrow) and will let you know their opinion then. I have spared neither myself nor that of which I wrote:— in a sense I feel I have expressed dramatically the modern South: what will be the merits of the play [1] I cannot attempt to say.

Please let me hear from you soon and I hope you will make no hasty and ill-considered return home.

I am well and have gained slightly in weight. Please watch over your own health and take all possible action to secure your comfort

Affectionately   Your Son,

Tom

(March 31, 1923)

DEAR MAMA: I am very, very sorry I have delayed so long in sending you an answer to your postal which you sent to me from Spartanburg, en route to Miami. I am sending this letter to Asheville, on the guess that you will have probably returned by the time it gets there. I hope your business ventures in Florida real-estate have turned out profitably. I have no doubt of your great financial ability; I sometimes wonder why you gave me so

[1] *The Mountains.*

little of it. I think if I had money of my own to invest I would rather let you handle it than deal with it myself. I have started a letter to you twice, but have never finished either. My play goes on here May 15 and I've been terribly rushed. It's the most ambitious thing—in size, at any rate—the Workshop has ever attempted: there are ten scenes, over thirty people, and seven changes of setting.

Mama: get down and pray for me. Prof. Baker is having Richard Herndon, the New York producer, up here to see the play when it goes on. Of course this means nothing more than that he's sufficiently interested to come and look it over with an eye to New York production.

As I may have told you Mr. Herndon is the man who gives the prize every year for the best play written in the Workshop. The prize is small, $500, but it carries with it a contract for a New York production within six months.

Last year's prize-winning play, a comedy named "You and I" was put on at the Belmont Theatre six weeks ago and is a hit. Herndon told Baker in New York last week that the play ought to run through hot weather:—that is to September or later. This means over 30 weeks for Philip Barry the author, and his royalties are at present about $700 a week. The contract reads that the movie rights are split equally between producer and author: they average around $15,000—so young Barry—he is three or four years older than I am—stands to make a tidy little fortune.

Of course I'm going to enter my play which is in the competition on which I'm now at work. Baker has heard the first act of the second play and says it has an "epic touch." Two plays are as much as any one is allowed to enter. I try not to build my hopes too high, but I can't help feeling I've more than a good chance.

I won't talk more about my play: I only know that it's the best

I've ever done, and that I've [*paper torn*] myself as an artist. [*paper torn*] no one in this country writing the plays I want to write! I feel the sap rising in me, I cannot with all humility, help but feel that the thing is bound to come, and come with a rush when it does.

I am a slave to the thing; my mind is filled with it night and day. I find I have become an eavesdropper, I listen to every conversation I hear, I memorize every word I hear people say, in the way they said it. I find myself studying every move, every gesture, every expression, trying to see what it means dramatically. It's impossible to be a dramatist and a gentleman; I gave it up long ago. Well, there are lots of gentlemen—only a very few dramatists.

Mama, in the name of God, guard Papa's letters to me with your life. Get them all together and watch them like a hawk. I don't know why I saved them but I thank my stars now that I did. There has never been anybody like Papa. I mean to say that all in all, he is the most unique human being I have ever known. I am convinced there is nobody in America today anywhere like him. When I am on the streets of this city, among the crowds, I try to burn myself into the "innards" of everyone I see, I listen in on everything I hear, I get their way of talking and looking, and, you know, the amazing thing, is how much alike, [*page torn*] commonplace, and unin- [*page torn*] most people are. With what I know now about them I am convinced that if I had never known my father, and that if one day on Washington Street, Boston, I had passed him, talking to someone, gesturing with his big hands, denouncing the Democratic party, wetting his thumb every now and then on his mouth—I say, if I saw this man, wholly absorbed in his conversation, seeing no one on either side of him, I would turn [*page torn*] and try to

find out [*page torn*] about him. So, for [*page torn*] sake save
those letters, and add to them any of your own you may have.
He is headed straight not for one of my plays, but for a series.
He dramatized his emotions to a greater extent than anyone I
have ever known—consider his expression of 'merciful God'—his
habit of talking to himself *at* or *against* an imaginary opponent.
Save those letters. They are written in his exact conversational
tone: I won't have to create imaginary language out of my own
brain—I verily believe I can re-create a character that will knock
the hearts out of people by its reality.

But I must break off here. I am just recovering from a severe
cold,—the second in this damnable, accursed, misbegotten winter. March came in like a lion; it is going out like a sabre-
toothed tiger. A day or two ago all past or present N.E. weather
records for this season were broken when the mercury here fell
to 2°. In Maine it went to − 12°. Today is still cold—but much
better, there is a high wind. I am through most of it now save for
a little cough.

Prosperity and health and success attend you all, and aid me
in your thoughts.

Say nothing about the new business: there will be time to talk
if anything comes of it. I have six weeks before the production;
they will be the busiest of my life, and I may come in this summer on a shutter but the God of my Grandmother—the nice old
gentleman with the long whiskers—has so far been good to me.
Love and prosperity again to you all.

Your Aff. Son

Tom

2 P.M. 21 Trowbridge March 31, '23
P.S. I am busy revising and condensing my first play: the one
that is to be produced. The scene designers already have descrip-

tions of the seven sets: Baker is announcing a set competition this week. He starts rehearsals April 22 and from then on—slavery, slavery, slavery!

May 1923

DEAR MAMA: I am sorry I have been so remiss in writing you but my time has been packed for three months now with my play [1] and its aftermath. I went to New Hampshire with Prof Baker last week after my play. We had a good time up at his Silver Lake Home and I got a day's rest. He wants me to go up there June 1 and finish writing my new play but I think I'll be here until June 15 since I need the library. Prof Baker wants me to send my play to the New York Theatre Guild.

He said he thought it had a much better chance of success than "The Adding Machine"—a play, like mine, written in scenes which went off in New York last week after 3 months run. Of course if I could only get a 3 mos. run I would make from eight to ten thousand dollars and be on my feet. If I could do this I would go to Germany in the Fall where I could live for one-quarter what it costs here.

I met a man the other day who lived last year in Munich and bought a house there for $50. He was living on the fat of the land, had a two room apartment for which he paid $1.00 a month and though living in princely fashion spent only $7.50 a week.

Of course the German mark is shot to pieces—you get now over 50,000 for a dollar.

It is terrible for the Germans—poor people—but fortunate for us. I was talking this morning to Prof. Langfeld of the psy-

[1] A play entitled *Welcome to Our City* which barely failed of production in New York, after a successful showing at Harvard's 47 Workshop.

chology department who is going to be in Berlin this summer
and who lived there for 7 years. He is a great admirer of the
Germans, thinks them far superior in every way to the French,
and a race which can't be crushed. The terrible things of the
war he called Prussianism—the work of a few autocrats—but the
people are kind, intelligent, artistic and friendly—a great race.

Of course, some of the most interesting things in the theatre
are being done in Germany—where our laboring people and
middle-class are going to see Bill Hart shoot 17 bad men, or
C. Chaplin throw a custard pie, or Norma Talmadge in "Passion's
Plaything," Germans with not enough to keep food in their
mouths are saving their pennies to see Faust performed or
Wagner's operas. If I sell one of my plays, I say, I shall do this.
Prof Baker is in New York to-day. He is going to see the
Theatre Guild in my behalf. He is a wonderful friend and he
believes in me. I know this now: I am inevitable. I sincerely
believe the only thing that can stop me now is insanity, disease,
or death. The plays I am going to write may not be suited to the
tender bellies of old maids, sweet young girls, or Baptist Ministers but they will be true and honest and courageous, and the
rest doesn't matter. If my play goes on I want you to be prepared
for execrations upon my head. I have stepped on toes right and
left—I spared Boston with its nigger-sentimentalists no more than
the South, which I love, but which I am nevertheless pounding.
I am not interested in writing what our pot-bellied members of
the Rotary and Kiwanis call a "good show"—I want to know life
and understand it and interpret it without fear or favor. This, I
feel is a man's work and worthy of a man's dignity. For life is
not made up of sugary, sticky, sickening Edgar A. Guest senti-
mentality, it is not made up of dishonest optimism, God is *not*
always in his Heaven, all is *not* always right with the world. It is

not all bad, but it is not all good, it is not all ugly, but it is not all beautiful, it is life, life, life—the only thing that matters. It is savage, cruel, kind, noble, passionate, selfish, generous, stupid, ugly, beautiful, painful, joyous,—it is all these, and more, and it's all these I want to know and, by God, I shall, though they crucify me for it. I will go to the ends of the earth to find it, to understand it, I will know this country when I am through as I know the palm of my hand, and I will put it on paper, and make it true and beautiful.

I will step on toes, I will not hesitate to say what I think of those people who shout "Progress, Progress, Progress"—when what they mean is more Ford automobiles, more Rotary Clubs, more Baptist Ladies Social unions. I will say that "Greater Asheville" does not necessarily mean "100,000 by 1930," that we are not necessarily 4 times as civilized as our grandfathers because we go four times as fast in automobiles, because our buildings are four times as tall. What I shall try to get into their dusty little pint-measure minds is that a full belly, a good automobile, paved streets, and so on, do not make them one whit better or finer,— that there is beauty in this world,—beauty even in this wilderness of ugliness and provincialism that is at present our country, beauty and spirit which will make us men instead of cheap Board of Trade Boosters, and blatant pamphleteers. I shall try to impress upon their little craniums that one does not have to be a "highbrow" or "queer" or "impractical" to know these things, to love them, and to realize they are our common heritage, there for us all to possess and make a part of us. In the name of God, let us learn to be men, not monkies.

When I speak of beauty I do not mean a movie close-up where Susie and Johnnie meet at the end and clinch and all the gum-chewing ladies go home thinking husband is not so good a lover as Valentino. That's cheap and vulgar. I mean everything which is lovely, and noble, and true. It does not have to be sweet, it may be bitter, it does not have to be joyous, it may be sad.

When Spring comes I think of a cool, narrow back yard in North Carolina with green, damp earth, and cherry trees in blossom. I think of a skinny little boy at the top of one of those trees, with the fragrant blooms about him, with the tang of the sap in his nose, looking out on a world of back yards, and building his Castles in Spain. That's beauty, that's romance. I think of an old man [1] in the grip of a terrible disease, who thought he was afraid to die, but who died like a warrior in an epic poem. That's beauty. I think of a boy [2] of twenty-six years heaving his life away, and gasping to regain it, I think of the frightened glare in his eyes and the way he seizes my hands, and cries "What have you come home for." I think of the lie that trembles in my throat. I think of a woman who sits with a face as white and set as if cut from marble, and whose fingers can not be unclasped from his hand. And the boy of eighteen sees and knows for the first time that more than a son is dying, that part of a mother is being buried before her,—life in death, that something which she nursed and loved, something out of her blood, out of her life, is taken away. It's terrible but it's beautiful. I think of the devotion of a woman of frail physique to a father, I think of the daisy meadows on the way to Craggy Mountain, [3] of the birch forests of New Hampshire, of the Missisippi River at Memphis—of all of which I have been a part—and I know

[1] This refers to Tom's father, whose illness and death are recorded in *Of Time and the River*.

[2] The reference is to Tom's brother Ben whose death from pneumonia is recounted in *Look Homeward Angel*.

[3] A favorite place for picnics near Asheville, N. C.

there is nothing so commonplace, so dull, that is not touched with nobility and dignity. And I intend to wreak out my soul on paper and express it all. This is what my life means to me: I am at the mercy of this thing and I will do it or die. I never forget; I have never forgotten. I have tried to make myself conscious of the whole of my life since first the baby in the basket became conscious of the warm sunlight on the porch, and saw his sister go up the hill to the girl's school on the corner (the first thing I remember). Slowly out of the world of infant darkness things take shape, the big terrifying faces become familiar,—I recognize my father by his bristly moustache. Then the animal books and the Mother Goose poetry which I memorize before I can read, and recite for the benefit of admiring neighbors every night, holding my book upside down. I become conscious of Santa Claus and send scrawls up the chimney. Then St. Louis.[1] A flight of stairs at the Cincinnati rail road station which must be gone up,—the World's Fair, the Ferris Wheel, Grover at the Inside Inn, the Delmar Gardens where you let me taste beer which I spit out, a ride on a bus-automobile—over the Fair Grounds with Effie—it is raining, raining—the Cascades in the rain—a ride in the scenic railway—scared at the darkness and the hideous faces—eating a peach in the back yard (St. Louis)—I swallow a fly and am sick—and one of my brothers laughs at me. Two little boys who ride tricycles up and down the street— they dress in white and look alike—their father injured or killed in elevator accident (wasn't he)—I "commit a nuisance" on the narrow step of side yard and the policeman sees me and reports me—the smell of tea at the East India House—I'll never forget

[1] Because of the opening of the World's Fair in St. Louis in 1904, Mrs. Wolfe took all her children there and conducted a rooming house at Fairmount and Academy Streets called The Carolina House.

it—Grover's [1] sickness and death—I am wakened at midnight by Mabel and she says "Grover's on the cooling board." I don't know what a cooling board is but am curious to see. I don't know what death is but have a vague, terrified sensation that something awful has happened—then she takes me in her arms and up the hall.—Disappointed at the cooling board—it's only a table—the brown mole on his neck—the trip home—visitors in the parlor with condolences—Norah Israel [2] was there—Then it gets fairly plain thereafter, and I can trace it step by step.

This is why I think I'm going to be an artist. The things that really mattered sunk in and left their mark. Sometimes only a word—sometimes a peculiar smile—sometimes death—sometimes the smell of dandelions in Spring—once Love. Most people have little more mind than brutes: they live from day to day. I will go everywhere and see everything. I will meet all the people I can. I will think all the thoughts, feel all the emotions I am able, and I will write, write, write.

I won't say whether my play was good or bad. Some people in the staid Workshop Audience were shocked, most were enthusiastic, and a great many said it was the best play written here. Good or bad, win or lose, [*The fragment ends here—Ed.*]

NEW YORK, N. Y.
June 9, 1923

DEAR MAMA: I am writing you in haste from Pleasantville New York, 25 miles from the City. I am down here with George

[1] Grover, Ben's twin, came down with typhoid and died on November 16th. The events of this summer are recorded in *Look Homeward Angel* and Grover's death is also the basis of a story, "The Lost Boy," contained in *The Hills Beyond*, published by Harper & Bros., New York.

[2] A neighbor, and mother of one of Tom's childhood playmates.

Wallis a graduate student of Harvard, who drove me down here yesterday from Boston. I had my examination—only one—on Wednesday, and being dead tired from that and the play I accepted his invitation. We are staying at the home of George's friend, Hal Duble, here at Pleasantville, in beautiful Westchester county. George is down here buying a house: he intends to live here and write. He is married and has two boys. Duble, who runs an advertising agency in New York, is married and has three fine children. My trip is costing me nothing—I will be here for three days in all. We then go back to Cambridge where I am writing my second play and touching up the first. I enclose without further comment a letter from the New York Theatre Guild. They are the greatest play producers in America and if my play gets done I would rather they would do it than anyone. I must shorten it to the usual two and a half hours before I send it to them. Please say nothing about this. It means merely that the play has been recommended to them and they are interested in it. If I don't sell this one I'll sell the one I'm on now.

Baker thinks I'll sell it, however. He says it's a better play than the last they put on and ought to have a greater popular success. Their last play was "The Adding Machine." They are now doing Shaw's "Devil's Disciple."

Prof. Baker thinks if I gave my name a German or a Russian ending the Guild would take the play in a minute. Most of their plays come from Europe. Please have hope and pray for me. In my valise is a twenty page letter which I wrote you before I left Cambridge in a heat of excitement and enthusiasm. But I won't send it: this is calmer and more temperate. I know this, however. No one in this country is writing plays like mine. Good or bad, they're my own. The play the letter refers to may or may not win success but it's the only honest, sincere play that has ever been written about the South. I know for I've read all the rest.

I will be at work in Cambridge when I go back until the latter part of this month. Then I'm going to try to peddle my two plays in New York—sending the first to the Guild as requested. Please say nothing and have hopes that I will yet crash through. I think I am inevitable. I believe nothing can stop me now but insanity, disease, or death. These are human risks. I am in full bud and this thing inside me is growing beyond control. I don't know yet what I am capable of doing but, by God, I have genius and I shall yet force the inescapable fact down the throats of the rats and vermin who wait the proof. Well, they shall have it, and may they choke upon it.

Let who will call it conceit:—I will do it or die in the proof. Nothing else matters to me now; the world's my oyster and I will open and know the whole of it.

I am tired and overwrought but this trip is putting me straight. Keep this letter for yourself: it contains matter that concerns you and me chiefly, and let me hear from you when you are able.

If I sell my play I am going to Germany and the continent for 10 months. When I come back I train my big guns. With all my love and affection, I am

Faithfully your son
Tom.

[From post card enclosed in letter]

I wrote the letter last night in Pleasantville and was a little inspired, I'm afraid, by some of Hal Duble's home-made wine. However I've read it over and I think I'll let it stand on the whole. I'm in earnest about the plays. One of them, I feel, I know,—is going to be sold. I'm sending you this from New York. I came in this morning and have spent the day at the Metropolitan Art Museum. It is glorious, wonderful, beautiful. I find my 3 days have cost me less than $8.00 including food, and that costs in Cambridge. So it hasn't been a bad trip.

Baker took me to New Hampshire for a day the week after the play. Outside that I've stuck to Cambridge the whole year. I go back to Pleasantville tonight with George— We spend tomorrow—Sunday, there and drive back to Boston Monday. Am sending this special so it will go faster.

Love to you all—

TOM

[Post Card]

PORTLAND, MAINE
Aug. 4, 1923

DEAR MAMA: I'm on my way to visit my friend Henry Carlton at Madison, New Hampshire about 3 miles from Prof. Baker's. I've finished two acts of new play and have revised the other which I'm sending to Theatre Guild this week as they asked. I'll write you at length from Madison.

TOM

NEW YORK CITY
Aug. 31, 1923

DEAR MAMA:

I am writing you from the Remington Typewriter Agency on Lower Broadway, New York. I had to have my play retyped, as the old copy I had was a very bad carbon, and I had done much revising in pencil. I am busily at it and giving it to the Theatre Guild tomorrow or Monday—Monday I expect. Tomorrow is the 1st and I believe Labor Day. After that I am going down to the docks and try to find employment on an ocean-goer—preferably to England for the time, until I can hear from the play. I am daily more conscious of my debt to you, and it preys on my mind. At the present time I could stand the loss of anything except what faith you may have in me. I asked Professor Baker to write to you concerning me and I hope he has done this. I wanted it done because he is not given to enthusiasm, and I know he will give you a sober, straight-forward account. Everything I have is staked on this play and of course when you consider how many people are writing plays it seems a long, long chance. I dare not think of failure. What I want—what would satisfy me—seems so little. If my play were not wonderful—if it were put on and ran for only six or eight weeks—it would be enough to start me.

I can offer no excuse for having sold no plays before this, but I do submit this to your consideration: A young man in any other profession would be earning a salary—would have achieved some financial reward ere this—here, your heart is broken over and over, but once successful the rewards are usually swift and large.

This great town roars around me in a never-ending pageant of glitter, show, false-front, and vulgar wealth. Women—cheap, vulgar women, the parvenu wives of soap manufacturers, usurers, grafters, politicians, hog-butchers, and God knows what else, put thousands on their backs, while the artists, the poet, the man with a mind, sensitive to beauty and nobility, longs in vain for a few of the wonderful books displayed in the windows. It seems at times that this pushing, boosting, trading, manufacturing, buying and selling American civilization will not be content until it has destroyed its artists—and when it does God help it, for no society can survive without them. All that lives of Greece is a few great poems, a few great books, a few great pieces of architecture and sculpture. All that lives of Egypt is a few great temples, half-sunken in the desert. These are the lasting and eternal things. What will remain of a civilization that reverences a man above all the poets because he can make a cheap automobile at $500 each? Perhaps God, as is some times the case, will become bored with these foolish little men, and their foolish little skyscrapers and flivvers—factories—and erase them, out of simple mercy.

Of course when you begin to talk to these people of Greece and Egypt they will wink at each other and snigger behind their hands, and nudge each other. They will even call you "imprac-tical"—the crowning curse of all. Yet, I know of nothing more practical than profiting by what the past has to teach us, and one thing it does teach us is that if man lives for bread alone—his social order is doomed. If they only knew more history they would perhaps be shocked to know how similar in many respects was Rome in its decline, to this country. There was the same vulgar display of wealth, the same vulgar waste, the same wor-ships of cheap, low, trivial things. The great poets of an earlier day were gone—freaks and degenerates had replaced them—the great rulers were dead—the bad Nero instead—but Rome had lasted for several hundred years, and Romans thought that Rome was eternal. Nothing could destroy it. Today we feel much the same, I think, and we have lasted hardly 150 years as yet. I do not know if you can observe it at home—possibly not—for the South is still conservative, and for the most part of undiluted stock; yet the signs of unrest up here are appalling. For one thing our constitution has perpetrated the most damable political theory ever conceived—namely that men are created equal. Now, I appeal to your judgment, to your good hard sense—did you ever see two people who were equal in any respect? In intelligence, in physical strength, in imagination, in courage, in judgment, in any of the things that help us through this tempestuous world? Furthermore, we Southerners, more than anyone else, recognize the falsity of the doctrine in practice at any rate, while defending it hypocritically in practice. Do we admit the equality of the negro? Do we give him the vote? Yet no one is better at whooping up equality than one of our quack Congressmen on the stump. It sickens you. Yet yearly we are bringing hundreds of thousands of inferior people, the Latin races, undeveloped physically, dwarfed mentally, into this country. From them we grow the American of tomorrow—"the hope of the world." It is impossible to regard them without a sinking of the heart. How can anything good come from it? I am no pessimist, but why try to side-step the facts? True ants we strut.

If you have any communication send it care of Harold Doble, c/o The Holland Advertising Agency, 244 Fifth Avenue.

I moved in from Mountain Lakes because it was too far out and cost me $2.20 a day to commute. A friend is coming in town tomorrow or Sunday and I hope to work him for a room. I feel fairly well, but, at the present, am hot and dirty. I hope you are all well and that you take care of your health, and don't overwork during the summer. I send you all my love and sincere regards.

Affectionately your son

Tom

HOTEL BELLEVUE
BOSTON
Xmas time, 1923

DEAR MAMA: I got your letter this morning and I am writing this in haste as I intend to go to Boston at five o'clock on the Fall River boat. I waited over here a few days in order to hear from you as my future address is so uncertain as to make immediate delivery of your mail improbable.

This is what I have decided to do. Several of my old Harvard friends are here in New York,—one, in particular,—a young man named *Dow*—is an instructor here at New York University—an instructor in English. He informed me recently that they would need a new man the second semester—which begins in Feb. I was unable to get in touch with Dow yesterday or today but another friend—George Nollen—who lives here—is going to get in touch with him and have him speak for me. Meanwhile I'm going up to Cambridge and get the Harvard Teacher's Bureau—which once before, you may remember, got me a job at Northwestern, to send all my letters of recommendation, and my scholastic records, and so on, to N. Y. U. If this fails, I am going to ask the Bureau to place me in New York or Chicago, if possible. It is not likely that I will get placed anywhere before late Jan. or 1st of Feb—that is, until the beginning of a new semester—and my plan is to spend the interim with Carlton[1] in New Hampshire. In that one month I can take my last fling at success in the only occupation I love—writing.

The•Guild has returned my play—but they first told me I was the best man the Workshop had yet turned out and the coming young man in the theatre. This was their play-reader, Lemon. The night I got their final decision, he took me out to dinner, and not only dined me, but wined me, with a bottle of his liquor, in order that I might not break down, I suppose. There was no danger, for I'm ready for anything now. He told me, among other things, that the Guild was afraid that I would hold this against them, and that I would not submit my other work to them. He then told me that Langner, a prominent director on

[1] Henry Carlton, a student in Professor Baker's 47 Workshop, whose play, *Down the Line* was produced in New York.

the Guild board was "crazy about my play" and wanted to see me before I left town. When we got back to his office he called Langner and *he* suggested that I come right up. Langner is a very wealthy Jew—a patent lawyer—and lives in an enormous apartment—I talked to him two hours. He told me I was a fool if I gave this play up now. He said in a week's time I could make it into a play that will sell—It needs no re-writing, he said— the stuff's all there—it needs cutting—i.e. shortening. The sum total was this: If I would go off somewhere—to the woods or the country and work a week on the play—cutting it down thirty minutes, and from ten scenes to eight, and "tightening" it up,— that is making the main thread of story, the plot, more plain in every scene,—he would handle it for me—put it before the Guild for me, and if they couldn't produce it this season, he knew other producers here that he felt would take my play and give it production. At any rate if I'd do this he'd push it for me. I had a play and a half at present—he wanted me to cut to playing time. The Guild—through Lemon—had intimated before this that they were somewhat afraid of my satire against the Northern negro, and the Northern Societies for Improving the Colored people, and the Northern sentimentalist—people who have great influence here. To Langner's credit he did not ask me to retract a thing—I can keep all this—all he wants is a shorter, simpler play. Well, I will take one more chance and give him what he wants, in spite of the fact that Professor Baker will throw up his hands and say that I have "prostituted my art," and so on, when I see him. Well, "my art" has kept me ragged, and driven me half mad; —I will see now if prostitution can put a few decent garments on my back and keep me housed. My good friends, Professor Baker included, have told me for two years now of "my great talent," "my artistry," and so on—they have told me it would be a terrible thing for me to do anything else but write. They have said "You have it—it's bound to come"—but not once has anyone given me advice on the simple little matter of keeping the breath of life in my body until the miracle does happen. That I can write better plays than most of those on Broadway I have no doubt—God help me if I can't—but to write such filthy, sexy twaddle, rot, and bunkum as this, I must cast all conscience to the winds. Well, I can and will do even that, for *money, money, money*. After all what will it matter to anyone—except myself. To the people at home? A lot they would care for "art." All they would know, and see, and care about is that my play was on Broadway. Baker will raise h—l when he hears of my decision to teach, but as I have not yet learned the secret of living exclusively on wind and water—there's no way out. My money's almost gone—I have fifteen or twenty dollars left—enough to get me to Boston or New Hampshire and the Univ. owes me a little more. I am going to try to borrow two or three hundred dollars in Boston, to buy clothing and tide me over until I get to work. If I fail in this I may have to ask you for an advance.

I forgot to tell you the best story of all. While I was at Langner's the phone rang, and Lemon, the play reader, called to ask if I was there. He then asked Langner to tell me to come back to the Guild offices when I left. I did so, wondering what it was all about. It was about ten-thirty when I got back, and Lemon asked me to have a seat, and hemmed and coughed nervously a moment. Then he said: "I know you are sensitive and proud about these things—but you mustn't be. I want you to take this—you can pay me back at any time—don't say another word."

Before I knew what he was doing he had put two five dollar bills in my palm and closed my fingers over it. I was pretty dirty, and ragged, for a fact—but I still had a $50.00 check from the University, which I showed him, telling him I wasn't quite hard up enough for a "handout." He said: "Then wait a few minutes and we'll take this ten and blow it in somewhere." So at eleven o'clock he closed his office and we went down to Greenwich Village—New York's artist colony. He found a little place there where you give three longs and one short on the door, and where they peep out at you, and let you in if they know you. It was a little place with a few tables and crazy looking people dancing about and we stayed there, and smoked, and ate, and drank, until five o'clock. He spent considerably more than his original ten, I'm afraid. I told him a great deal about myself, and I know I have at least one good friend in New York. And I have the additional satisfaction, if it be one, of knowing they believe in me. Langner, being a Jew, gave me the most practical advice of all. There are thousands of bank clerks, and real estate men everywhere making $35 or $40 a week, he said. But there aren't three people in America who are doing the same class of writing that I am. Therefore, it was a matter of pure business, artistic considerations aside, to stick to it. The best plays made the most money in the end.

I don't know where I'll be for Christmas. Perhaps in Boston or Cambridge—if my good relatives or Professor Baker invite me to share their feast—if not in New Hampshire. I shall manage to eat somewhere and get full—even if at a restaurant—but, God knows, I am still young enough to have a horror of Christmas by myself.

The meanest, most persistent cold I ever had is slowly breaking up. Otherwise I feel well. I was sorry to hear of your trouble with influenza; we seem to have encountered a minor epidemic. But I am relieved to hear you have recovered. Please keep warm; in your house that's the main thing.

Uncle Elmer hasn't appeared on the scene yet. I shall probably miss him. Perhaps that's best,—in my present condition. So meticulous a dandy as I hear he is would no doubt be shocked by such a ragamuffin as myself. As a matter of fact I almost have an aversion,—natural or unnatural, to seeing any of my old friends,—unless, by God, I know they are friends whether you bloom, or if you wither. But such people aren't friends—they are saints—and I have stopped believing in heaven. I couldn't stand Asheville now—I couldn't stand the silly little grins on the silly little drugstore faces. I couldn't stand the silly little questions of "What're you doing now?"—And the silly little "oh" and the silly little silence that follows when you say you are writing—as if they could know—stupid little vermin as they are—the tragedy, and the heartbreak, and the travail of mind and spirit—that has kept me ragged. And for what—a dream—a poem. And what do they care, in their mean little hearts for a dream or a poem? Oh I know them—know them—know them to the bottom of their base, greedy, money-loving little souls—I know how the vapid sneer will change to the fawning smile once they hear you have prospered and that it has gone well with you. If such people ask news of me,—be silent, or say that I am dead. Let me be dead to them as they are dead to me.

Meanwhile may you all prosper and grow happy, and enjoy the merriest Christmas of your lives. I will wire you greetings— it is all the plenitude of my purse will permit me to give—along towards Christmas—and let you know where I am. With great and sincere affection to you all—

TOM

P.S. I will write Frank as you suggest—I had wondered about Dietzie and am much relieved to hear he is recovering.

I am glad to hear of Frank's success, and appreciate his good wishes. He has always had mine and he ought to know that that is true of the whole family.

10 TROWBRIDGE ST
CAMBRIDGE MASS
Friday Jan 4. 1924

DEAR MAMA: I am writing this in haste and sending it to you, special delivery. I hope you will answer immediately in the same way as I must act quickly. First of all I hope you enjoyed your Christmas. I spent the day at Hilda's with Lester Bottomly, Uncle Henry and Aunt Laura, Elaine and Harold Gould, and their children. I had a very pleasant day, and a full dinner. I got your check a day or two later and this helped me to be happy. As I told you in my letter, it was likely that I might be forced to draw on your account. I got $10.00 before I left New York, and on arriving here, not knowing of your later gift, I got Uncle Henry to cash a 50.00 check out of which I purchased a suit, being in rags. I got a good suit for 35.00 and have just purchased an overcoat for 34.50 The coats I looked at were as low as 19.50, $25.85, and $29.50, but all struck me three or four inches above the knees. I also purchased a hat, shoes, and a couple of suits of underwear. I now have about $35.00 left. Everyone here, including Professor Baker, have been most cordial and have had me out several times. Prof. B. had me out to his house a few days before Christmas, where I dined, and talked over my plans with him. He said he didn't intend to let me spend the next four months as I had spent the last, and that I had to settle down and get busy writing again. He hit the ceiling over the teaching proposition and said it would never do; that it would give me no time to write and that it would perhaps impair my talent—since it is critical work, where writing is creative. I told him this might be very true but that I had no money now, and was faced with the prospect of earning my own living,—finally, that I did not intend to ask you for more support. He couldn't or wouldn't understand this, and seemed to think it was pig-headedness on my part that kept me from asking you. He said I was still developing, that I hadn't matured yet, and that what I did at this period was of critical importance. Finally he made me promise not to do anything "rash," as he expressed it, until he returned from New York. He got back a day or two ago and, as I told you, I lunched with him yesterday. What he said was substantially the same as before. I told him I knew perfectly well the conditions under which I could write best—that perhaps leisure and freedom were best—but that, unfortunately few of us can create our own conditions in this world, unless we have wealth to support them. I believed in myself, I told him, and I believed in my rapid development this next year or two, but I could not reasonably ask help from you or any other practical person unless I had something definite,—a Broadway production—to offer at that time. Not being a prophet I could not promise this. He told me again if I had not been "pig-headed"—he thinks me stubborn and self-willed—if I had taken his advice four months ago and shortened my play he thought it would be sold by now.

During the holidays my friend Geo Wallace wrote me and told me there were going to be two or three teaching vacancies at New York University in Feb, and that Dow, a former Harvard man, who knows me, and who teaches there, would speak for me and advised me to get busy through the Harvard Teacher's Bureau. If they're still open it looks as if I can have one.

I have decided to start negotiations with them tomorrow through the Bureau. I don't know what else to do. I may run up to Carlton's in New Hampshire for a few days, but not for long. I may try to shorten my play during the few weeks of grace yet left to me, as the man on the Theatre Guild desires, but, my life being so up in the air, lacking any centre and balance, as it has for the past few months, I find it hard to accomplish anything I want to write,—I have two or three new plays bottled up—but I must get some sense of security and comfort again.

I think I telegraphed you that my play has been written up in a new book on the theatre. The book's name, I believe, is the *New American Theatre,* and is written by Oliver M. Saylor, an authority on the drama. Professor Baker called my attention to it when I got here. I was blue and despondent and told him art could be damned,—that I would turn my play into a musical comedy if there was money in it. He told me I couldn't,—that he and the Workshop and myself had all been written up to-gether, and that my play was described as the "most radical experiment ever made in the American theatre," etc. If I changed it, I went back on myself publicly, and on him, and on the Workshop. He doesn't mind my cutting it—he agrees that it is too long—but he doesn't want me to change the essential structure of it. So, you see, I am getting famous as I get poor.

If I could find some benevolent old gentleman, with more money than brains to finance me; or if I could go in debt even, I think I would take the chance. But I know of no other way out; I'll have to fly in the face of Baker's opposition and take the teaching job. I feel confident of my ability to fill it capably.

I want you to write at once because I need your advice. I am staying at 10 Trowbridge St, Cambridge, just a few doors from where I was last year. Write me there.

Uncle Henry tells me he has written you. I hope you are well, and that the real-estate in Miami and Asheville continues to boom. I have more confidence in your business judgment than anyone I know, and I believe you cannot fail to make good profits on your investments. I wish I had but a gram of your shrewdness in this respect. But please watch your health and see that you are comfortably housed and fed. I send you my love.

Your Son   TOM

P.S. I have just thought that Special Del. is useless since the only address I know is "Gen'l Delivery."

HOTEL ALBERT
11th Street & University Place
New York
Feb 6, 1924

DEAR MAMA: I have heard nothing from you since I sent my telegram announcing my final decision to take the New York University offer. I came to town last Friday, Feb 1, and met Ralph Wheaton here on Saturday; he had just returned from Bermuda and had had a large time, from his account. We talked over long distance to Mabel that night, and she had been ill, she told me. She said that you, as well, had been sick, and I was distressed to hear of both your illnesses.

This is February 6, the beginning of the new term; but my classes will not begin until tomorrow. They have given me a schedule of eight hours a week, which falls on Tuesday, Thursday, and Saturday. I have a class on these days from nine to ten; another from eleven to twelve; and on Tuesday and Thursday only I have a class from four to five. This gives me Monday, Wednesday and Friday free, although there will be corrections and gradings to be made on papers. I am somewhat nervous, of course, when I think of my first appearance, but I shall do my best, and I feel that I am going to get along. I have looked around for a room, and have seen many, but nothing that suits me. Of course, I don't expect to find anything decent for less than $10 a week, and that will be small. Possibly I will have to pay as much as $12. It would open your eyes to see in what cramped conditions these people live. I am at present stopping here at the Hotel Albert,—a quiet family hotel a few blocks from the University. They have given me a rate of $12 a week on my room, and they want me to stay. A number of the University people stop here, I believe, but I am not sure I should like it as a permanent residence. If you come back from Florida soon why don't you pay me a visit? You have never been to New York, I believe; at any rate, not for a number of years, and everyone ought to come once. You could stay down here where it is quiet, but within reach of everything, and we could go over the city together.

Now is the best time, as it gets hot in summer, and you might find it disagreeable.

I draw my first wages on March 1; until then I must continue on your bounty. The die is cast, at least for seven months, and whether for ill or good, only the gods can tell. Write me here at the Albert; my room number is 2220.

Meanwhile, I hope you recover your strength and are able to be out and at your business again. I shall expect to hear from you soon after you get this; until then, I am

with much love,

Tom.

HOTEL ALBERT
11th Street & University Place
New York
Wed. March 12, 1924

[Note at top of first page]: I shall take what money is left in September and go to England.

DEAR MAMA: I have just finished reading your letter. I did not know where you were, whether to write you at Asheville or at Miami. I had a letter from Uncle Henry a day or two ago. He was somewhat concerned about you, because, when I last wrote him, you were sick in Miami. You can surely have very little winter now in Asheville. I should suppose spring would be upon you in a week or two: the year looks early. We are having a nasty spell of wet and snowy weather here, at present, but the winter has been remarkably mild. Spring comes in April.

I have settled down to the round of my work. I have about 110 in my three classes, somewhat more than I bargained for,— more than I was promised. This means I have a paper from each one once a week, which must be graded and corrected. That part of teaching is drudgery. The class work I enjoy; most of us, you know, enjoy hearing ourselves talk and, I believe, my students are quite astounded that so young a head can know so much. At any rate, if I'm not always accurate, I'm fluent, and it produces its effect. Yes, it is true I have girls in my class,—eight or ten in each, but I maintain the proper distance. As to my *dignity*, and so forth,—I do not know if I convey the impression or not:— dignity at 23 looks somewhat foolish, you know. However, I maintain order, and the boys and girls tell me they like me; a boy told me Saturday that everyone was trying to get in my class, —but you must take this *cum grano salis*

You must remember that some of my associates here have been teaching twenty years; that almost all have been teaching four or five years: and that I am a greenhorn, so far as actual teaching experience is concerned. Furthermore, God or Satan has not given me the temperament of a teacher; I am rather a bit of a poet and an artist who has had to bow to inexorable circumstances. Don't think I'm unhappy. On the contrary I regret nothing. I am getting a new and intimate contact with certain elements of existence which should be of the greatest benefit in the end.

I was brought here, you may remember, on the promise of

$1800 in 8 monthly instalments. Well, I still get my money,—
only they pay me in 12—$150 a month. This means I shall draw
pay five months or so after I finish in September; but it means I
shall have to practice rigid economy on my present income. As
you know, I am a poor economist. It is not that I am given to
foolish extravagance. It is merely that money never has, or never
will, I fear, have any intrinsic value for me. Its ownership means
nothing: its only value, so far as I'm concerned, is to make me
forget the fact I ever wanted it: to allow me to buy a few of the
beautiful, mind and body satisfying things I want,—as pictures,
books in hand-tooled bindings,—and good food and wine for the
belly.

How, or why this is, I can not tell. I only know that one Tom
Wolfe, a queer looking person, some six and a half feet high—
by which I mean he does not look like the average good Presbyterian, Rotarian, Kiwanian, Booster, or Realtor—that is to say, he
is not commonplace—was born some 23 years ago in a community
which bought and sold real-estate, and which was convinced that
it was the finest, the purest, the cleanest, the greatest place upon
the top of the earth, in which to live. Of course, the town had no
literature; it had no art; it had never heard of Ibsen; Keats and
Shelly were vague names to it; and Shakespeare was a fellow they
dosed you on in high-school. All that the human heart and brain
and spirit had fashioned into eternal loveliness throughout the
ages; all that separated and distinguished man from the pig; all
that was deathless and immortal was held in contempt. A person
who cared for these things was "queer," or actually "immoral,"—
that is to say he cared for art which, to those crude minds, suggested an unending succession of pictures of naked women.

Well, I do not condemn these people. I do not denounce them.
I have a very deep affection for the place of my birth. The

provincial, the middle-class, the bourgeois, are to be found everywhere; they are necessary, I suppose—only, when you differ from
their own narrow moulds, they may try to crucify you.

Now, don't you see that, so far as my "friends" in Asheville
are concerned, it matters little whether I succeed or fail:—they
are utterly incapable of understanding either. That is, if I really
succeed, by the only standard that counts,—my own,—namely by
writing a fine and noble play or book, worthy of my best, they
would not understand what I had done, and would no doubt
be a little bored by the result,—preferring *Parlor, Bedroom, and
Bath,* or the poetry of Edgar A. Guest, or Dr. Frank Crane, and
so on.

If I failed, they might consider that failure a brilliant success,
for I might write a cheap and meretricious play which would soil
and degrade my talent, but which might make me a fortune.
And, after all, that is all that matters in Asheville, isn't it.

I have had very little time to write so far,—but I have written
a little. Professor Baker, I suppose, is angry because I came here.
I haven't heard from him. However, bread is not growing on the
trees this year.

Tell Mabel I can find her reasonable accommodations at any
time,—a room with bath here in the hotel at $2.50 or $3.00 a
day. It is silly, of course, to come to New York, and ruin your
bankroll with the rates at expensive hotels, when there are quiet,
clean inexpensive places elsewhere.

Tell her I know of two or three good little Italian restaurants,
where the food is inexpensive, and the cocktails are fifty cents,
and wine seventy-five cents a pint.

Take care of yourself, and keep the house warm until the
weather is milder. I wish you any amount of success in your
Miami ventures. Only remember this, Mama:—life is brutal and

has a tragic underscheme: we mean nothing in the Great Plan, and the health may be crushed from us at any moment, by the same careless, unseeing fingers which have flung billions of men before us into the earth to rot. Look at the facts squarely, and don't blink them. When you talk of "being on easy street" in five years, of enjoying the fruits of your labors, be sure that meanwhile you do not lose the capacity for enjoyment, which is the important thing; be sure that five years is not an excuse, and that, at the end of that time you may not wait for five years more. Remember that we shall all come to "easy street" in the end; only we shall not know, we shall not care, for our houses on that street will be all one—six feet in length, and two feet wide. Live a little now, I entreat you; for we are as the men of former time—no different; and in the end we, too, shall turn our faces to the wall, and the light will go out; and we shall go into a place where there is darkness,—nothing but darkness.

Let me hear from you as soon as possible. Love, and health, and happiness be with you

Your son

Tom

P. S. Yes, I need the shirts.

April 4, 1924

Dear Mama:

Just a few lines are all my time allow. I must go back to the interminable work of correcting papers—like the brook, *that* goes on forever. On three days a week—or four—I can sleep late, and generally do, because on my teaching days I am so worn by nightfall that I sleep as though drugged. I don't know how to conserve nervous energy; I burn it extravagantly. However, I am not unhappy. I believe I am learning much, although I am doing no writing. What time I have is usually spent at the theatre, or at the library, or in the open. When I am through grading papers, and writing my comments on the back, I don't feel in the mood for composition of my own. You can't serve two masters; I have elected to serve one, and I must see it through. Hereafter, I believe, I shall be able to do my work more quickly—I yet strain my Presbyterian conscience; and I believe I do too much.

The shirts and socks have not come; I hope I get them soon— I am ragged. I must get a suit of clothes, too. This one is beginning to flap in the wind. I got Mabel's telegram. I am sorry she can't come now. I had hoped to see her. However, a little later the weather will be milder. My late predictions of spring were false; there was a heavy snowfall here on the first of April. Now, I believe spring is here to stay. It is a fine, blue, spring day— no wind. I am off ten or fifteen pounds since coming here; but, then, I was growing fat and lazy in Cambridge. I shall try to hold onto what is left.

I live for September when I shall try to collect the remainder of my salary and go to England. I should have six months' pay dating from Sept. 1st. Perhaps I can get away with seven or eight hundred dollars. I shall sail third class, steerage, a fast boat does it in five days, and I can hold my breath that long. I shall go down to the south of England, where, I am told, it is beautiful, and bury myself in a little village there; at one of the old inns where you can get good English ale and beer. It will be cheap; perhaps forty or fifty dollars a month. I can write there for two months—away from the world I know. Anywhere, anywhere,— out of *this* world.

How large, how golden seems that little sum of money. Yet how pitifully small it is. And how much wealth there is which has been got by dishonesty, trickery, and blind luck. They tell us in Sunday school to be industrious and saving, and steady;—we will be rich. It is not true. The world is filled with bookkeepers who have all these qualities; who work twice as hard as their employers. They shall die in a bookkeepers bed, and go to a book-keepers heaven or hell where there are no interesting people.

The golden years of my life are slipping by on stealthy feet at nightfall; there is a foot-print in the dark, a bell strikes twelve, and the flying year has gone. My life is like water which has passed the mill; it turns no wheel. And all of which I thought myself a part drifts by like a painted picture. The great play is yet unwritten; the great novel beats with futile hands against the portals of my brain. Proud fool! I have eaten of the Lotus and dreamed too deeply; the world is at me with its long fingers, and must have its payment There is not time! If I but had a hundred years there might be some realization of my dream. But I shall not live so long; and shall my dust taste better than a peddler's, when the worms are at me?

I had to draw on you at the end of the month—this month I shall do better. Please watch your health; don't overwork.

I send my love to you all.

TOM

HOTEL ALBERT
Eleventh Street & University Place
New York
April
Monday—21, 1924

DEAR MAMA:—Written in haste and therefore short. Thanks for news of Koch. Called him yesterday: had breakfast with him this morning. He wants to put one of my old Carolina one act plays in a new book—*Return of Buck Gavin*. It was hastily written in three hours at one sitting when I was 18. Honestly, I don't think I can afford to let my name go out over it. But we shall see.

Pained at the implication in your letter that I was ashamed of North Carolina—only what is N.C. willing to do for me? I don't think there is a place there now for anyone who cares for anything besides Rotary and Lions and Boosters Clubs, real-estate speculation, "heap much" money, social fawning, good roads, new mills,—what, in a word, they choose to call "Progress, Progress, Progress." The only Progress is spiritual; the only lasting thing is Beauty—created by an artist. And N. C. has forgotten such as I.

N.C. needs honest criticism—rather than the false, shallow, "we are—the—finest—state—and—greatest—people—in—the—country"—kind of thing. An *artist* who refuses to accept fair criticism of his work will never go far. What of a *state*?

I love N.C. more than any other place in the country! But what has it to feed my spirit, my mind. Last week I saw plays written by an Englishman, a German, an Italian, and an American. This is universal culture. I'm not crazy about New York, but I love the theatre. This, I hope, makes it plain.

N.C. will be ready to welcome me with trumpets if my plays are acted on Broadway—above all, if they make *money, money*. You know that is quite true. Look around you in Asheville. Are the most prominent people there the finest—by education, personality, culture, and general character. By no means. After all, haven't you all worshipped the long bank roll too much. Grove is a great man because he sells more pills than anyone else; Mrs. Vanderbilt is a great woman because of Biltmore house and twenty millions.

Be honest: You know I have never been a snob. And it is because I respect my family so much, knowing you were as good as any, to see you bend a supple knee at any time to the Asheville Goulds and Astors. If any of them patronize me— telling you I am a "bright boy"—for God's sake, don't look grateful or humble. Tell them I am pleased to hear of their interest and that I should be glad to give them a few moments of my time when they're in New York. This last is meant humorously —none the less seriously.

I can't honestly fall on my knees before Asheville's Four Hundred. I know people already who are socially and nationally prominent, Prof. Baker, for example,—so damn their condescension.

I've just had a four day Easter vacation and got almost an entire act done on my new play. Now—back to the grind. It's useless to say "don't work too hard." I've got a great deal of my Presbyterian conscience left, and I can't shirk the job.

I'm sorry about the money. I've enough left to do me two days longer—then I'm broke to the first. Not extravagance, Mama. But next month I'll do it or bust. I'm sorry to hear of your financial difficulty. I've no doubt of your ability to come out with profit and honor.

But don't overdo it, Mama. Life doesn't last forever. And, in fairness to yourself and everyone, don't say it's "for the children." I'm sure they would not be slave drivers. If you do it, admit that it's for your own pleasure and prosperity. Understand, Mama, if I seem to sneer at money and money getting it's not because I despise it—I acknowledge gratefully now all that you have been able to do for me because you had it. I can never forget it. Only, money is not an end—it is a means.

You show some contempt for my $150 a month. It's not much

after Harvard, is it? I shall not argue the point. No doubt you know many High School graduates who are doing better. It depends on what your standard of success is.

I shall live within my income hereafter. I could live now if I drew on my advance but I'm looking to the $750 that comes to me in September as a passage to Heaven—I'm going to England steerage and write and write until I'm broke or my fortune's made. Tell the Philistines that Samson bids them "Go to H—" And for you all, much love—

TOM

HOTEL ALBERT
New York
June, 1924

DEAR MAMA: Just a few lines for the present. Examinations have just ended at the University and I've been up to my ears in work—marking exam books and making out grades. Now the second semester has started, and I will not be done until mid-September.

The work for the summer should be easier—my classes are not so huge. I "flunked" about ten, and about ten more dropped out. I hope to finish my play before September. It goes well when I have time to work on it, but, thus far, I haven't had much time. I have made a good reputation with the faculty because of my work—and they keep asking me to come back. God knows! God knows! I am not and never will be a schoolteacher. But I must live somehow. During the past four or five months I have broken away from everything and everybody. Professor Baker hasn't written a word. I think he's bitterly disappointed because I began teaching, but he never told me by what means I could live.

I suppose I am one of the loneliest people in the world—not that I do not know people, for I meet them continuously, women particularly—who seem to like me. I don't think I have ever quite understood myself, and I have never found anyone who understood. That's why I'm lonely. I am falling in love every month or so, but it never lasts more than a week or two.

God knows, it wouldn't be pleasant at home, with people crying all over you, and running in and out of the room, and so on. However, I do not think of death to-day. I am a trifle dizzy, but on my feet.

There is only one thing that a brave and honest man—a gentleman—should be afraid of. And that is death. He should carry the fear of death forever in his heart—for that ends all his glory, and he should use it as a spur to ride his life across the barriers. I hate people who say they have no fear of death. They are liars, and fools, and hypocrites.

Well, I have written more than I intended. I am not unhappy. This great city has fed my imagination—it has allowed me to dream.

Koch of Chapel Hill keeps insisting by letter and telegram that I allow him to publish my first one act play, and his publisher, Holt, called me up the other morning and invited me to a dinner party at his home, to which a number of writing folk had been invited. I didn't go because I didn't have a dinner jacket, and I hate these affairs, anyway.

I shall not allow the play to be published. I wrote it when I was seventeen and it is pretty crude. I wrote it in three hours on a rainy afternoon. I would be unfair to myself. I'm glad you made the trip to Louisville; glad that Frank is really doing well.

HOTEL ALBERT
11th St. & University Place
New York
[Letter undated. Envelope dated 7/25/24]

Postcript at top of first page: It is broiling hot here— My brains are baked— Thank God there's less than two months left before freedom.

DEAR MAMA:—Will you cover a check for me—a check which I drew yesterday? It was made payable to the Hotel Albert and was for $76. Meanwhile I have directed the University to send you half my check of Aug 1—for $75.00—and it should get to you not later than Aug 3. As you may know I let the hotel act as my banker and give them my check the first of every month. If I run out of money they have been kind enough to advance whatever cash I needed. The check therefore covers meals (mainly breakfast) room rent, and cash loans. I drew it because the manager told me it was not customary to let bills run two weeks in excess of rental. I did not know the manager before, but I was very much offended, as I trust the hotel with all my money each month, and cancel all indebtedness promptly. What money was ever advanced to me by the hotel was purely at the suggestion of the members of the desk force—the cashier and head clerk. I felt, and still feel, very bitterly toward the manager who is a way-down Easter from Maine. He apologized profusely. Said he had not known of my arrangement, and insisted that I might wait to Aug 1, or pay at my own convenience. I was hurt, I think, because I felt I had found a home in New York—these people have been nice to me—and the appearance of the low-down, suspicious, get-the-money instinct made me half sick. Consequently, after thinking the matter over for a night, I decided that I would rather ask a favor of you than of a way-down-

Easter. I hope you don't think so badly of me now as not to expect the money immediately after I am paid. I am fairly honorable, I think, and I have made it a point of honor to live, *so far as possible,* within my income, which, as you know, is $150 a month. That I have not always succeeded, that I have occasionally gone to you for aid has meant simply that my money was out. Mama, you know as well as, or better than, I that I am not a good economist. Unfortunately I have not your saving instinct. I could not honestly, therefore, tell you that there is no one in New York who lives on $150 a month. I am sure that there are such people, and a great many. Most of them live in the suburbs, where it is cheaper; a great many, I suppose, live on the East Side. But I don't feel that I have been extravagant—I have bought one cheap suit of clothes—which, of course, set me back —and my appetite is as large as usual. That is my big extravagance—my ravening gut. I suppose I could eat less, but I have a big body, and a devouring mind which will never let me rest. The damned thing grinds, grinds, grinds all the time—it gives me no rest save when I sleep. Perhaps that makes you smile, but I feel at times as if I have developed a powerful monster, which will someday destroy me. And when that mind has worked a few hours on books, papers, Creation—it calls for a different sort of food—meat, potatoes, pie. Yes, it eats even more than my body. Within me somewhere terrific energy is generated—I must always be going—either attacking a book or my play furiously, or teaching furiously, or racing around, as fast as I can go, even in the sun. I take things with too great intensity; I can never do things by halves. As a result, during this terrific spell of weather I have become desperately tired—not bodily, but mentally.

I get a little time to write but my friends tell me I have written a great play—the new one. God knows. I have a prolog, two acts, and part of the third finished. If I had only time enough! When I finish in September—my classes have final exams Sept 15th—I'm going to New Hampshire for a few days, and then as quickly as possible to England. From September 1, I have six month's salary due. Money, money!

Good God! What couldn t I do with it. I have had a wonderful experience. In June a young fellow I knew at Harvard—by name of Olin Dows [1]—wrote from Cambridge and asked me if I could get a room for him here in the hotel near me. I knew the boy slightly—he's just twenty—and he saw my play at Harvard, and was enthusiastic and painted me—he's studying art. So he came, and we've been together a great deal. He never spoke of money or of his family—but I knew he was very wealthy because he would try to give me $15 and $20 books of art. He invited me up to his father's country place up the Hudson two weeks ago—at a colony for millionaires, a very old Dutch place, called Rhinebeck. His people are fabulously wealthy—as wealthy or wealthier than the Asheville Vanderbilts. They live on a great estate of 2000 acres overlooking the Hudson, with gatekeeper's lodges, and a wonderful colonial house. Next door are the Roosevelts—Franklin D.—and the Astors and Delanos are farther up. The boy's grandfather lives on a great estate adjoining and all this the boy inherits. The grandfather married Oliver Harriman's daughter. His people are wonderful—left me absolutely free to do as I pleased—put me at ease. His mother, on hearing I was from Asheville, asked me if I knew Cornelia. I told her that I did not. I think they understand my position—but they liked me and insisted that I come back as often as possible. He

---

[1] A young painter Tom came to know while in Harvard, whose parents had a large estate at Rhinebeck on the Hudson. Tom describes his visit to their home in *Of Time and the River*.

goes up every Friday and stays to Sunday, and he wants me to go back with him tonight. But I can't. I have papers, mid-term reports, and what not.

They have six thousand volumes—beautiful expensive books in their library which no one reads. Money, money! In addition, he has a sister about nineteen who is one of the most beautiful and wonderful people I've ever known.

I'd be alone this week end if I went, and I could rest. His family, except his father, have gone to Newport. His mother told me she was to visit Alice Vanderbilt there—they are related, I believe.

His father comes down to the city now and then, and has taken us out—to expensive restaurants and the theatres. They are unhappy—I caught that while I was there. His father is fifty—his mother forty—but his mother will always be young— that's the trouble. She always has young people around to play golf, or swim, or dance with—there were several boys and girls when I was there. His father is as old as his years. The boy talked it over with me quite frankly—of course his sympathy is all with his mother, yet his father is crazy about him. He told me his father's father died when the son was in college and left the boy one of the wealthiest bachelors in the country.

That's all for the present. Only, if I had one tenth what those people have, I'd be a great man ten years quicker. Life is so damned unfair.

You never write. You never think of me. If I should die here you'd forget me in two months. You will say you wouldn't, but you would. I'm not bitter. Only I know you've for the most part, forgotten me. Life teaches us. Nothing endures. Nothing lasts except beauty—and I shall create that. You don't know me, Mama. I'm not important to you—I've become a man, and you

will never realize I'm older than I was when you took me around
with you—when I was eight. I shall never forget, or be lacking
in gratitude for what you have done for me—but I shall repay
that some day. I shall be great—if I do not die too soon—and you
will be known as my mother. I say that seriously—I believe it.
There is no one like me, and I shall conquer. Fools will call this
conceit, but let them say what they will—they are fools.

I am utterly lonely; there is no one in all the world to whom
I can talk, but in my loneliness I am strong. I shall survive and
triumph.

I hope all your affairs are meeting with success, and that you
find happiness in directing them.

Your son—

Tom

HOTEL ALBERT, NEW YORK CITY
Thursday, August 14, 1924

Dear Mama: I had intended much earlier to answer your
letter, but until the last three days heat—heat for which this
world has no name—choked and stifled and beat me down. And
during that terrible time I had to go on teaching, grading papers,
spending my strength and energy, recklessly. I thought I should
go mad. For three days now the weather has been cool and
pleasant. But I do not know if God is good enough to finish the
summer with coolness. Thank heaven, there is less than one
month here for me now. I meet my last classes on September 5,
and give them their examination one week later on September
12. I am through, then, so soon as my grades go in; and I should
not be above two days in this. Olin Dows has invited me to
Rhinebeck to rest and write for a week or two before I sail, to

rest and write, and I shall probably go; but then, mama, I sail, and Heaven and Hell shall not prevent me.

I have become like some mad beast who sees through famished eyes a pool of forest water; I have only one thought in mind, to get away—anywhere, anywhere out of this world about me—and finish my beautiful play. It is maddening! The thing is done, finished and chiselled in my brain, but Time, my work, and the weather have entered a deadly conspiracy to prevent my writing. I have two and a half acts, and no time to finish. It is simply maddening. I have worked too hard, giving my brain and my heart, to these stupid little fools; talking like an angel or a God in language too few of them will understand. And yet, there are rewards. This morning I got a letter from one of them—a girl—telling me that the only thing that keeps her in college now is my class; that her other instructors are narrow, bigoted, and intolerant; that I have taught her to try to be "big like myself." She is honest, and what she says heartens me. And I believe the others understand and appreciate a little:—they say they do. And, of course, the college wants me back. The Dean and the head of the department have been most friendly; they come around and talk to me, tell me to take as long as I want to decide—they have given me until December to answer—and promise me a *princely* raise in salary—two *whole* hundred dollars a year. But the truth of the matter is, as I have told them and my classes many times, I am probably the world's worst Freshman instructor. I haven't the teaching temperament—and the Freshman instructor temperament, I believe, is one of little imagination. I have too much. Details and the teaching of mechanics—the rules of grammar—torture me; yet I have so much conscience that I see it through to the bitter end. God knows what I shall do, unless I sell my play—my new or my old one, or both. The old one went to Europe with a wealthy woman producer, and she wrote back very enthusiastically, saying it was "unusually fine," "promised well for young America," and did I have another with not so many characters. What she intends to do I don't know. I'm sick of praise; I want money.

From September 1 I have six month's pay due me—$900. If I am fortunate, I *may* get away to England with $700. Passage on the cheapest one cabin boats, one way, is $115. If I can raise $400, exclusive of passage, I may live for four month's or more, as I understand it is cheaper, much, than America.

I shall have to ask you to wait until September for your money—I can barely get along this winter on what I have. I am tired and can't write much more. But I must go, Mama; my life has turned to dust and ashes in my mouth, and I find myself unable to do the only thing I care for—the only thing I ever shall.

Don't worry about me—I'm not like Frank. I am young and strong and, with a week's rest, full of courage. I shall never be a weight around your neck. No one regrets more than I do the necessity of my calling on you at all this year; but remember, Mama, this has been my first year of self-support; I was desperate and took the first thing that offered, and came to live in the most expensive city of the world on a small salary. Don't worry, I say. I am still fairly decent and honorable, and you can depend on me to come through somehow—yes, even if I have to teach my life away; although God grant I may escape that.

I can say nothing about Frank's latest trouble except to express my sincere grief, disappointment, and astonishment. But weeping and wailing, and cursing and reviling will do no good, Mama. We've tried all that, and it has been no go. Surely we should learn something from tragic experience. Yet I doubt that we do. We blunder through the jungle desperately, seeing nothing, learning nothing, and all we tell ourselves is lies, lies, lies.

Mama, let us face the terrible truth. I have come to know that the miracle rarely happens in human affairs; Lazarus is uncured and bleeds from his sores.

I have never known Frank well—he left home when I was a child, and my memory of him since has been mainly of a series of escapades. Yet I think I know all the essentials.

When misfortune strikes Frank, as the result of his own conduct, he will accuse the world which "owes him a living," his parents, his brothers and sisters, who are "down on him"—in short, everyone and everything but himself.

Yet, if Frank has even a modicum of success, he becomes vain, boastful, arrogant, and goes around giving himself ridiculous airs. He reforms the affairs of the country, gives pointers to J. P. Morgan, and says he guesses "Little Frankie showed them"—whatever that may mean.

The underscheme of all life is tragic. Only fools and stupid swine rush about bellowing and squeaking about their happiness —something no one ever had; something that never existed; something weaklings are always whining about. But some of us may do something with our lives before our flesh must fill the mouths of worms; others are born into Hell and carry Hell with them like a torch, until some merciful power destroys them.

I am all nerves, but in fairly good health. I've lost fifteen pounds this summer, but I shall be all right by October.

Someday, before we all die, perhaps I shall get from home a letter in which all the news will be pleasant. I never have thus far.

Affectionately.   Your Son,

                                              Tom

Sunday, August 18, 1924

DEAR MAMA: When I make application for my passport at the Custom House here, it will be necessary for me to present, along with my application, a certificate of birth. I am sending this certificate to you. Since you are busy, I know, will you get Fred or Mabel to take it to Fred Sale, or to someone with power of notary, to have it filled in and certified with a notary's seal? It should not take over four or five days, I am told, to have my application approved and returned from Washington, whither it must be sent. But, I wish to get these matters straightened out *now*, so that I may not be rushed in September. For your own information when you go, I will tell you that you pay the government $10 for a passport to a foreign country, and you pay each country you visit an additional sum which varies from five to ten dollars but which is usually five I believe. To England it is ten—France (I think), five.

I have been making enquiries and getting information about the fare to England, and find that it varies greatly. If you travel first class on one of the crack boats, your passage of course, is expensive. But I find that there are many good smaller boats— "cabin boats" they are called, because there is *one* class of passengers—where the passage is much cheaper. For example, on the North German Lloyd cabin boats, passage to Plymouth, England, including meals and stateroom, is $115 and $120. *Third class* passage on these boats is $103.50, plus the customary government tax of five or ten dollars. These boats do not race across in five days—they are slower, and require nine or ten days for the trip. But you may see how reasonable this is when you consider that passenger fare to San Francisco must be almost, if not quite, $115, and this does not include pullmans and food. I shall most probably go on a boat like this, as I should prefer the slower trip and the saving in money. There is no reason why a person may not go abroad for a year now and return, having spent much less money than a year's living in America would require. I shall limit myself to $100 a month while over, and I am told this should be quite enough if I exercise only a little care. In the small villages in the South of France, for example, one can live on next to nothing. A German at the North German Lloyd offices to-day told me that German laborers are being paid not over $4.50 a week—if they can live on that, I should live on $15 or $20; of course the big cities—London and Paris—are more expensive, but my friend, Jack Withrow, who came back last month from a year in Europe, told me he lived most of the winter in Paris, in the Latin quarter, at a pension (boarding house) where his room and board cost only $1.25 a day. This is only $9.00 a week. One could probably live in Paris on $75 or $80 a month.

I am finishing this Sunday. I do not feel well; I have a slight head cold, and something is wrong with my eyes. I hope it is the cold. I don't know. If I read any length of time my eyes smart and burn—I noticed this only two or three days ago. I hope to God they are not going back on me now—I have used them so much grading papers, sitting up until one or two o'clock that I am worried. If they don't get better in a few days I'll have them examined.

I am enclosing the certificate of birth which must be filled out. You may read it, and see what is required. Apparently it must be stamped with a notary's seal. Have it filled out and returned to me just as soon as you are able.

Meanwhile, I hope this finds you all well.

Affectionately,

Tom

Post mark August 24, 1924

DEAR MAMA:—

Will you please have the birth certificate attended to and sent back to me as quickly as possible. I must make haste. I finish here the 12, and much preparation is before me.

I'm pretty well but praying for the end of the term.

Love

TOM.

[Hotel Albert, New York City—dated some time in 1924, evidently in September, at end of summer term.]

DEAR MAMA:

Just a few lines in answer to your last letter. I had my last classes on Friday, and give my first examination on Friday, the 12th. I want to get away as quickly thereafter as possible, as New York eats my pay right up. I am going to the dentist and must pay him $30 or $40. Have five months' pay coming to me, and shall try to get paid in a lump. I shall buy one suit of clothes and a large bag; both the bags I took away from home—the little one and the big one—both old and cheap, are burst beyond repairs. If you could find one at home, not in use, that makes a decent appearance you would save me the expense of buying one.

As to expenses abroad, I probably know quite as much as 'Dine, as most of my friends of the last four years have been over as many times. Expenses in all the big countries abroad are much lower than here; in some countries very much lower. Rich and vulgar Americans, however, do their best to increase expenses for others by throwing their money loosely around, and almost begging for the privilege of being swindled. However, as a friend of mine secured board and room at a pension in Paris not later than June, for $1.25 a day, I presume the experience may be duplicated now. It is my intention to keep within $100 a month, *once over*, and some people assure me the estimate is liberal. It does not mean, however, expensive hotels, first-class passage wherever I go and association with damn fool pork packers and chewing gum manufacturers from Peoria, Illinois. But I am ready cheerfully to forgo the companionship of these delightful swine for a few months. When I am in France, I shall keep just as far away as possible from all natives of this broad land of freedom and from everyone speaking or abusing the English language. In this way I hope to acquire a speaking knowledge of French in about two months.

I am looking forward to Mabel's visit; it would be a terrible disappointment to me now if she postponed it. Tell her, for God's sake, to let nothing forestall it. If I thought there was a chance of your coming I should urge that, too, but I know there is very little chance of your getting away at this time. If I have any available socks or shirts, send them on. Of course, I should like to see you all before I go, but a trip to Asheville would be expensive—not worth while, and I honestly have no desire to see Asheville, aside from members of my family.

Write me as you are able; chances of communication may become scarcer for a time.

Your son,
Tom

HOTEL ALBERT, NEW YORK CITY
Oct. 20, 1924

SUNDAY NIGHT

DEAR MAMA:

Fred went home today. His feet were sore from the walking he has done, but I believe he enjoyed the trip, and that it has benefited him. My boat, THE LANCASTRIA, did not sail this Saturday. It goes next Saturday. Meanwhile there is business I must attend to. I am putting my play in the hands of an agent and tonight I begin work on a short story which I intend to finish before I leave and send to Mr. Jackson at Asheville so that he may market it. I am going down to the University tomorrow to get, if possible, the $300 still due me. Passage on THE LANCASTRIA will cost me $130 to London. The boat takes nine days. She is a fine vessel. I went over her today. Library, smoking room, lounge, veranda cafe, dining saloon and so on. I went through the kitchen—everything clean and shining, and bigger than a hotel. Originally a three class vessel converted into cabin boat.

I shall write 1,500 words a day from now on. If I do this I believe I can sell enough stories this next year to support me.

I want to hear from you before I go; I want to know that all is well. I am alone now; I am embarked on a desperate venture—do or die: but I believe my course is right.

Take good care of yourself, and see that you get to Florida before the weather grows cold.

With much love to you all,

TOM

[*Telegram dated Oct. 24 P.M. 5:03 New York, N. Y.*]

MRS. JULIA E WOLFE

48 SPRUCE ST   ASHEVILLE N CAR—

SAILING LANCASTRIA CUNARD LINE NOON TOMORROW LOVE TO ALL

TOM.

[*Telegram dated Oct. 25 P.M. 1:08 New York, N. Y.*]

MRS. JULIA E WOLFE

48 SPRUCE ST   ASHEVILLE N CAR—

AM OFF   GOT LETTER AND PACKAGE   GOD BLESS YOU ALL

TOM.

ON BOARD THE CUNARD R. M. S. "LANCASTRIA."

Mailed from Dock (*Envelope dated 10/25/24*)

DEAR MAMA: I'm off— Got your letter last night, and got package with shirts this morning at hotel as I was packing.

This looks like a good boat and I know I shall be comfortable.

I can say very little just now except that I shall work as never before, and try to get wonderful experience and education from this trip. I feel very well.

Mama, the world is small, and I can come from any quarter almost upon the wings of the morning. God bless you and keep you all.

I send my deepest love,

TOM.

P.S. I paid the hotel as I left with a cheque on Wachovia, as I wanted to keep all my Express Cheques intact. I got the extra $300 from the University.

I shall economize, work, learn, and someday I'll ride to glory. God bless you all!

CUNARD RMS "LANCASTRIA"

P.M. one o'clock

Tuesday, November 4, 1924

DEAR MAMA: I am writing you this in the middle of the English Channel, about two or three hours away from Cherbourg, France, where this letter will be mailed from the boat. After an hour or two at Cherbourg where the ship lands passengers bound for France, we cut back across the Channel to the mouth of the Thames, where we proceed up the river to London and the end of my journey, which we should reach by noon to-morrow if we are quick enough to make the early voyage.

Last night at ten o'clock it was announced that the beacon lights of England were on our left, and I rushed on deck in the face of a howling wind to look on the lights of England—old England—on the Scilly Isles and on Land's End. This morning at six o'clock we slid into the beautiful little harbor of Plymouth, England, and I caught my first glimpse of English soil. A beautiful little town of 30,000 people lay off in the distance, and round smooth green hills with little vegetation sloped down to the water. The tender came out to the boat to take off passengers in a hurry to reach London 200 miles away. I shall stay on the boat, for my fare is paid, and they must feed me, and the train fare from Plymouth is $10.00.

No one who ever made a voyage has got as much from it as I have. The passenger list was small, only 96, and I got to know them all; and they included knaves, fools, aristocrats—Englishmen who have beaten up and down all the coasts of the world, and who think not as much of a two week's trip to America as you do of one to Miami. I have put it all on paper, day by day, the tragedy and the comedy, the beauty and the mystery of the sea; and the courage and courtesy of these Englishmen who have made the sea their slave.

I shall send it back from London tomorrow to *The Citizen*, if they care to publish a real piece of creation, and you may read at length what I have seen.

All my dreams are coming through. I am assured that I may secure very comfortably in London board and room for £2–10 sh a week—a little over $11.00; and that I may live comfortably in London on £5 or £6 a week—less than $30.00. The South of France is far cheaper; already I have recommendations to pensions at rates of 16 or 18 francs a day—80 or 90 cents.

I shall stay in London two or three weeks—then I may go on a walking trip through the beautiful country villages in Southern England. An old Englishman named Adams, and his wife, have invited me to visit them at their home in Rye, England. Adams is mayor of the town—a very beautiful and famous village—and he is returning from the States where the Rotary Club has feasted him. He is a Rotarian.

At my table is young Hugh Tennant, aged 32, who is of one of the greatest families in England; he is cousin to Lady Asquith. He is returning to England after five years at the British Embassy in Washington. He knows Asheville very well: when he got on the boat he told me he had just come from a visit to the Vanderbilt's—the Cecil's. He was Cecil's best man. He has offered to write letters securing admission for me to the Houses of Parliament, and other places.

The weather is lovely—a terrific wind across the Channel,

but blue skies and a flashing sun. I can see the coast of France before me now—from the writing room.

We came across with an injury to the starboard engine, and we are two days late. The weather was lovely most of the time, good most of the rest, and rough only two or three days. I made the trip very well, although I felt sorry for myself once or twice when the boat began to pitch and roll. Seasickness is a kind of head giddiness accompanied by a vast indifference to everything in the world. I feel very well this glorious day, but am glad the sod of England will soon be beneath my feet.

I must finish this, having said not one tenth as much as I wished. I shall conquer the world on this journey; this voyage and this new world has changed my life. I know I shall be lonely and disheartened often, but a wonderful experience is before me. We are fools to live in a narrow cage!

For God's sake, all of you must watch your health, and send me news. Always tell me the truth, but no worse than that. I may cable you my address and my safe arrival from London. But rush mail by *fastest boat* to American Express Co, London, —Love to you all,

TOM.

[*Post Card:*]

LONDON NOV. 14, 1924
Send mail to Am. Express
Know you have my letter sent from Cherbourg now. Writing at length in day or so. Paying 5 shillings a day for bed and breakfast. This is a magnificent city and the English a fine people. Writing it all up.

Got Fred's letter.

[*Card: View of Bath, England.*]

Nov. 29, 1924

I have been here two days in the West of England, 107 miles from London, in this famous old town, which goes back to Roman times, and whose hot waters have called the great and fashionable of the last 3 centuries. Have $275 left—go to London —straight to Paris in a day or so—much cheaper there. Then to South. Writing it all up. Have heard nothing from you.

New address Am. Express, Paris.

This is the most beautiful town I've ever seen.

[*Post Card:*]

ST. MARY REDCLIFFE, BRISTOL

This is considered by critics as perhaps the finest parish church in England. In one corner of the church yard is a monument to Thomas Chatterton, a great poet and a great genius, who could make no way in the world and killed himself at the age of 17. Today I go to Paris. I mail this from London. Write me American express, Paris. No mail from home for weeks.

[*Christmas card:*]

"Joyeux Noël!" "Les meilleurs voeux pour un Joyeux Noël" to you and all the Family.

Tom.

FROM PARIS

Your most welcome letter arrived, sent over from the London office of the American Express Co. The address here is: American Express Co., 11 Rue Scribe.

I am giving this to some young Americans who are sailing tomorrow on *Leviathan*. They have promised to mail it in New York to insure quick delivery. New Year's is the great holiday here; I do not think they make a great deal of Christmas, but I shall celebrate the day with you in my heart.

But remember, when you sit down at two o'clock to eat your dinner, it will be seven o'clock here and I shall be sitting down to supper.

This, along with a letter, which I hope get to you in time for a joyous Christmas, is the only token I can send you across the seas, but it carries all my affection and regard for you and the family. I am living in the Latin Quarter of Paris in a room which costs 12 francs a day—about 60 cents—but I am comfortable, learning the language, and a great deal else, I hope; and although a bit lonely, losing myself in my work, and finding some joy there.

Tom.

Paris. Jan. 20, 1925

Dear Mama:—I am sending this to Asheville with instructions to forward, because I am not sure how long you would stay in Miami, or whether you had gone, or whether you had returned. I got your money, cabled in answer to my cable. There was a draft here the following Tuesday for 2300 francs—as I figured it up, about $124 at the present rate of exchange.

What happened was this:—I got your check in January. It was made payable to you and drawn on the American Express, Paris. It was signed by *Branch*—an employee, apparently, of the American Nat'l Bank at Asheville. Your name was *not* on the back. I went to the American Express Co here to cash it. They explained that it could be cashed by no one but *Julia E. Wolfe,* and not until her endorsement was on the back. They thought perhaps I could get the money if I had a friend with an account at another bank here who would guarantee the endorsement, could stand for the loss if there was one. I know a lady here—about whom I shall tell you—went with me to her bank here—Morgan Harjes and Co. (of New York) They told us the check was absolutely worthless as it stood, that it must be sent back to America for the missing endorsement; that the only way I could get money was to have $100 transferred from the lady's account. As this meant simply borrowing $100 from her, I decided to cable.

Somewhere, somehow—where, when, I don't know—I lost your check. It may be somewhere in my room now, among my papers, books, clothes,—but I am quite sure no one has it; and if they have I am quite sure no one can cash it, because I notified the American Express immediately—they assure me no one had tried to cash it, and that it could not be cashed any way; that, in a word, you are quite safe. I have asked here twice since, and nothing has turned up. Of course, they have instructions to stop payment, if any is attempted.

Now, about myself, and why I have not written more and longer letters. I told you in my cable I had finished my play— for four weeks, I wrote until three o'clock in the morning, and I have lived in hell; now I am all right again. Here is what happened. I came to Paris early in December, knowing no one. My first two nights here, I stayed at a hotel near the station where I arrived, the *Station of the North* (Gare du Nord). As it was too expensive, 30 francs a day, (about $1.50) for the room, I went the third day to a small hotel in the Latin Quarter across the Seine,—where artists and writers live, and where it is cheap.

There I found a room for 8 francs a day—a dingy little affair up five flights of winding stairs. I told the proprietor that I was going to the theatre—this was at six o'clock—that I should return after the theatre with my baggage. After the theatre I went to the first hotel near the station, got my three bags and a taxi, and went to my new room. I arrived at ten minutes to one o'clock, the place was locked, but I pressed a button, and the concierge (the porter) admitted me by pressing an electric button which opens the door. I paid the taxi man and went in. The concierge, a man about forty five years appeared, pulling on his trousers. He asked me if I had a room; I told him its number, and he looked at my bags, giving a great groan, when he saw it was very far up, and that my bags were heavy. He began to hobble around painfully, and told me that he was *mutilé* (wounded in the war), that it was very hard to carry the bags up at that hour of night. I told him I would take two—my little one, and the good one,—that he could keep the third one—the old black one—and have it brought up in the morning.

Well, Mama, to make a long and painful story short, when I came down in the morning, and asked the proprietor and his wife for the bag, they looked worried, and told me the concierge had gone out for the day—that he would return that evening. I was not worried, I simply concluded the man had put the bag somewhere for safekeeping. That night, about six, when I returned, the concierge had come back and the proprietors were giving him hell. They came out with it—the concierge, instead of putting the bag in his room, had left it out of sight in the hall, around the corner. At about three o'clock, so they said, a man had called, had asked for a certain madame who formerly stayed at the hotel, and as he went out had taken my bag.

I almost went crazy for an hour or two—not because of the

value of the bag, or the clothing it contained, because the bag was about gone—the lock was gone, the straps were broken, the buckle wouldn't hold; it was not worth $1.50, and the little maid at my London lodging had transferred most of my clothing to my big one. But what could never be replaced was the manuscript of my new play, with which I have lived for over a year, and which had become a part of me. I don't think you can understand my feeling quite, but nothing has hit me as hard as this since Papa's death. I went immediately to the Commissariat of Police, and told my loss. They asked me to give a description of the contents in my valise—this I did as well as possible—they called up the concierge, and questioned him carefully; they told me nothing could be done, that the valise was stolen and could not be found; that my only recourse was to make the hotel pay. The next day I left the hotel, and went to another, where I have stayed since, and been very comfortable. Just a week had gone by since I arrived in Paris; I knew no one. I had taken a terrific cold in the foggy weather, and I had only one thought—to lock myself in and write until I died or had written my play over, and finished it. I swore to myself that I should write a certain amount every day, and never go below it. The hotel people before I left got very nasty; they said they would pay, but only what they thought they should. How did they know I had in the valise the things I said I had; furthermore, after sticking to the story about the man who had called and asked for the woman for two days, they changed suddenly, and said the man had called and asked for me. They were suggesting, you see, that I was in conspiracy with someone, and that my plan was to defraud them. Then they gave me the paper which they asked me to sign in exchange for the 500 francs they offered me. The paper was an insult—it contained some rot about "the wounded soldier"—they were trying to work up sympathy for the imbecile of a concierge. I refused to sign the paper or to take the money—when they tried to deduct my bill for three days from the 500, I insisted on paying separately. I told them I would find out what my rights were and decide what I should do. The next day I looked up the one person I knew of here—a boy I had known slightly at Harvard, George Stephens. He has been here 16 months, and speaks French well. He advised me not to accept the money, but to go with him to the Justices officer (*Justice de Paix*) who is in France an official city officer, with an office in each ward of the city. We went to the Justice for our *arrondisement* (district) and entered a civil complaint against the proprietor of the hotel.

To make a long story short, the case was called up a week ago, I went in with the concierge before the Justice—the Justice heard me very kindly, told the Concierge he was responsible, and asked me how much I demanded. I told him 1200 francs—about $60—really a great deal more than the clothing and valise was worth, but I was determined if possible, to make them pay. The Justice told me he could not award 1200 francs, that the highest award he could make was 500 in his court, and that I should either go back to the proprietor, get my original 500, or go to a higher court where the process was long, and would cost me another 500, with victory doubtful. I decided at once to go to the hotel and get the 500, if I could.

I took George with me, went back, and found the wife of the proprietor there. She broke out into a stream of abuse—during the interval she had thought of new lies; she declared that I had gone out to talk with someone outside the hotel, after coming in the first night, and so on. I kept quiet, pretending to understand no French, and let George do the talking. But I told him to keep cool until we got our fingers on the 500. Meanwhile her husband returned from the Justice. He also was abusive, but I think they had told him he must pay, and after saying he had been an honest man all his life, but that he would never be honest again; and that we had not been in the war—which, I told him, had nothing to do with my valise—he produced 500 francs and made out a release for me to sign, this time with no nonsense about the wounded soldier. I made a copy for myself, signed both, got the money in my pocket, and told George, then, to tell the man he was a dirty scoundrel, and the woman that she was dishonest. He did this, word for word, and they followed us to the door, their faces contorted with rage and hatred.

So it ended. Now, Mama, you mustn't accuse me of undue carelessness. One is generally told that articles are safer in the keeping of the management than in one's room—what I did anyone might do. Five hundred francs is equal to about $27 or $28, but this buys a great deal more in France than in America—one can buy a new suit here for 300 or 400 francs. What I had in the valise was about one dozen of my oldest shirts, two or three suits of light underwear, a suit of pyjamas, the old blue suit, which was worn out, and, what I needed most, a good many socks. I don't believe an American second-hand man would have given me $25 for the lot—it was the play that killed me, and, of course, I could put no price on that.

At any rate I finished the new play about Jan. 3; it is "bigger and better" than the old one—I believe the best thing I've done. Since then I've been re-working it. On New Year's Eve I ran into one of my closest friends, Kenneth Raesbeck, who was Professor Baker's assistant. He is over here for a year. We went out, and for one night I forgot my sorrows, wading all over Paris in working-men's and communist dance halls, in the slums of the city, seeing wonderful and incredible things. The next day I met his aunt and a woman from Boston about 35 and 30 years each, two very fine and charming ladies, who have a studio here. They have rented a big car for three months, and are going to tour all over the South of France; they want me to go with them. I have about decided to go—I was sick and weary and worn out when they met me; they have put me on my feet again. The things I have seen here, the places I have been, in this beautiful and magnificent city, during the past three weeks, I will have to tell you in another letter. Don't be unhappy about me. I came to write, and writing was forced on me—I am glad now the thing was stolen. I have gained a tremendous lot from all of this. I had intended to send my experiences of England home long ago, but this happened. Now I am all right, I have friends, and I am seeing new things—I have learned enough French in six weeks to go anywhere; to get anything I want. My friends have taken me in the car to Versailles, St Germain, and to Rheims where the great cathedral is. By myself I went to Chateau Thierry and the Belleau Wood, where the Americans fought so well.

As to money, if you could manage to help me with as much as $100 a month, I will have enough. By myself, I could travel a little cheaper; with these people it will be a little more expensive, as I will not be another sponge; and I will see a great deal more. Meanwhile I shall get my play ready to send back to America, and I shall write other things, of which I am full.

Continue to send mail to the American Express, Paris—I don't know what route we shall follow, but I will leave or send forwarding addresses here. This is the best plan. Please write and give me all the news; I will tell you more next time.

I hope you got my cable Christmas, I saw no one Christmas day; I went out to a restaurant for food twice; I wrote all day, and I hoped very much to hear from some of you.

Shall write you all later.

With Great Love,

Tom

PARIS, Jan. 28, 1925

DEAR MAMA:—I received a letter from Fred to-day which distressed me very much, because it contained the first news I had heard of Mabel's illness. I have written them both, and I am now writing you; by the time this letter reaches you you will be in possession of the other which will give you most of the news of my activities since I came over from England. You need not worry about the check you sent, which I lost; it is quite safe—I stopped payment at once, but I had already been informed by the American Express here and by another bank that it would be impossible to cash it. I am only sorry for the trouble it caused you; sorry, too, that I was forced to send you such a long cable, but I did not want you to worry, or to think I had wasted the money. I told you in the last letter about the valise, and also that I had shut myself in and finished my play. I am now going over it, reworking it, and making it as good as I may, before I send it back to America. Then I settle down to the business of writing stories—cheap stories, if necessary—in order to make money.

I am going South to-morrow, to a little place on the Mediterranean called St. Raphael, where there are some people from North Carolina, a professor [1] from the University and his family. He has wired me that he could get me a room. There it will be cheap, quiet, and I may work.

I told you in the last letter that I thought I would go South in a big touring car which some friends of mine have hired. This would be very pleasant, and I should see a great deal of the country, but I have decided against it, mainly because I would have very little time to work travelling around; and because all these people have a great deal more money than I have, and I fear it would prove too expensive. By the time I arrive in the South, a long journey of 600 miles, I shall not have very much of the

[1] Professor Arnold of the University of North Carolina.

money you cabled left. But I promise you absolutely that I can live on less than $100 a month there, on $70 or $80, if necessary; for I shall not be travelling around, and living is cheaper.

I have not wasted money; I have traveled some, you must remember, in England and in France, and I have lived in London and Paris most of the time. It is a matter of deep regret that I should have to ask you for anything, but if, within the next five or six months you could let me have as much as $500, I could see Southern France, Italy, and do my work.

When I left home, you may remember, the understanding was that I should go as far as I could on my own, and that I should ask you for help when that was gone. I want you to understand, Mama, that I am giving myself one last desperate chance before I return to teaching. I believe I can earn my living teaching at any time, but I want to avoid doing it if by any possible chance I can succeed through what I write. I have nothing in the world except two manuscripts, and the will to go on. *Please*, if you are able, stand by me a little longer.

I should like to point out to you that there is a certain advantage in knowing French well enough to speak it. In seven weeks, I have acquired enough to get around, and to make myself understood. I believe that in another two or three months I shall speak with some fluency. At any rate I should know enough to be able to teach elementary French at a preparatory school or a university.

I am told that money may be sent by cable at the rate of $100 for 90 cents. If you can, do this when you get this letter, if you have not already mailed a letter with money. It has been about three weeks since I cabled for money; by the time I make the long trip South, most of the money you sent will be gone. I shall hang on there until I hear.

I think the best and quickest arrangement will be for my mail to be sent to the American Express Co here; it will be forwarded immediately to me where I am.

I am tired and worried; I hope Mabel is on her feet again. At any rate, I am convinced the wisest thing for me is to stay on here and work, at least for three or four months longer. All I have is my belief in myself; you must try to help me to keep it, if only for a little time, in the hope that things may brighten.

I believe honestly I have written a good play; now for the stories.

Please decide, Mama, if you can afford to help me to the extent I mention; and let me go on for a time without the additional shadow of money hanging over me.

I send you my deepest hope for your good health, and for your success in all your ventures.

With much love,   TOM

If it were convenient to send me money in two instalments of $250—the first to last two and one half or three months—we might avoid difficulty and delay of forwarding; particularly if I went into Italy, and travelled about there.

TOM

CHARTRES, FRANCE. Feb. 24, 1925

DEAR MAMA:—Your money arrived safely— Sorry I had to cable, but for a few days I had been living on kindness of a woman I met in my little hotel. I am on my way South, stopping at interesting places on the way down. Here at Chartres is perhaps the finest cathedral in France—perhaps in the whole world. I am writing you a letter in which I give you all the news. My mail is being forwarded from American Express, Paris.

Love,   TOM

THE AMERICAN EXPRESS CO., INC.
11 RUE SCRIBE

Visitor's Writing Room
PARIS, March 16, 1925

DEAR MAMA: Just a short letter written in haste the day of my departure for Marseilles. Both your checks came by way of the Nat. City Bank. I was away in Touraine—the chateau country—for two and a half weeks—and found the last when I got back here practically broke.

Good news for you! Don't worry. When I got back, in addition to your letter, I found a letter from Professor Watt of N.Y.U.[1] begging me to come back in September as a member of the regular teaching staff at a salary of $2000 to begin. I am answering and accepting, *hoping to God* in my heart, that I may escape by Sept. in some other way.

Meanwhile I am writing like a fiend. I have written, in addition to my play, what amounts to a short-sized novel in length called *Passage To England*. It grew out of my notes on the voyage. I am sending the first instalment off to Mrs. Roberts to-day to give to George McCoy[2] of the *Citizen*. I don't know if they will take it—but if they will they may have it—I *must* get published. After that stories of England and France—and Mama, some wonderful things have happened.

In Tours, Mama, I met a real countess and spent the day at the magnificent chateau of a real marquise, both of whom had worked for the American soldiers, during the war, both of whom were pulling the leg of every American who could give them publicity. They laid themselves out for me, thinking I was a

[1] Homer A. Watt, Chairman of the English Department, Washington Square College, New York University.
[2] One of Tom's best friends from boyhood.

great American journalist, who would tell all the American papers about it. I have one of the funniest stories you ever heard.

I have a letter from Professor Arnold this morning from the South of France—St. Raphael. He has returned from Italy and wants me to come down—he has taken a cottage for his wife and kids. Says they can fix me up "for a few days." I'm going tonight to Lyon, in a day or two to Marseilles, and afterwards to St Raphael. Remember I've accepted N.Y.U. If the *Citizen* is afraid to publish my voyage (which may get them in a libel suit) Mrs. Roberts will give you mss. The thing now is for me to get it all on paper.

Write me at once; I shall write you all from the South—but write now. And forgive the haste of this 11th hour letter.

Send all mail to Am. Express Co, Paris—it will be forwarded.

God bless you all—I wish I could enclose the fine letter of Professor Watt. It made me feel a little proud—at any rate, as if I were of some use to someone (although I don't believe I'm worth $2000 a year to anyone). He said, "Please come back, Wolfe. Send me a special delivery and say you will."

I am reading a great many French books, and speaking badly, but with some fluency at any rate. I talk to anyone and get what I want.

I'm going to drown Mrs. Roberts in MSS. beginning right away. If you're at home, warn her.

And love, a great deal of it, to you all. Don't worry if I've told you little about England and France. It's coming in the MSS.

Spring, thank God, is beginning. In a week everything will be out. The winter here was wonderfully mild—not nearly so cold as Asheville; but considerable rain.

Love to all

TOM

For God's sake, write.

SAINT RAPHAEL
April 14, 1925

DEAR MAMA:

I have been here in Saint Raphael a little village of 6000 or 8000 in the South of France for two weeks now. I came down slowly through France from Paris, stopping midway at Lyon, the great industrial city, at Avignon, and at Marseilles, the great sea port. I am here on the Riviera, within two hours of Nice and Monte Carlo and the Italian border.

I received your $200 when I got here and I have $175 of it left. I am writing hard, and shall stay here another month, rewriting my play, and sending some stories to Mrs. Roberts, which she will keep or dispose of, as she sees fit.

At any rate, all I want to do for the next month is write. I was very lonely, but I have met five English and American people here who have been and are being very kind to me. This part of the world is beyond dreams beautiful. The Mediterranean is flowing in not 100 yards from my room; behind along the whole coast is a range of rocky mountains, sometimes of grey rock, mountains of red. This, along with brilliant sunshine, a glittering blue sea, and a blue sky is the Riviera—the playground of the world.

Along the rocky slopes, or occasionally in the little valleys or plateaus, formed where the mountains bend away from the sea, are built the great white villas of the rich; they are creamy-colored with roofs of brilliant red tile—and the rich soil around them is bursting with a heavy growth that is half tropical—half northern—scrub pine, palm, cork, and flowers of green and red and gold so brilliant that they seem to be painted or embroidered, but not to grow.

If you look at the map you will see that the South of France is still very far North of Florida—it is about level, I should say, with New York, but it is, of course, vastly warmer. But it is not so warm as Florida in winter; you need your overcoat in the shade, and the nights are cold.

I think I told you that I had received an offer from N.Y.U. for September, and that I shall probably be back there. I have a story about an old countess which I believe will be good enough for almost anyone. I shall send it in two weeks.

If this letter is not long, know that every other thing I write and am sending to Mrs. Roberts is for you. You will understand this. What I am doing, beyond my play, is to make a fairly complete record of my journey. It will at any rate be vastly useful to me later. This has been a tremendous expense for me. You will be glad to know that I am reading French like a streak. I have lost weight, but I feel well.

My plans are briefly this: here for another month, followed by a short trip into Italy, and a return through France to England. I want to go to Southern England in warm weather for exploration. After that, home.

Don't worry; you will never regret this trip. It has been a treasure house to me.

I am writing this letter briefly and rapidly in order to get it off this afternoon. God bless you all, and prosper you.

I am most happy to hear of your success in Miami; you are a great business woman, but I have inherited none of your talent.

With My Deepest Love to All

TOM

I hope you can read this. Continue to send mail to American Express, Paris

ST. RAPHAEL
May 26, 1925

DEAR MAMA:—

Your letter came yesterday, containing the check, which I have deposited at the bank here until my departure tomorrow or next day. I am going into Italy for a week or ten days, returning after that to Paris, and then back to England, which I want to see in summer—particularly the southern part, Cornwall and Devon, which is particularly lovely at this season.

Since coming to this little town I have done considerable writing; I am thoroughly tired as I write but I hope to be about my work again in two or three days. It has grown hot here—most of the English and Americans have departed, and my sole companions have been two very kind and wonderful women—a mother and her daughter, lonely like me. These women are great ladies; they are the wife and daughter of a very famous actor, Louis Calvert, who died two years ago in New York. He was an Englishman, but he loved America so well that he took naturalization papers. These women, thanks partly to my persuasion, are going back to the city they love in another week—New York. I look forward to their companionship there next year.

Mrs. Calvert's mother is an immensely rich old woman; she— Mrs. Calvert—was born and lived for eighteen years on their great sheep ranch in South America. They had there—have there now —100,000 acres and over a half million sheep. There are eight children, and each of them is given a set income of £1000 a year out of the profits of the business. This would seem to be enough to support two women—it amounts to about $5000—but Mrs. Calvert is a very generous and extravagant woman, and she can hardly pull through. She came here to save—her mother, who is now 78, is a little woman, half paralyzed, with a streak of cruelty in her: she has promised to help her with extra gifts, as she helps her other children. But so far she has done nothing. Usually, if wool gets a good price, the income is greater: last year she got £1400. She has already borrowed in advance, so that she has only £300 of her income left for the next year. The other day, however, her mother wrote from London, saying she was giving her £200 extra. This gives her about £500 for the next year, and on the strength of this, she is leaving this hole, and sailing from Marseilles to New York.

I can not tell you how beautifully good these two women have been to me. I came here almost two months ago, desperately lonely, and suffering from a bad attack of heartbreak. I think we liked each other from the start, because we were all lonely, and the place was filled with cheap third rate English and Americans, who could not afford the more expensive resorts such as Nice and Monte Carlo, and who loaded the air with poisonous gossip.

I was staying, I still am staying, at a wretched little hotel without a bath, just over the kitchen; hot, smelly, dreary—the two women had rented a little villa high on a hill behind the town overlooking the sea. They came down in the evening to the café to eat and, finding that they were sometimes accosted, frightened, or followed by the particularly low breed of French-and-Italian population which infests this place, I began taking them home at night, staying late, reading, talking. I shall never forget them; I believe they will never forget me. I have never read them a line I have written—they have taken me solely on my face valuation which, ragged and unkempt as I am, is not very great, perhaps; but they have done me the honor of believing there is something of goodness and greatness in me, and I shall try not to disappoint them.

This voyage has done a great deal more than show me places: it has shown me people, three or four very fine people, and I believe I have grown immeasurably. I have been terribly lonely; but that has been good for me; and I have learned to work day by day. I shall not fail from lack of effort, and I am willing to work indefinitely to do my best, to secure some recognition.

I look forward with joy to my return to England:—I have loved London ever since I first saw it, and somehow or other, cold and insolent as they sometimes are, I believe in the character and honesty of the English.

I cannot tell you my feelings concerning the French in this letter:—it's too long a business. They have some very attractive qualities, but I do not trust in the depth of their feelings, or in the honesty of their friendship. There is something false about their amiability: they are always waiting for a tip, or a purchase, or a donation.

Of course, at the present time they do not like my country. They are very indignant because our government has asked them to pay the money they borrowed during the war. They print insulting cartoons in their papers and magazines depicting Uncle Sam as a money lender and a usurer, who will grind the blood out of his victims in order to make them pay. American vulgarity and American Philistinism is a source of much satire and jest; also the American tourist who spends his money here.

I suppose, like all nations, we have our vulgarities; but I have seen no group of people more vulgar in its manners, its speech, and the tone of its voices than the French middle class. And no matter how materially-minded our own people have been, or are now, there is a certain satisfaction in knowing that, at least, they wash themselves with some regularity.

I shall never go about waving my country's flag—I believe I recognize a great many of our faults, but the faults I recognize are not the faults Europeans accuse us of. That is what sometimes annoys me. They may curse us all they please if they only curse us for sins we have committed; but they are forever cursing us for things we are not guilty of.

For example, one of the great superstitions about Americans is that they love the dollar—that they will sacrifice anything to get it. And yet, nowhere, I believe, in the world, will you find sheer greed, sheer miserliness, so much as among the French peasants, who have been known frequently to bury money in the earth, hoarding it, keeping it, loving it, piece by piece.

There are ten thousand things I could tell you about places, people, events; but a letter is too short, and I would not know where to begin or stop. Suffice it to say that I have enough to keep me busy writing long after I get home; and that in the meanwhile I may put a little of it on paper to send to Mrs. Roberts. God knows what may become of it, but it may be of value to me in later years.

I read with great satisfaction of your success in the form of human activity you like best. It seems an irony that I, who have been boosted, praised, and believed in by many people am as yet obscure, unknown, and may continue so; while you, who never had such advertisement, are able, when you are past sixty, to carry to success almost anything you undertake. Certainly, if final judgment had to be passed on our lives to-morrow, there could be no doubt as to which of us had succeeded or failed. I appreciate your belief in me, and for the sake of the happiness of us both, I hope we shall both live to see it justified, but I know that at the present time I am far more dependent on you than you on me.

I am delighted to know that you are really going to build a house of your own at Miami; I believe, however, you will continue to find Asheville a good place to spend Summer and Autumn.

You speak of a voyage to Europe next summer, with Mabel. Nothing would give me greater pleasure than to conduct you, and I might be of some slight service in showing you about—not that I have by any means an encyclopedic knowledge of England and France. Few people have. I do not think you would find it expensive. I believe $150 a month would see you through comfortably. What I do advise against is the usual American tourist's two or three months' voyage, in which they try to visit all the lands and cities on the face of the globe. These poor devils who go in the tourist parties are driven like sheep from place to place, returning exhausted at the end of what was to have been a voyage of pleasure and exploration, with a dim nightmarish recollection of cathedrals, ruins, hotels—God knows what. Life is too short to kill yourself and your pleasure in this way. If you come for two or three months, don't put more in the pitcher than it will hold. Stay a month or so in England, seeing a few of the best things slowly, and so with France, Germany, or Italy. You will not only know far more when you return, but you will have enjoyed yourself without killing yourself.

A great many people feel it is their duty to spend a great part of their time visiting cathedrals and art museums. If you are not interested in pictures or in cathedrals, why go? I am, rather, but I should certainly not go to them if I liked something else better. The only satisfaction a great many people get from a trip to Europe is the ability to say "I've been there" when a great many places are mentioned. This means very little as they remember vaguely what they have seen.

To come as I have come, to study, to watch, to observe is an intensely valuable but intensely saddening experience. Hatred, suspicion, and dislike is abroad in the world, sowing the seeds already of another and more destructive war. The French, of course, like no one but themselves. Needless to say, they hate the Germans; they are jealous of the Italians who are growing rapidly in size and power; they fear and hate the Russians, who have spread communist propaganda throughout their country; they are, and have always been, the enemies of the English; and they dislike us, because we are rich, prosperous, because they owe us money which we are asking them to pay. Of course, we are paying the penalty of being too prosperous in a world impoverished by an idiot and ruinous war. Very few people like us, and very few would be sorry to see misfortune fall upon us.

I sometimes grow impatient with America for being a damn fool sentimentalist:—our money goes for hospitals, libraries, reconstruction work over here, and we are repaid with insults and mockery. We are accused of having entered the war to make more money, of having come in at the end to save our faces and our hides, of having sent Wilson, who is pointed to as a fool and a scoundrel who made a peace that has ruined them. Of course, poor Wilson had very little to do with it: the peace that was made, and for which they are now paying, was the work of the rogues who ran their governments at the time.

Of course, I feel rather sorry for the French. They are a feminine race, with the jealousy and the bitter tongue of a woman. They are the most provincial of peoples, rarely travelling beyond their country, because they are convinced they have the only country fit to live in, the only art and literature worth knowing. As a result they simply welter in the most absurd prejudices about the rest of the world; and they are steadily alienating the affections of all their former allies while they clank a big sword about, many sizes too large for them, in an effort to intimidate and crush Germany.

Germany, of course, has twice their population, and a dozen times their vitality. I am afraid that this poor, vain, egotistical little race will one morning awake to find themselves alone in the world with the Prussians coming down across their borders like a river. If that ever happens, and France is alone, she will be wiped out. She has neither the strength nor the stamina to go it with Germany on her own.

In spite of France's professed inability to pay her debts, everyone is at work here. There is by no means the unemployment one finds in England: there is, in fact, no unemployment at all. Of one thing you may be assured: she will not pay her debts if she can avoid paying them, and if she pays it will be because she knows she would lose in commerce, currency, and business if she refused to pay.

We are taught in America to dislike the English, and to believe in the French. It is simple madness. The English are often insolent, and frequently jealous of our commercial power, but they have character and, I believe, down below all the rest, a certain feeling of kinship with us. Moreover, they have a fundamental honesty.

I am wiring the American Express Company tomorrow to hold my mail until I return to Paris from Italy. That may be two weeks. I shall visit several of the Italian cities, Florence, Milan, Genoa, and Venice, but I shall not get to Rome this time. This is the Holy Year in Rome, and thousands of rich American Catholics are making pilgrimages there. I understand that rooms are hard to get and that one must pay cutthroat prices. I may stop off at Nice and run over to the Island of Corsica, Napoleon's birthplace, for a day or so. It is eight hours by boat from Nice.

I have received letters from Mabel, Fred, and Frank recently. Ask their indulgence if I do not write until I return to Paris. I have written acceptance of the N.Y.U. position and had a very nice, a very flattering letter in answer. All told, things might be worse. I shall send some more stuff to Mrs. Roberts, I shall come back to New York with a play, very bad or very good, and I shall have some means of feeding myself if heaven does not suddenly begin to rain green backs.

God bless you and keep you all in safety and happiness.

TOM.

CRANSTON'S IVANHOE HOTEL,
BLOOMSBURY STREET,
LONDON, W.C.I.
Monday, July 27, 1925

DEAR MAMA: I received the money you cabled last week, but thus far I have had no letter from you. I have been in England a month now, since my return from France and Italy, and I want to come home about the middle of August—in a little more than two weeks.

I have sent Mrs. Roberts no more MSS., partly because I have been travelling a good part of the time, partly because she told me some of the packages were damaged; and I have been unable to discover whether all I sent arrived.

I have made a great many more notes all during the past ten days and have been writing again. I shall send her three or four more batches before I sail; and I am bringing a valise full home with me, including my play.

I am going up to the English Lake Country today and shall be gone a week. It is one of the loveliest parts of England, I am told; it was also the home, for a long period, of the poets Wordsworth and Coleridge.

England, London especially, has been damnably hot until the past day or so; now, with true British changeability, the weather has become cold and rainy.

I took cold shortly after my arrival, and for the better part of three weeks I was a great deal more dead than alive.

I was in Italy for three weeks—until my money was gone, and I had just enough to take me from Venice to Paris. I knew I could not afford an extensive tour of the country; I confined my travels to the Northern part—to the cities of Genoa, Milan, and Venice.

The Italian police, including the secret service, did me the honor of keeping a very close watch over me; in Milan, the largest city in Italy, I was stopped by plain clothes men twice at night, searched, examined; and my passport read backwards and forwards. I haven't the faintest idea what it was all about, but I enjoyed it hugely, and I like the Italians tremendously. They are a lovable, witty, pleasant, affectionate, and unrestrained people, with infinitely greater sincerity than the French; and their country is as beautiful a place as God has created. Venice remains for me not as a city, but as a dream floating upon an enchanted water. I cannot go off here on any attempt to describe that magical place, where there is no traffic, only the dark, innumerable little side canals slapping gently under your window, leading into the Grand Canal—the Broadway of Venice—flanked with beautiful palaces centuries old. Once Venice was a republic—and she was mistress of the seas, and the commercial head of the world. That was over 600 years ago. She has since decreased both in size and wealth: the population now is about 170,000.

At night, the lagoon, the Grand Canal, and the side canals are thronged with the most beautiful boats in all the world, the gondolas, which come curving out of the water like carved smoke.

The gondolier stands behind, upright, propelling the boat with a single oar, which he uses on one side only, but with a skill you would not believe possible. They go around corners in the narrow side canal grazing the walls or another gondola by a fraction of an inch; but they never touch.

I can't go on—I should keep on forever. I have, I think, the idea for a fine story about Venice—I shall start it before I come home. I was in Paris a little more than a week when I returned—it, too, is beautiful now, save for the presence of a hundred thousand tourists.

I returned from Venice to Paris—second class—in order to avoid the expense of a French sleeper. I broke the journey in two by spending the night in Switzerland, at Montreux, a famous resort on Lake Lucerne, a mile or two from the Castle of Chillon. The mountains rise like sheer walls above the bluest water in the world—but I'll tell you of that, too.

I'm very sorry my expenses have increased these past two months; but I bought some clothes—a suit, hat and shoes; it was necessary to buy an Italian visa to enter the country, and I have traveled possibly 2500 miles. In Italy, not knowing their beautiful language, I spoke French, which a great many of them understand. I tried to economize on lodgings, and so forth, but I was under a disadvantage—moving in haste, and not knowing the country.

London seems terribly expensive to me after France: in fact London seems almost as expensive as New York: but I believe thoroughly in the honesty of the English, and I know that I am charged no more than an Englishman, despite their very desperate economic condition. So much may not be said either for the French or for the Italian.

I am anxious now to economize in every way possible, until I return to work. I have done considerable writing, and acquired a million ideas; I have come alone, wandered alone, almost without plan,—indeed, in an insane fashion—but it has been right *for me*. I venture to think I have done and seen things one in a million never do. I have known some sadness, a great deal of loneliness, but I am older, more matured,—I believe, more of a man. Do not despair: at least someone has enough faith in me to offer me a small wage for my services; and presently, I think, I shall come partly into my own kingdom. I know that I have something to say now; it twists at my brain and heart for expression. If God would only give me a hundred hands to write it down.

Mama, do you want me to come home before I go back to New York? I want to see you all tremendously, but there is the expense of the fare from N.Y. home and back again. I am going to look up third class passenger going home—it is about $90; and if I can avoid going through Ellis Island for detention or inspection, I shall come third.

If you have not written me by the time you receive this, I suggest you cable a word or two. I have $140 left of the $200 you sent—I had borrowed money from a friend—a girl I knew at Cambridge. There are thousands of Americans here, but I stay by myself mainly, going through old book stalls, prowling around old parts of London, or striking up acquaintances with Cockneys, bums, and other interesting people.

The English have been recently amused and interested by the great "Monkeyville" trial at Dayton. All the papers carried leading articles day by day; every one wrote letters and editorials, and the opinion seems to be that intellectually our population is about 60 years behind their's. I have something to say about it in something I'm writing now.

This must stop. My train leaves in an hour or so. Give Mabel, Fred, and everyone my love; and let me know in time what you think I should do. I think perhaps I must be back in New York by Sept 15.

Tom

This hotel is a very good place, cheap, clean, and comfortable —if you ever have occasion to use it. I have been here two days; before I was at a lodging house near by—a shilling cheaper, and a thousand times worse.

HOTEL ALBERT
ELEVENTH STREET & UNIVERSITY PLACE
NEW YORK
Saturday

DEAR MAMA: Here is a short letter to thank you for the telegram you and Mabel sent me on my birthday; I am writing her, too.

I have been extremely busy at the opening of the term: my work thus far has given me no time for writing, or for anything else. My friends, however, have flocked around me, and have given me much entertainment.

I spent the week-end at Olin Dows's—the big place up the Hudson; Henry Carlton was in town, and we were together for three or four days—his play is to be produced here next month and he returns soon; and a very beautiful and wealthy lady,[1] who was extremely kind to me on the boat, and who designs scenery

[1] Aline Bernstein, the distinguished stage and costume designer.

and costumes for the best theatres in New York, and supports another with her money, has seen me daily and entertained me extensively. In addition three theatres have sent to me for my plays: someone or something has boosted my stock during my absence. Kenneth MacGowan, who, in company with Eugene O'Neill, our foremost dramatist, and Robert E. Jones, our best scene designer, runs the Provincetown Theatre, wrote me the other day asking for my old play and for my new one. The Theatre Guild has also sent for them. The old play was in the hands of the Provincetown and the Guild once before: they kept it several months, and rejected it; but they are now asking for it again. All this means nothing, remember, save that they wish to see it and reconsider it: and that they have come to me this time.

I hope to God one of them goes on: at the present writing it seems that I shall have little time for writing this year, and that if I market anything, it must be something that I have already written.

The weather here is clear and bright; but during the past day it has taken an extreme turn towards cold. I got out my overcoat to-day; it is wrinkled and stained with something the French dropped on it, but it is warm.

I continue, thank God, in excellent health, with an expensive and growing appetite; my pay, which was due Oct 1, was delayed because of failure to give my address, or for some other reason: I got it to-day—$166:66:66, which, multiplied by 12, makes $2,000. I don't know what I shall do with it, but my mind is divided between a case of Scotch whiskey and the first instalment on a Ford sedan. What is your opinion: do you incline toward the liquor or the Ford? I have bought no clothes yet: there has not been time. But if my present social triumph becomes permanent, I am going to get very very gay.

Mabel spoke of coming to New York in "two weeks." Persuade her, in God's name, to come before I grow old and toothless, and try to persuade yourself to come along. Most of the real estate here has already been bought, but I am told you Florida people are very clever at buying and selling property that does not even exist: New York should give you a wide scope for your talents.

At any rate, write me a word or two between operations: I hope above all else for your health and happiness and long life, and for any success you believe in for yourself, whatever its purpose, whatever its use. I can no longer grow excited over any of the things that ever seemed to me excellent and pleasant and wise: whether it be the color or length of God's beard, the fame of a poet, the future of the race, or the accumulation of treasure here or in heaven. The only thing I do believe in, in this universal futility and emptiness and oblivion, is getting all the entertainment and exhilaration we can out of the whole bad business: let us do what we will and can and enjoy, whether it be the making of little patterns of words on paper, or the buying or selling of clay in North Carolina, or sand in Florida.

Both, I assure you, are equally useless. God bless you.

Том.

HOTEL ALBERT
11th Street & University Place
New York
Sunday, Jan. 31, 1926

DEAR MAMA:—

I have been extremely busy with examinations since I returned —this is a breathing spell.

Last week, after giving my examinations here I went up to Boston to visit friends. While there, I went in to see Uncle

Henry at his office. He has asked me to communicate to you the sad news that Aunt Laura is dead: she died on Wednesday, I believe, about two weeks ago at a hospital from heart's disease. As you know, she has suffered from this trouble for years:—the condition became acute only a few weeks ago.

Uncle Henry was in a great state of emotion: he broke down and cried, said the "light of his life had gone out," told me that he had re-joined the Church during the past week so that his spiritual union with his wife might not be broken, and finally got me to read a letter he was writing to all of her friends, which amounted to a Eulogy of his services as a husband. He said in it that he "had *idolized* his wife for fifty years, and that now he *idealized* her."

It was very plain to me that Uncle Henry was anxious now to put on a good face before the world. He told me that I probably never observed the close affection that existed between him and his wife, but that it was there all the same, and he said that this affection had become stronger than ever during these two years that I have been away. In proof of his great affection, he said that all his goods and possessions and all his money during the past fifteen years had been held jointly with his wife. I am telling you all this not to attack Uncle Henry, for whom I feel some sympathy, but to give you the very plain facts of the matter. He will not suffer much, I think. He will spend another week or two in his present state of self-pity, and after having convinced himself that he was a generous, tender, and devoted husband, and that no friction or lack of loving understanding ever separated him from his wife, he will continue on his way as before.

I think you had better write Uncle Henry as soon as you can: express your regret and sympathy. Of course you will say nothing of all this.

I have worked hard; the Theatre Guild has my play yet; I am

working on the other, revising it; I am in good health; and I have no other news for you.

I wish you great fortune in your investments, and I send all the family my love. Write me when you are able.

Let us all be decent and fair and generous to one another; let us not talk over-much of our generosity and nobility; let us not curse and revile and abuse one another: let us not be torn by jealousy and ill feeling. We do not become great people merely by whooping it up and saying we are, nor generous people by calling our selfishness and our lust for praise generosity. At any rate, pretense and dishonesty does not deceive me any more. I was a thousand years old when I was born; I can, I am sorry to say, see through most people as easily as I see through a window pane. About the greatest desire I have at present is to step as hard as I can upon cant, hypocrisy, and twaddle where I see it. There are few heroic lives: about the only one I know a great deal about is my own. This is boastful, perhaps, but as it is also true, I see no cause to deny it. Year after year, in the face of hostility, criticism, misunderstanding, and stupidity, I have been steadfast in my devotion to the high, passionate, and beautiful things of this world.

To you all, now, I can give nothing perhaps that you value except the assurances of my loyalty and affection. This, strange as it may seem, is one of the things that cannot be valued—not even at $2000 a front inch. And I shall probably go on being loyal and honest in my affection as long as I live—I can't help it— whether it is deserved or not.

Again, with great affection and with sincere wishes for your health and prosperity, I am

Your son

Tom

FK NEWYORK NY JUN 22 26

MRS. JULIA E WOLFE

48 SPRUCE ST   ASHEVILLE N CAR—

GOOD BYE MAMA   SAILING ONE OCLOCK TONIGHT BERENGARIA

WRITE ME AMERICAN EXPRESS CO LONDON   GOOD LUCK HEALTH

AND HAPPINESS   LOVE TO ALL

TOM

815 AM

On Board the Cunard R.M.S. Berengaria

June 23, 1926   1:00 A.M.

DEAR MAMA:—I am writing this on the boat at the time she is scheduled to sail—one o'clock in the morning.

However, for one reason or another—probably the tides—we may not sail for another hour or two. I instructed a friend to send you a telegram and I hope you get it. I have had, of course, no news from any of you.

I wish you what we have perhaps never been able to get for ourselves as a family—happiness, repose, and comfort. I want you to know that I am doing what I think best for my happiness and my success. I shall work hard: I shall hope for much—there is nothing to be gained now by attempting to explain what can not be explained, what must be understood.

I must tell you that my belief in any affection my family bears to me has been severely tried—but I give back to you all, without cant or hypocrisy or pretension, the deep feeling I continue to hold for you all.

I believe we are worshiping different Gods, but if we can't understand, let us try to be loyal. And so, God bless you all.

TOM

I am going to Paris for a week. After that,
American Express Co., London

Written from THE PUMP ROOM, BATH.

Britain's Historic Spa.

Sunday, July 18, 1926

DEAR MAMA:—I am writing you this note from the famous old Pump Room, Bath, the centre of England's fashion a century ago:—all of the great lords and ladies came here to take the waters and enjoy themselves. It is perhaps the most beautiful town I have ever seen; it climbs a hill, and is surrounded by steep beautiful green hills. It was built on a uniform plan by one architect.

I was in Paris 10 days, and have been in London a week. Now I am on my way North to the Lake District; in the country there I shall settle down to work. London was very hot—this morning in Bath, however, we were treated to a gigantic deluge of rain—the most, say the natives, in 62 years.

I have no time to say more at the moment—I had a suit of clothes made in London—the best I ever had—for $40.00—two pair of trousers. Other prices are high. The country apparently has resumed its usual course after the strike, but there are a million and a half unemployed.

I shall write you fully in a day or two, and tell you my plans. I got your letter in London; I was delighted to get a letter without bad news in it—one of the very few I have had from home in years. In particular I noticed what you had to say "not understanding" something or other. I can make no claim to great wisdom in understanding people—I doubt that many people can—but I believe I understand very well to what lengths the mania for property drives people: to the deception of one's self and others. The best thing any of us can do in this world, perhaps, is to speak up and have our say when the time comes—to be grateful for all love and kindliness, but to step bluntly on cant and twaddle and nonsense. I have no belief in your property or in anyone's property anymore: I have no hope or belief or expectancy of getting anything from it now or hereafter—and he who ceases to hope or believe ceases to desire. But I have not yet ceased hoping or believing that there may be left in some of you some genuine atom of affection, sympathy, and good will for me, in spite of our years of absence, and of the spiritual sea which separates our lives.

I shall write in a day or two. Meanwhile, God bless you all, and prosper you.

TOM

Write American Express Co, London

[*Post Card*]

YORK, ENGLAND
July, 1926

DEAR MAMA:—I am here in York in the North of England. Left Bath and Bristol, went to Lincoln, where the finest cathedral in England is situated and came here. The picture here is of Fountain Abbey, the finest old Norman ruin in England. It is 25 miles from here. I went there yesterday on my way to Lakes—

TOM

[*Card dated Aug. 6th, 1926*—AMBLESIDE]

DEAR MAMA:

Here is a little English village in the Lake District, N. of London, where I have been staying and writing, about two weeks. Hope to have news of you when I return to London. Much love and much health—
TOM

[Post Card]

LONDON, August 28, '26 [?]

DEAR MAMA:—Got your letter the other day—writing you— Living in London now writing my book— Have been in Scotland and North of England. Lived in this village in Lake District for two weeks. How is your property? Better I trust. Good luck—prosperity—

TOM

[Post Card]

BRIGHTON, ENG. Sept., 1926

DEAR MAMA:—This is England's great shore resort for poor people. That explains my being here. Writing you a letter. Good luck, good health.

TOM

[London]

Saturday Night
Sept. 11, 1926

DEAR MAMA:—I have been in London about a month since I returned from Scotland. I have two rooms in Chelsea, a quiet part of the city, where I have been hard at work on a book. I am alone—know few people, and therefore have to work.

England has had a warm sunny lovely Summer—a beautiful country, wretched with unemployment and labor trouble. I am going across the Channel to-morrow for two weeks—my address will be American Express Co, Brussels, Belgium. After that I return here: in October I may go up to Oxford University for a month or six weeks.

I am sorry to hear of the trouble at home—Frank's illness, and so on. It is no new matter—I have nothing to say that would help or affect the matter in the slightest way. I hope by now he has recovered, or, at any rate, is feeling better.

The Summer is over—I sometimes hear from you in the winter, but never in the Summer—that's the time for business, I suppose. Well, I trust you have been successful, but a letter from Robert Bunn, who occasionally writes me—since the black sheep must stick together—tells me things have gone pretty dead. I don't know whether you have lost out or not—if you have, try to be content on what you have, feed and house yourself properly, and forget about it the rest of your life. Money in our family has been a deadly poison—for it you have lost comfort, peace, and in the end, money itself; it has been a breeder of suspicion, of jealousy, of falsehood among brother and sister— What you get is always under-valued, what the other fellow gets, over-valued. This sad bitter story is not new: it has been repeated millions of times over throughout the world.

I am very tired to-night—unable to write either an interesting, or a long letter. I am working very hard on my book—I hope something may come of it; whatever happens to it, whether it gets published or not, it will be dedicated to the best and truest friend I have ever had—the one person who has given love, comfort, and understanding to my lonely and disordered life.

I may go back to New York in the winter, if I finish the book, to get employment—possibly in the movies, doing scenario work. I hope that I shall never teach again.

My life here is quiet enough—certainly it is lonely enough, although people are very kind. When I am not working, I walk through the million streets of London, watching the eternal parade and pageantry of life that passes by. My health is good— I have had a cold, but it is better.

Good-bye for the present. I shall try to write you at length from Belgium. God keep you all well, bringing to you some greater measure of happiness than you have known.

Whenever possible, write me cheerfully.

With love to you all,

TOM

[*Post Card*]

BRUSSELS
Monday, Sept. 20, 1926

DEAR MAMA: I am in Belgium for two weeks. After that, back to England. Think I shall be at Oxford in November. Working all the time on my book. This is Brussels, a city about the size of Baltimore—very gay. They call it "the little Paris."

Good luck, good fortune to you all.

TOM

HOTEL BRISTOL & MARINE
9, Boulevard Botanique, Bruxelles

ANTWERP Sept 25 1926 (envelope)

DEAR MAMA: I am writing you this from the city of Antwerp in Belgium, altho the letter head is from my hotel in Brussels. I came here yesterday from Brussels, 25 or 30 miles away—tomorrow I am going to Bruges—a city of canals, like Venice—and from there back to England. I have been working all the while.

I have read in the Paris editions of the *New York Herald* of the great tragedy in Florida. I hope that no one for whom I care has suffered loss of life or limb in the disaster: I am reasonably sure many of you have lost money.

I am beginning to learn pity for human weakness—I have a compassion for all of the poor blind fumbling Creatures that inhabit this earth—a compassion I did not have at twenty, for young men are thoughtless and cruel. People are driven to avarice, meanness, ungenerous living for themselves and all about them, but somehow I don't feel the loathing for it all I once did:—We are all, to a certain degree, little and weak, and we don't know it; we wish to appear great, we convince ourselves that the course of our lives is right. We build up our dreams of wealth, congratulating ourselves all the time that we are perfectly business-like, that nothing can go wrong: the place is bound to grow—we can't lose.

And so we, the wise ones, figure on everything but thunder, lightning, earthquakes, and the storm, two years away, that will gather in the ocean against our money.

I am happy to see in the papers that the first reports of the loss of life were exaggerated. I can not see that much else matters greatly, if you are all safe. I believe you can better sustain a loss than Fred—I understood he had invested money down there: I am very sorry to think it may be gone. The possession of money—a competent sum—may be of great importance to a young man: it may mean independance, marriage, a family—a sense of security he could not otherwise have. Therefore, if anything can be done to retrieve what he has lost, or to assist him in any way, you should, if you are able, give him help freely, and at once.

People certainly learn some things through misfortune. In

this little country of Belgium, which was entirely occupied, a bloody battlefield, with its inhabitants either held prisoner, or driven into flight, during four years of war, there is so much gaiety and mirth—in spite of the fact that their wealth was destroyed, a sense of knowing what life is for. Brussels and Antwerp are fine cities—the size of Baltimore and Washington: they are filled with many ancient and beautiful buildings, churches, and museums: there are thousands of cafés—blocks in which there are hardly anything else—the population sits outside and drinks beer. These people are more Saxon than the French—they are not so dark, nervous, or talkative. French is the language generally spoken in business and commerce, but among themselves they speak Flemish—a language similar to German.

In spite of the lowness of the Belgian franc—it is as low as the French, everyone seems to be busy: there are few people out of work. Certainly they have not the terrible condition of unemployment and economic depression that faces England.

They are very fierce and proud about their war-record, declaring they owe no one anything, have never been defeated, held off all Germany, and man for man are superior to anyone on earth.

I am all alone. I talk to no one save waiters, strange travellers, and so on—but my life is used to loneliness. I get on.

My address is the same—Am. Ex. Co. London. I may go to Oxford in October for a month. I hope to find mail from you in London telling me you are all well and safe and, if possible, that the loss is not as great as it seems.

When you get this I shall be twenty-six years of age. There is nothing further I care to say about it.

Good-bye, good luck, God keep you all.

TOM

OXFORD, FRIDAY
Nov 19, 1926

DEAR MAMA:—I have been here at Oxford almost five weeks—
I am leaving to-morrow, and after a few days in the south of
England I am going to Paris, and from there on a short trip to
Germany. I expect to leave France for America late in Decem-
ber—I shall probably spend Christmas on the water and arrive in
New York in time for New Year's.

I have done a great deal of work here and am very tired. The
month of November has been grey, gloomy and rainy—true
English weather at this season, very depressing.

If you write me before I come home—if there's time—you'd
better write me to The American Express Co., 11 Rue Scribe,
Paris. I will be there by the time this reaches you.

I have gone about the university here a great deal—I have met
a great many of the young men who have been very good to
me. But I am not sorry to leave. I am tired and heavy. I shall
finish my book in New York; after that, I shall find employment
—perhaps in the movies.

I hope things are going well with you all—I am glad to know
that the Florida catastrophe was not as bad as we at first supposed.

The English coal strike still drags on—people hope it will be
settled soon, but the country is in a desperate position. Our
nation, because of a great number of things, but chiefly because
of our prosperity, and our attitude on the war debts, is very
bitterly disliked here and in Europe to-day.

What shall I write you? I don't know, because I am tired, and
because from most of you I do not hear at all, and from you only
once in two or three months. I suppose in every family there's
always a stranger, always an outsider. In our family Ben was
the stranger until his death—I suppose I'm the other one. I shall

spend Christmas alone this year, but wherever I am, I do not think I shall be more unhappy than I was at home last Christmas —I hope you will all be happier this one.

Goodbye—mama. God bless you all, and keep you well, and give you whatever you are after. If you write me before I return, send your letter to Paris! Good luck and good health to you all.

TOM

Saturday

I want nothing from any of you except assurance of your health and well being.

Tell Fred I'll write him from France.

[*Post Card*]

TORQUAY, DEVON
Nov. 23, 1926

DEAR MAMA: This is Torquay a seacoast town in the South of England—I left Oxford two days ago and am going to France later in the week. Hope things are going well for you, and that all are in good health.

Love,

TOM

[*Christmas Card*]

MUNICH, MONDAY
Dec. 13, 1926

DEAR MAMA:—I think I shall be in New York in time to wish you a Happy New Year by wire. The card wishes you a happy and merry Christmas in German, and that goes for me, in American, with all my heart.

God bless you all.

TOM

HARVARD CLUB
27 West 44th Street
Thursday Night Jan. 6, 1927

DEAR MAMA: I came back from Europe as a second class passenger on the *Majestic,* landing in New York on the Wednesday before New Year's. But I waited until New Year's Eve to send you greetings. I got Fred's wire New Year's day, and I had a letter from you yesterday, enclosing a check for $50.00, and another a few minutes ago, which had been sent to England, and back to me from Paris.

I am living in a dilapidated old building over a pressing club down in Eighth Street. I have no bath, but cold water, toilet, and a huge room with skylights—the whole floor, formerly a sweatshop, I believe. But I like the space and the light. If I can keep warm I'm going to live there and finish my book. The rent's only $35.00 a month—very little in New York. The University people welcomed me with open arms, tried to sign me for two years, and have offered me $2200 to teach seven months, beginning Feb. Three days a week—three hours a day. I have until Monday to answer. My friend stands by me, insists that I finish my book first, and that I can get work later with an advertising company she knows, which will give me more money. I do not know yet what I'm going to do.

I stayed in Germany about two weeks, returned to Paris for three or four days, and came back on a fast boat for New Year's. I want this letter to go to you tonight, and I will not attempt description. I'll do that later. I am very glad to be back—I have a few friends here who are faithful to me—the old wander-urge will come again, I suppose, but for several months I want to draw in and work. I like the bracing dry air of America, the vitality, the largeness of things—there are also things I don't

like—our loudness, our whoop-it-up methods, our childish boast-
ing, but I have faith enough to believe we'll get over these as
we grow a little older. And I couldn't be anything but American
if I tried. We have it in us to be a really great people, I think,
whenever we find what is sometimes called a soul. And I know
we have one somewhere. And that is more than I care to say
for the French at present.

I wondered if Uncle Henry would really do it—I see he has.
I am glad to know he has someone who will care for him, and
be his companion. I hope she makes him happy: I'm sorry to
think that his children may be cut off now from sharing in
what estate he has. They were certainly very bitter against him
after Laura's death, but there is probably a reason for such bitterness. But give him, at any rate, my best wishes, and ask him,
please, why he has never shipped my books to the address in
New York that I gave him. I handed him two or three dollars, as
I remember, for transportation. I may yet have to go to Boston
for them.

I am glad to hear of your lease of Market Street. It should
give you a steady income for your living expenses. I hope you
are right in your predictions for the future of Florida and of
Asheville, but I hope nothing resembling a boom ever comes
to either place again. I am sure we can all manage a living.
Somehow the N.Y.U. people are still anxious to have me—I hate
teaching, but it pleased me to see that I was wanted and that
they were willing to pay money for what I did. I am a very poor
teacher, but they seem to think I "inspire" the boys—God knows
what that is. I suppose I could get $2400 if I haggled, but I
can't haggle. I'll get along somehow.

I am rather tired, although physically I am in very good health.
But I have travelled hard these last 6 weeks and I had worked

hard for months before that. And I am just beginning to get adjusted to America again. It is cheerful to know that every one at home is in good health. May it continue so long years. It is news I almost give up hoping for.

Keep yourself well, warm, and fed. I send you all, in spite of this dull midnight letter, my love and my remembrances.

TOM

I think I shall continue to get my mail here for a time. Tell Fred I'll get off a letter to him before the week's out.

HARVARD CLUB
27 West 44th Street
Friday, March 4, 1927 [Envelope]

DEAR MAMA:—

I am on my way up to Boston for a few days in an effort to rescue my books. I have been working very hard and living very cheaply, cooking my own meals. I hope to get the book finished in the Spring.

My h alth is good, but I have felt rotten for two or three days, because there's a leak in the gas meter in my garret and I woke in the morning with a headache. I'll fix it when I return or call a plumber. No time for more now. I'll write when I get back— Tuesday or Wednesday—if you want to reach me for some unexpected reason before that time send message to the address of my friend—Mr. Frederick L. Day, 84 Garden Street, Cambridge, Mass. I won't be staying there—I don't know where (perhaps with another friend)—but that will reach me most conveniently.

Tell Fred I'm writing.

Goodbye, Good health. God bless you all.

Written in great haste at train time

TOM

[This letter enclosed in envelope dated 7/21/27]

HARVARD CLUB
27 West 44th Street
Monday, April 18

DEAR MAMA:—I have not heard from you in several weeks—or months—but suppose you have been well. I am going up to my friend Olin Dows's place in the country to-night for a few days—perhaps for a week. I have worked very hard and am played out, but a day or two in the open should put me right. The address—if you should want to communicate with me quickly—is Foxhollow Farm, Rhinebeck New York (c/o Olin Dows)

I hope all goes well with you, and that you are realizing from your ventures in real estate all you had hoped for. Don't worry about it too much if things are slow. You should have, at any rate, enough to get along with.

I expect to finish my book this Spring. I am chronically tired in my leisure moments, and unable to write long or interesting letters. It all goes into the book.

But take care of yourself and when you have the time, write a few lines. Give my love to everyone. I must go now for my train.

TOM

HARVARD CLUB
27 West 44th Street
Friday   New York, June 3, 1927

DEAR MAMA:—

I have been steadily at it since I wrote you last—the weather has not yet been severely hot and I have managed to stand it in my attic. I'm afraid, however, that it will be too hot to work there after the next two or three weeks. I am very tired but I can see no let-up until I get the thing finished: I find that if I stop writing even for a day, it is hard to get back into it again. I keep getting letters from N. Y. U. telling me of my appointment in September—had another one tonight saying it was all settled. But I've answered nothing definitely yet—I haven't felt free to until I finished the book. Don't know what I'm going to do; but I'm going to be very tired. My health is good—I've lost my appetite, which is sad news to me, but I find one can do with much less food than he thinks he needs.

I never hear from any of you any more—I believe most of you owe me at least one letter, perhaps more. I wrote Mrs. Roberts in care of Mabel because I had lost Mrs. R's new address. Will you ask Mabel if she has been able to deliver it? You congratulated me in your last letter on having "rich friends." I think I am more to be congratulated on being unwilling to use them or gouge them, because they have cared enough for me to help me. I have worked much harder this year than at any time in my life—much harder, I believe, than most people ever work—and I have taken enough to feed me. The garret (used occasionally by another person as a studio) has been given me. Certainly, I shall begin to live in much greater comfort as soon as I go back to employment of any kind. It seems to me that I am one of the few people in America I have ever known who has been faithful to the thing he wanted to do most and told the world to go to hell! Most of them never so far as I can see do anything they like. I have never valued enough I suppose the advantages of having or making money, but since one hundred million of my fellow country men have valued nothing else, there should be room for a few like me. I have—I am afraid this will shock you —very little patriotism. If it were not for circumstances, and the great affection I have for a few people, I should not hesitate to

leave the huge, loud noisy madhouse for a more pleasant part of
the earth. The few first rate Americans I know and value are
as fine as any people I have ever seen—in many respects, finer—
but for the most part we are a nation of overgrown and illbred
children, roaring our virtues out at the top of our voice, the loud-
mouthed men "who won the war"—insolent to everything but
money, servile, boastful, and cowardly, That, I am sorry to say, is
my free opinion of the great intelligent self-governing public of
this noble land—the amalgamated Boosters, Kiwanians, Lions,
and, in general, the Federated Half Breeds of the World. I hope
this does not pain you too much: as a matter of fact I do not
think other countries are much better off—the rabble everywhere
is much the same—loud, ignorant, and cheap, and if their leader
is not always, as is ours, a fool (I refer to that great, far-seeing,
divinely gifted, noble hearted statesman, the Abraham Lincoln
of the Babbitts, the Hon. Calvin Coolidge, who has never said
anything, and has certainly never done anything)—if their leader
is not a fool, I say, their politicians, like ours, are rascals. But at
any rate you can forget about them elsewhere over a glass of
beer or wine that will not send you home without your eyes.
They are not so loud, not so offensive. As a matter of fact I get
along beautifully with the few people I do like—and the others,
the hundred million who surround me, I simply ignore, unless
they begin to blow their bad breath and their superstitions in
my face, to shout and to swagger, to tell me who won the war,
what traitors the English are, and what fools the French, and
why the citizens of this earthly paradise are God's chosen people. Then, if I can't escape, I am forced to tell them the particular kind of swine I think they are. The Southerner on the whole
is a better fellow, I think, than the Yank. He is, God knows,
just as ignorant, he has the same superstitions, but he is quieter,

kinder, slower, and less offensive. New York I detest—it is the apex of discomfort and semi-barbarism. But I stay here because I care for a few people here, and because it is the only place I know of where I can find employment. There is a great deal of money in me if I had a good business manager. I am sure I could make it out of advertising, the movies, or some form of publicity (fat, juicy, sugar coated lies for our great Boob Public to swallow). I know a great deal about some things, (not as much, it is true, as most of my fellow country men who know almost everything), but I have read and studied much and observed abundantly. Perhaps I shall end up by persuading the morons that the way to live forty years longer is to eat yeast every day, or to keep the voice beautiful by smoking Lucky Strikes. There is no limit apparently to what they are willing to believe, if you say it to them long enough.

I trust your health is good, and that your real estate investments are turning out as profitably as you expected. I hope you have given up keeping boarders and roomers. Surely you have enough to keep you without going through that slavery again for third-rate people. Try to get all the comfort, pleasure, and happiness you can out of the life that remains to you. You have had a very hard life—full of pain and trouble—but I do not think you have done all you could to make it easier. I hope you all get along together more happily: there has always been a useless, wrangling, jangling, and quarreling of weary egotisms. Do not think too much of how good, unselfish, noble, and honorable you all are, and what a rotten cad the other fellow is. I have sometimes found that the person who talks the loudest about his honor knows least about the meaning of the word. Life dropped one of its big shells on us, and blew us apart. Life at home practically ceased to be possible for me when Ben died.

And I have sweated too much blood since. Yet I doubt that I am in the mind and heart of any of you as much as you are in mine. I think of my past life—sometimes—my childhood most of all—as a man thinks of a dream full of pain, ugliness, misunderstanding, and terror. But I know that none of us is to be blamed very much for anything. Strangers we are born alone into a strange world. We live in it, as Ben did, alone and strange, and we die without ever knowing anyone. It is therefore beyond the power of any of us to condemn, judge, or understand. I'm simply sorry for everyone. We all need it.

God bless you, and keep you all well, and bring you happiness. Write me as soon as you can. I don't know how long I shall stay here—when I get through I may go abroad again.

With much love to all,

TOM

HARVARD CLUB
27 West 44th Street
Monday night   July 11, 1927

DEAR MAMA: I am going to Europe to-morrow at midnight aboard the *George Washington*. My address will be the American Express Co., Paris (11 Rue Scribe). Mabel will doubtless give you the news in a letter I wrote to her yesterday. I will be back in New York in September to begin work at N. Y. U. and to sell my book if I can. I am very tired—both brain and body— and to-day has been terrifically hot. I'll write you a better letter next time. I went into the country for the greater part of June on the invitation of my friend, Olin Dows. He gave me the Gatekeeper's lodge—a lovely little cottage in a woody hollow by a beautiful little river, which fell over the dam a few feet away.

Below I could look out on the Great Hudson. I lived very simply, and cooked all except one meal a day. Dressed up and went out among the Swells a few times. I like Olin Dows very much —a great person.

If I get back a few days before the opening of school—Sept. 20 —I'll come down to see you. If not, I can perhaps come Christmas. The people at N. Y. U. have been very good to me: I have good hours and I hope my teaching will be easier this year. May do radio work with Henry Carlton, also. He wants me to. I've had a year of very hard work; I've learned a great deal about my craft, at any rate. What chance the book has I can not know until I put it into publisher's hands in autumn. I'm sorry to hear of Mabel's bad health, but very glad to hear of your good health. And I pray the family can get through one summer without ugliness and unhappiness among its members. Please guard your health and watch after your comfort. Surely you have enough left to keep you comfortably, and you must be tired of real estate after your recent sad experiences with it. Mrs. Roberts wrote me that you had lost much property and money. I hope this is exaggerated, for I do not want you to be unhappy because of it, but beyond that I do not think it matters very much. We have never had anything from the property but discomfort and worry; I do not honestly care very much for myself—not because of my altruism—but because I believe it's a myth, and that if I should outlive you, and be one of your heirs, there would be nothing for me anyway. I am not particularly gifted for business, as you may have observed, and by the time a somewhat bewildered creature of my temperament gets through signing papers, and having things explained to him by lawyers and executors and saying "Yes, I see," he sees nothing except that he gets nothing. I can understand money, but I can't understand property. You may say that my college expenses came from yours and Papa's property, but it seems to me it came from your bank account. Perhaps property gave you the bank account, but I think it's much more likely to eat one up.

At any rate, enjoy yourself and don't worry. It really doesn't matter very much as long as you have enough left to live well— and I'm sure you have. If we can only get a little wisdom from our misfortunes, the game's worth the candle, I suppose, but so few of us do. I wonder how much those self-important little people did learn: when I saw them last they were already counting their millions and convinced they had grown rich because of their shrewdness, business ability, and high intelligence. Now they will probably salve their pride with hopes for the future. We must be wiser than that: death's ahead of us. Let's have something for our pains now.

Good-bye for the present. Write me to Paris. I send you all my love and my wishes for your health and happiness.

TOM

[Card] (A street in Vienna—Graben, Wien) Aug 12, 1927

VIENNA

Saturday, August 12

DEAR MAMA: This is Vienna—one of the finest cities I've ever seen. I've had no mail in Europe. I presume I'll find some when I get back to Paris at end of month. Returning to New York middle of September. Love to all. Hope you're well.

TOM

[*Card*] View of Vienna (Wien I., Aüberes, Burgten mit Museen) Aug. 19, 1927

VIENNA, Aug. 19.

DEAR MAMA: I'm going to Prague (the Capitol of Czecho-Slovakia) this afternoon. Sometime next week I go back to Paris. Hope to hear from you there. This is a beautiful city: the life of the people delightful. Hope this finds you well and happy.

Love

TOM

[*Card*] View of Nürnberg

NUREMBERG, August 23, 1927

DEAR MAMA:—I'm back in Germany again after a few days in Prague. This is one of the prettiest old towns in the world—City walls and all the old homes intact from the Middle Ages. Going to Paris from here.

Love to all

TOM

[*Card*] Dijon, France: Avenue de la Gare
date illegible

DEAR MAMA: I'm stopping off here for a day or two on my way to Switzerland where I'm going to stay and work. This is the capital of the old Kingdom of Burgundy—now a part of France—where the good wine comes from. I hope this finds all well and happy.

TOM

[*Card*] View La Place de l'Etoile, Paris, France

Sept 4th, 1927

DEAR MAMA: I'm returning to New York in a week or so. I found no mail here from any of you. Do you think it's quite right? I hope you are all well and happy. Write me to Harvard Club.

Love,

TOM

HARVARD CLUB
27 West 44th Street
Sunday night   Oct. 2–3, 1927

DEAR MAMA: I was 27 years old five minutes ago. This is just a short line of greeting and remembrance to you. I shall write you at greater length later.

I saw as much of Mabel and Ralph during their short stay as I could: I thought she looked much better when she left.

I came down immediately after their departure with a terrific cold; but I did not go to bed and am now much better. Yesterday and today have been red-hot—I have been hunting a better place in which to live, and I am heat-exhausted. My work at University goes well. Tomorrow I begin to get my book typed.

I am 27 and, so far as I know, in good health. I have the friendship of a few fine people who think *I* am a fine person. I have done bad things and cruel things in my wild and lonely youth, but on the whole I have lived a decent and honorable life, without talking overmuch of decency and honor. I have hated what was cheap, common, and vicious—I have loved what was beautiful. I am grateful where gratitude is due, but I shall confess no obligation to anyone where none exists. It has taken me 27 years to rise above the bitterness and hatred of my childhood. I have no apologies to make for my life, nor any explanations to give to people who can not understand them.

As for you all, I shall continue to remember you, and to be loyal to my blood even when, as usual, no answer comes to me. I send you all my love and my hopes for your health and happiness.

TOM

HARVARD CLUB
27 West 44th Street
Sunday night, Oct. 9, 1927

DEAR MAMA:—I got Ben's watch a day or two ago. Thanks very much for the gift. It was probably the one thing I needed most. I confess it gave me a weird feeling to have his watch in my hand: I have not been able to use it yet, but I shall begin tomorrow. I wound it, and it seems to keep good time.

I am busier than I have ever been in my life. In addition to my teaching, I work four or five hours every afternoon dictating my book to a young man who is typing it for me—he is one of my former students, very intelligent, and a good typist. In addition, I have moved out of my filthy garret into a new apartment: it is a magnificent place in an old New York house owned by a wealthy old bachelor who is himself an artist. I have the entire floor—two enormous rooms, a big kitchenette, and a bath. I have a garden behind, and a quiet old New York street—one of the few remaining—in front. It is in one of the old parts of town, 8 minutes from the University.

The owner demanded a rent that would have taken almost

my whole salary: it was cheap even at that price (as New York prices go), but I told him I had only an instructor's pay and couldn't afford it. He wanted me to come in: he liked me, I believe, and he doesn't like business people. He cut off several hundred dollars. I now get the place for about $135 a month, half of which is paid by Mrs. Bernstein—about $65 apiece, you see, or no more than I paid two years ago at the Albert. In addition, we can sublet in the summer; if any place in New York can be rented this can, and I could without difficulty get $100 or $125 for it in summer. Thus, we get this fine place for $50 or $55 apiece. Mrs. B. is going to use the big front room as a studio, and room where she can meet her business associates in the theatre. She has had to find a place—she has more work this year than ever before, and my garret was too dirty to bring people to.

I shall be tremendously busy until Christmas, but I feel like working. If Fred comes up, I have plenty of room to keep him.

Write when you can.

Love to all

TOM

Sunday, Dec. 11 1927

DEAR MAMA: I have been very busy with classes and the book, and I am very tired. That is why I have not written you sooner. At present I am taking every spare minute for my book. I *must* finish it by first of the year and give it to a publisher for reading. Therefore, I am afraid I can not come home for Christmas. A trip home would cost me not less than $100—a big sum to me at present—and I would use time that I need very desperately.

I think I may come down in the latter part of January, during the examination period here. I would have a few days then, and I could use the time with a free mind.

I think of you all a great deal, and I want to see you all. I particularly want to see you. But I know you will understand my reason for not coming Christmas. I am trying to do something with my life—it is right that I make every effort to do something with it now. And I must finish what I have started.

I hope you can all meet this Christmas in love and happiness. I hope the New Year will bring you all health and joy, and a better life. As soon as I can come, I will see you.

This is a poor letter because I'm very tired. But I send you all my love and good wishes, with all my heart. I shall wire you at Christmas. Let me hear from you. Take care of yourself, be content, be happy, if you can. Love to all

TOM

SA NEW YORK NY DEC 24 1927
MRS JULIA E WOLFE
48 SPRUCE ST ASHEVILLE NCAR
I AM WITH YOU ALL IN LOVE AND REMEMBRANCE ON CHRIST-
MAS DAY BELIEVE I CAN COME LATE IN JANUARY IF EXAM SCHED-
ULE PERMITS WE WILL HAVE ANOTHER CHRISTMAS THEN WORK-
ING HARD   GOD BLESS YOU ALL MAY TODAY AND NEW YEAR BRING
YOU ALL HEALTH AND HAPPINESS

TOM

HARVARD CLUB
27 West 44th Street
Monday, Dec. 26, 1927

DEAR MAMA: I hope my telegram got to you on time Christmas morning. Thanks for your letter and for your gift. I shall make a very earnest effort to get away for a few days at the end of January. I must first see when my exams come. If I am lucky, and they are "bunched," I shall have more time. I am almost at the end of my book (and of my strength!). If I hold out I should finish by Jan 1, or a little later. I am writing the "big scene" at the end now. I haven't wasted my time by sleeping. I work until five or six o'clock in the morning. I need a day or two off, and may run up to Boston. I could possibly afford that trip.

I hope you had a nice Christmas, and got a good dinner. I got a card from Fred today, with a check attached. I am answering it in another letter. I shall save both your gifts until I need them most.

I am sorry your investments have gone badly. But let us hope the New Year will bring a change in luck, and let's not worry too much about it, anyway. I am delighted to know that your health's good—that is the main thing. The next time we get hold of money let's put it in the bank, or on our back, or in our bellies—where it will do some good. It is right to look forward to a "rainy day," but all life, if we pinch too hard, is likely to turn into a rainy day, and it's amazing to see how few people who have nothing starve to death in the gutter.

I hope you are all well. How is Mabel? Is she better? I shall write to her later. I sent Mrs. Roberts a telegram on Christmas day, and one to Effie and the children. I hope all got there.

I send you all again my love and hope for your health and prosperity this New Year, and all the months to follow.

TOM

I heard from Frank. Will write him.

27 West 44th Street
Sunday, Jan. 22 1928

DEAR MAMA:—I had meant to write you sooner, but the examination period is on, and I have been busy making out grades. I had my first examination Monday night, and did not finish with the grades until Thursday. Now I have another tomorrow night, and two more on Tuesday. It is unlikely therefore that I can finish before Thursday or Friday. Since the new term starts the week after, you will see that I have not time enough to make a visit. At the most it would allow me one or two days in Asheville.

My next chance therefore is Easter. I shall come then if I have time and money. I have very little of either at present. I am worked to a frazzle, and my left eye went bad about ten days ago. For a day or two I thought I had something in it, but I then discovered it was eye-strain—the result, perhaps, of night work and electricity. During the last day or two, however, it has become much better—I think it will be all right soon.

I am desperately tired, but I'm at the very end of my book, and in a few weeks I'm going to take a rest. I'm going to the theatre, and I'm going to try to give a little time to a few of my friends. Perhaps you feel I do not need a rest. When I was in Boston (for two days) Hilda told me she had heard from Fred, that he had described my easy life, my getting up at noon, and that he wondered what I'd do if I had to do a little work. I wonder if he forgot to add that I worked until five or six every morning. I should like to assure all my good friends who never use their heads, except as something to put a hat on, that the brain that works too hard gets tired just as does the tongue which talks too much.

I want to tell you something very plainly: I am not trying to avoid seeing any of you. I have given you a straight story of my difficulties—I always have. There has been no evasion, and, in spite of an ugly and rancorous feeling towards me which may exist in the family—a dislike which most of us feel for anything that is strange to us, remote from our experience, and living on a separate level of thought and feeling—I want to see you all very much. For I am loyal to you all, and still care for you very much—no matter how much pain and ugliness I may have to remember. And I know I am tarred with the same stick as the rest of you—whatever I may have of intelligence or talent came with my inheritance, just as did the other things, good and bad —the vitality, the strength, the weakness, the taint in the blood, the sensuality,—all the rest of it. I do not think I am to be blamed if I have tried to make use of the assets, and control or do away with the liabilities. Well, it is just as well to talk plainly when we have something to say, isn't it? Part of the trouble and confusion of life would be avoided if people spoke out now and then.

I was in Boston two or three days for a rest—but I worked all the time. I wrote all night, visited two or three of my friends at Cambridge and Concord, and saw Hilda and Elaine.

Elaine threatened to hate me forever if I spent more time with the other one than with her, or saw Hilda first—and so on. When I got through with them I had no rest and no strength left. I was in no condition to visit Uncle Henry, and I didn't go. I have no apology to make: funerals come high, and I haven't money enough to pay for my coffin.

We have had a mild winter here until the last two or three days when it has been bitterly cold.

I hope this finds you in good health, and keeping warm and well fed. Also, that business is better.

Write as soon as you can, giving me the news. My health is pretty good, but I am tired, tired.

Love and good health to you all

TOM

P. S. They have already asked me to come back to N. Y. U. next year—I believe I am the first they spoke to. I have given no answer yet.

HARVARD CLUB
27 West 44th Street
Saturday, March 31, 1928

DEAR MAMA: I finished the book[1] on which I have been working for the last twenty months a few days ago, and I sent a copy to a publisher for reading Monday afternoon. What their decision will be I do not know and will not for another four weeks. It is a huge book, but not too long, I hope, for publication. My friends are very hopeful about it—more so than I, because I am too tired to be hopeful or desperate, or anything else at present. I have six weeks more of teaching at N. Y. U.—it seems to me to be six years, but I will do my work thoroughly and finish up.

Whether this book succeeds or not, I think we can both have this hope—I have always finished any job that I have begun. It seems to me most of the failure comes to people who give up half way. In spite of the fact that I know nothing of the book's ultimate fate, I have a feeling of victory: I have done a tremendous piece of work—it took up over a year and a half of my life, and almost drove me crazy at the finish, but I *did* it. I know now that if I had given up, I should have done great damage to myself—I should have had an ugly fight to wage with myself at some other time in my life. At any rate, I have at last learned how to work—and that's a big thing.

[1] *Look Homeward Angel.*

Now, Mama, I need a rest desperately—but there's nothing doing for a short time. The Easter holiday comes next week—but for me it means nothing. At N. Y. U. the students are given only three days—Thurs, Fri, and Sat. Since my classes for the week are over Thurs. night it means I have only one extra day. If I come home, this means I would have to leave after 9:30 Wed. night and be back before 6:30 Monday night. I am therefore coming home in May—examinations begin May 14—I should be through by May 25. If I have a week or more between exams, I may come home then. If not, I shall come down after everything is over. I shall probably go away again this summer. My plans, as usual, are undecided. The University people want me back and have offered me a raise in salary—a small one, all they can give. But everything depends on the book: if any one takes it, I shall drop everything like a shot, and write another one I have in mind. If not, I think the time may have come for me to get out of teaching any way. No one can ever tell me again that teaching is "easy" work: it takes the marrow out of your bones if you try to do it well. Since I have never intended to be a teacher, and since it represents a compromise whereby I may live while I write, I think I may try to compromise hereafter in a more profitable direction—advertising, for example. In other words, if I'm going to wear myself out, I see no reason why I shouldn't try to make some money out of it. Do you? I'll have more time to write hereafter. I've heard nothing from you in a long time. Please let me know about yourself at once. How is your health? How is the family? How is business? Tell Fred I am writing him. The Boston episode didn't bother me at all—I mean Hilda's gossip. Both Hilda and Elaine waste themselves in idle gabble. That's one of the troubles of the world—people get nothing done because they spend all their time in foolish gossip. I've begun to find that the only thing to do is to stick to your job, grit your teeth, and let them talk. When I was a child I day-dreamed about having five or ten million dollars and spending it on steam yachts, automobiles, great estates, and swank. Now I know that happiness is not to be got at in that way: the only way I know is to find the thing you want to do with all your heart, and to work like hell doing it. I may never be happy even so, but if I did nothing I'd be ready for the keepers in six months.

I am going into dry dock for repairs for the first time in almost two years. I have been to the dentist, and think I shall see some one about my eyes. One of them is bothering me, but I think a few days' rest will fix it. As a matter of fact, I think nothing much is wrong with me, except my feeble mind: my brains feel like a plate of cold scrambled eggs. I thought the dentist would find me ready for grinding, yanking, and shiny false teeth, but he found only a broken filling and a small cavity.

So I may have a few more months of life in me yet.

Tell me if the wonderful mountain springtime has begun yet. It began here, but changed its mind a day or two ago—We have had rain and cold since. But, thank God, it can't be long now.

Write when you can. Give my love to everyone.

Your son,

TOM

HARVARD CLUB
27 West 44th Street
Thurs, June 7, 1928

DEAR MAMA: I got Fred's letter yesterday, but have had no news from the rest of you for several months.

I finished my work at N. Y. U. about a week ago, as tired as ever I was in my life, but I have had a week with little to do and

I feel much better already. I thought I was about ready to be measured up for a wooden overcoat, but there may be life in me yet. I've put into dry dock for repairs—eyes and teeth. Went to see one of the best eye doctors in the country about my left eye—it hasn't hurt much, but for two or three months I've felt as if there was something in it. He went over me with a dozen machines, and reported that I had very good eyesight and that he could find nothing wrong. Said feeling of foreign body in eye might be caused by having had something in it which had left a little scar when taken out. My own feeling is that I was just plain tired and nervous—he gave me something to put in, and today it feels as good as ever. I'm also going to a fine dentist—the first time I've ever had a good one—who is repairing some of the mistakes others have made. I was taught nothing about the care of teeth as a child, but I have taken good care of them since. My front ones are still good and regular, but my back ones are full of silver. I don't know how much it will cost to pay these specialists, but I'll never again fool with cheap mechanics when there are good doctors around. I'd rather go in debt for the privilege of keeping my eyes and my teeth.

I resigned at N. Y. U.—but they gave me my job back any way, and told me I could have it any time I got broke. But I'm ready to try something else—if I'm going to work as hard as I have, I want to be paid for it. The J. Walter Thompson Company—the largest advertising company in the world—has offered me a job writing advertisement for them. I got it because of my book—they read part of it. They want me to begin in October—but they also want me to promise to stay for three years. If I do, they say, I can make a great deal of money. I don't like the three year business—haven't given an answer yet. A publisher has my book—I have had a bit of good news from it: they say it's too long, and will have to be shortened but that there's some fine stuff in it. I'm to see them and talk about it. Also, a well known woman writer and critic said she would be my agent for 10%— she said it was too long, also, but that she thought she could find a publisher.

I have enough money to go abroad—it's cheaper there than here—and live cheaply for a few months. I need a rest and I've also got a new book—a short one this time. I want to get away soon—within two weeks, if possible. I think I'll come home for a few days—I'll drop in unexpectedly, perhaps, the first chance I have to come down—perhaps at end of this week or beginning of next. Don't talk to me of staying at home and *resting*. There's no rest for me there—I've tried it before. I want to be alone for a time where no one can get at me. I want to see you all very much, but I'm not coming to see the whole damned town, including relatives. So don't try to drag me around or tell me I "ought to go to see" any one. I'll make one visit, and no more—to Mrs. Roberts.

God knows how my money will hold out—it will cost $100 to run down and back for a few days—if I don't get out of the country soon I'll have none left.

This is all for the present. I hope this finds you all in good health. I'll try to send you a telegram before I come. Love to all,

TOM

HARVARD CLUB

27 West 44th Street

Monday, June 25, 1928

DEAR MAMA: I'm still here because the dentist had to make an extensive operation on my tooth and mouth. He's about through now, and has done a fine piece of work, but God! How it hurt. The whole tissue around the tooth was full of pus: it had been discharging into my blood for several years and had attacked and eaten away part of the bone structure about the tooth. He punched a hole through the jaw the other day and let it drain, and he cleaned it out this morning. I didn't know what I was in for! He went down to the naked bone with a knife and scraped and cut away all the diseased tissue. Says I'll be all right now. I'm going Saturday, but I don't know yet on what boat, I'll go on anything they can get me on: this is the rush season and it's not always easy to get passage. I've made all the other arrangements, and have only to pack and get on.

Saw various people about my book: a member of a publishing firm says it's a good book, a fine and moving book, but that I must cut it. We agreed on a length it must not exceed, and he said if I would get it down to that length he was sure it would get published. Meanwhile, another firm—a new one just starting—have asked me for first option on my second book. They say that if the writing is as good as in the first, and the book is of *a reasonable length*, they will publish. So maybe I've started somewhere at last. But I've got to learn one of the hardest things of all—to say a great deal in a little space.

I feel a great deal better than I did a month ago, but I want to get out of New York and start work on a new book. I was still somewhat tired and nervous when I came home, and worried because of all the things undone here, and I am sorry if I ever showed it. But it did me a great deal of good to see you all, and I am very glad I went down.

I want you to promise to write me a letter that will arrive in Paris—American Express Co.—*before* July 15, no matter how busy you may be. I am also asking five or six other people to do this. I know that one of the ugliest feelings in the world is to be alone in a foreign country and to come away from the mail-window emptyhanded. And one of the happiest feelings is to get a letter. It keeps you from that terrible feeling of being cut away from everything you have ever known. Therefore you will be doing me a great service if you try to write once in a while. And I promise that I shall always answer as soon as possible.

It is hot here today, and it was hot here yesterday—that sticky sweltering heat that only New York can furnish. But before that it was cold and rained almost constantly. My place on Eleventh Street is the pleasantest place in the city—it gives me almost my only reason for wanting to stay.

The advertising people have given me additional time in which to answer: I'm going to ask for a month or two leeway and finish the new book. Then I think I may go to work for them.

Great crowds of people are going to Europe—more this year than ever before. I'm not glad about it, because the more space you have on a boat the more fun you have. I'm trying to go on a German boat—the *Albert Ballin* of the Hamburg-Amerika—because I like their food and beer. If I could, I would drink at least a quart of good beer every day. It never hurt anyone, and its evil effects existed solely in the minds of the fools and scoundrels who have foisted Prohibition and rot gut gin upon the country. Upon second thought I shall not drink a quart of beer a day while I am gone—I shall drink a gallon, and raise three hearty cheers for all who drink more.

I was glad to find you so well and lively when I went home. I should like to think I may be as well and vigorous forty years from now. And I believe your affairs will not turn out badly in the end. At any rate, nothing is to be gained by worry over them.

I would get plenty of good food, and not work very hard for the people in the house.

I missed Olin Dows in Washington but had a long talk with him the other day here at the club. He is a fine person, and a true friend.

I wish I could tell you where I am going this summer, but I don't know myself. I shall be in Paris only a few days, but that is the most convenient mailing address. I wanted to go to Vienna, but I discovered the other day that a great music festival is on there, the city is full of Americans, and the prices, of course, have gone sky high. So I must go elsewhere—somewhere quiet and cheap.

I should like to tell you more about myself, but during the last few years, I have discovered the value of silence. And I find that I can no longer chase around the neighborhood blabbing out the things I feel deepest. An insane desire to gossip and tattle comes from a lack of anything worth while in our own lives: when we are bored by ourselves we try to live on the experience of other people. That is the thing I noticed about Asheville this last time. Everyone is touched with this disease a little—to my great surprise I discovered traces of it in my good friend, Mrs. Roberts, and it made me cautious.

All of us talk too much and, perhaps without meaning to be, are disloyal to one another. But I am learning honor on this point, at any rate.

I send you all my love, and I hope this finds you all in good health. Please don't fail to send the letter as I asked before July 15. With much love,

TOM

[*Card*] Boulogne-sur-Mer, France, Statue of Frederic Sauvage

BOULOGNE S.-MER

July 9, 1928

DEAR MAMA: I landed here today after a comfortable trip in a slow Dutch boat. Met many of the Dutch and have invitations enough in Holland for all summer if I choose to go. Staying here for night to get good sleep and stretch my legs before going to Paris. Write me—

TOM WOLFE

[*Card*] Venice, Italy: view of St. Marks

July 18, 1928

DEAR MAMA: I came here all the way from Vienna yesterday. I'm going on to Florence today and will send you a letter from there. Coming back to New York in two weeks.

Love

TOM

[*Card*]

(A view of the Arno River, with Bridge of St. Trinity)

FLORENCE, ITALY

July, 1928

DEAR MAMA: This is a part of Florence. I've been here several days and am going on to Rome today. Will be in New York for New Year's.

Love

TOM

[*Card*] View of Notre Dame, Paris

July, 1928

DEAR MAMA: Here's a picture of Notre Dame, and the island is the river which was the ancient city of Paris and surrounded by a wall. Now it's the seat of the city government. It has been terribly hot here—I've been almost laid out. Got your letter here —I'm leaving Paris in a day or two but continue to address me here. Writing letter—

Love to all.

TOM

HOTEL BURGUNDY
8, Rue Duphot, Paris
Monday, July 23, 1928

DEAR MAMA: I got a letter sent from the Harvard Club and another sent here. I have been in France two weeks; I had a comfortable trip over on a slow Dutch boat, and met many Dutch people who invited me to visit them in Holland. I stopped off for a day in Boulogne—the French seaport town—and for another day in Amiens, where there is a beautiful cathedral.

The weather here has been very hot and dry, and for a few days it was terrible. Never felt such heat in my life. Paris is full of Americans, English, and Germans. There are a great many Germans, and they all seem to have plenty of money. The French themselves seem prosperous—much more so than they have been. Prices, particularly in the tourist sections, are high, but it is still possible to live very cheaply farther away from the centre.

I was here during the French National Holiday—July 14— which is like our July 4. The heat was blistering, but the French made merry for three days. The streets were full of people dancing, eating, and drinking—autos and buses had to stop until the dance was over. This is a beautiful and fascinating city—cut by grand boulevards, and beautiful parks. There are of course hundreds of old narrow streets coming in from all sides, but it is the most beautifully constructed city in the world.

There are literally thousands of cafés with tables on the sidewalks, and from what I can see the French spend hours of each day in these places. They come to drink and talk—but they talk a great deal and drink very little: they are a very temperate race in all their pleasures—they know more about enjoying life than we do, and they take their time. They are a remarkable people, intelligent, witty, industrious, and practical—but they distrust everything and everybody that is not French. Thus they do not like foreigners, and they regard Americans as their legitimate prey for all manner of cheating. On this account I do not like them a great deal—although I have learned to protect myself; I have more in common with the English and German races.

I have gone to see a great many pictures, and have looked at a great many books, and bought a few—while here. I think I shall go from here to Brussels, and from there to Germany, settling down to work in Munich or Vienna. I am leaving in a day or two. But continue to address me Am. Ex. Co. Paris—mail will be sent on until further notice.

I got a long but somewhat despondent letter from Frank. I am writing him. I hope this finds you all well and happy. The hot weather keeps me from writing you very much: I would like to give you an adequate picture of this wonderful city—but all I can do is to mention magnificent boulevards, interesting old quarters with narrow streets full of people, dozens of churches, museums, and parks, and crowds of gay people who go surging back and forth incessantly while others watch them from the tables of cafés.

I was down along the Seine this afternoon: the high stone walls of the river are covered for two miles with the little stalls of the booksellers—they sell you everything from books to old pictures, pottery, and coins.

I'll write you a better letter next time.

The heat almost laid me out, but I'm all right now. Love to all

TOM

GRUBER & CIE
Hotel Des Boulevards
Place Charles Rogier
Bruxelles

BRUSSELS
Wednesday Aug 2, 1928

DEAR MAMA: I came up here to Brussels a week ago from Paris. I wrote you from Paris and sent you several post cards which I hope you received. I'll try to tell you about myself, and about Brussels, and about my plans.

I have had to do a great deal of writing, as my friends came through with letters as they promised. And I have recently begun work on a new book. I got a letter from Mrs. Resor, the head of the J. Walter Thompson Advertising Company, and she told me that their offer remained open indefinitely, and that I should come to see them when I got back. Also that she knew a charming lady of 38 who had made a great deal of money in business and wanted some culture. Would I be interested in giving her instruction? I answered that I had a great deal of culture and no money; and that if the lady had a great deal of money and and no culture we ought to make a trade. At any rate I feel as if something is open for me when I go home.

Brussels, as you know, is the capital of Belgium and was occupied by the Germans almost the entire length of the war. It is a city about the size of Baltimore or Boston, and is about the same distance from Paris that Baltimore is from New York. I came up here on a fast train in three hours and a half. We passed right through the battle field—through Compiegne, and Saint Quentin, and finally Mons, where, you might say, the war began, for it was at Mons in 1914 that the little British army made its famous stand and its famous retreat in the course of which it was practically annihilated. There are few signs of war now, save that, in these very old countries, one notices every-where the *newness* of the buildings. They have built everything back—little homes of red brick or white plaster. Occasionally you pass the ruins of a building destroyed by shell fire, but these are few. The wheat was ripening in the fields and was being harvested, the canals and rivers were filled with big barges; the country looked fat and rich and peaceful.

Brussels is a fine city, and calls itself "the little Paris." In some respects the place is more elegant and luxurious than Paris—it out-Parises its mother. There are wide boulevards, great parks, and huge buildings and arches of triumph with boulevards lead-ing up to them in the French manner. The people are very gay and stay up until all hours: they have a form of prohibition here which prevents your ordering anything but beer, wines, and champagne at [sic] café. If you want anything stronger you must go to a store and buy at least two quarts. This kind of Prohibition seems to work. There are literally blocks of cafés and wine shops, with nothing in between, all crowded with people drinking, laughing, and talking. But I do not see any drunkenness.

The country is divided into two races—the Walloons, who speak French, and the Flemish, who speak Flemish (the same language, save for accent, as Dutch) This causes a great deal of trouble, and there is constant talk of separation. The Flemish want to keep their language, their customs, their traditions; the Walloons insist that there be only one language in the army and schools—French. All public announcements and the names of all streets, and so on, are printed in the two languages. The spirit and appearance of Brussels and its inhabitants is predominantly French. The architecture, the cafés, the boulevards, the public monuments and the language is French. But 25 or 30 miles away is Antwerp, which is an ancient Dutch city, and which still remains Flemish. The people are more stolid and heavier, the prevailing language is Flemish, and so on. It is a strange situation. I don't know what will come of it.

Of the two I like the Dutch better. The Belgian Walloon apes the French in every way possible; it is French civilization and French culture he wants to belong to, but the other people stick to the traditions of their own civilization. The Belgians on the whole are a surly and unfriendly people: they still hate the Germans—which can be understood—but they dislike the English, who came and saved their necks, and I cannot understand that, unless we sometimes dislike those people who have done us a great service.

Finally, living here is cheap—much, much lower than it is in Paris. You get 35 Belgian francs for a dollar, and only 25 French ones—I have a good room in a good hotel here for a dollar a day, and I can eat and have a bottle of wine for seventy five cents. The food and drink are good, the people are well dressed and seem prosperous enough—in fact, all of Europe that I have seen this time seems to be on the up grade.

I do not know how much longer I shall stay here; I think my ultimate goal is Munich in Germany, and Vienna in Austria. I shall probably go from here to Cologne and take the celebrated trip up—or down—the Rhine. I want to see a few places in Belgium before I go—the distances here are so short you can go anywhere in an hour or two.

Please write me to the American Express Company in *Paris* —the mail will be sent on.

I hope this finds all at home well and happy. Give my love to everyone.

TOM

[*Card:*] A view of the Place Rogier and the North Station

BRUSSELS, BELGIUM
Aug. 4, 1928

DEAR MAMA: Here is where I have been living while in Brussels, but they must have taken this picture at five o'clock in the morning as the place is six times as busy during the day as you see it here. I live in the hotel a corner of which I have marked at the left. Railroad station at the back.

TOM

[*Card*] View of Cologne, Germany

KOLN—August 11, 1928

DEAR MAMA: Here is a part of the fine city of Cologne. They claim about 750,000 inhabitants—I am not sure it is so large. The Germans look prosperous and up-and-coming. The town is

full of magnificent new buildings and fine residential sections—
all built since the war. There are enormous restaurants, enormous
beer houses by the score, and literally thousands of small ones.
And the Germans eat and drink, it seems, most of the time. I am
glad to be among them again. We are more like them than the
Latin races. Things here are spotless and clean and efficient, and
they do not try to cheat you.

TOM

[*Post Card*]

BONN
'28 (?)

DEAR MAMA: Here is a piece of Cologne with the Cathedral. I
stayed there a week, and I am writing you this from *Bonn*, a quiet
university town on the banks of the Rhine two and a half hours
away by boat. I am going on to Munich presently.

TOM

[*Card*] View of Bonn on Rhine

DEAR MAMA: This is the chief market place in the old town of
Bonn on the Rhine where I have been staying the last week. I am
going on to Munich in a day or two and I hope to have a letter
from you there. Hope this finds all at home well and happy.

TOM

[*Card*] View Rolandseck

WIESBADEN, Aug. 25, 1928

DEAR MAMA: This is a view of the Rhine—I made the whole trip
up from Bonn to Mainz the other day. It is a beautiful thing and

deserves all that has been said about it. I stayed in Mainz which is occupied by thousands of French soldiers for two days, and I am writing this from Wiesbaden, a great bathing resort a few miles away. This place is occupied by the English.

TOM

[*Post Card Date Unknown*]

WEIMAR, GERMANY

DEAR MAMA: This is Martin Luther's living room in his house in Wittenberg—I stopped there yesterday—Am in Weimar today —the town Goethe lived in. Germany is a very beautiful and interesting country—Have seen many things and will tell you of them when I get back.

Love

TOM

[*Card*]

FRANKFORT

Sept. 30, '28

DEAR MAMA: Here is a bird's eye view of the old and interesting city of Frankfort on Main—a half million people here. You can see some of the famous old houses in this picture which shows the old section of town. The upper stories hang over and kiss each other, and you meet yourself going backwards.

Going to Munich tomorrow.

TOM

[*Card*] View of Munich—Neuhauser

1928

DEAR MAMA: I came here from Frankfort almost three weeks ago and got your letters. I have written no one since; I have been at work but I'll try to get a letter off soon. If not, I'll say as much as I can with post cards. This is one of the most beautiful and fascinating cities in the world—also the famous *Beer City*. And God! how the people eat and drink! Hope this finds you well.

TOM

View: Wien I Opernring

VIENNA, Oct. 26, 1928

DEAR MAMA: I have been unable to write you sooner. I was injured in Munich and had to go to the hospital for several days.[1] My nose was broken and I had several deep wounds on my head and some small ones on my face. I'm going to be all right now. Going to Budapest (Hungary) and to Italy from here. From Italy home.

Love to all.

TOM

[*Post Card*]

BUDAPEST,

Wednesday, Nov. 7, 1928

DEAR MAMA: This is as close to the Orient as I've ever been. The people here—the Hungarians—were originally Asiatics who

---

[1] Tom received these injuries when attacked at the beer festival known as The October Fair. This is recounted in *The Web and the Rock* in chapter 47, "A visit to the Fair" and chapter 48, "The Hospital."

settled here hundreds of years ago. But a great many of these Asiatic traits they have never lost. I have just heard that Hoover got in. I'm sorry. My heart was with Al—and the Pope.

Love,   Tom

[Card]

STRASBOURG, Tues, Dec. 7, 1928

DEAR MAMA: This is Strasbourg the capital of Alsace-Lorraine that the French got from Germany after the war. But they all speak German yet, and look more German than French. I'm on my way to Germany. Will be in New York by New Year's.

Tom

[Card] View—Temple of Saturn, Rome

Sat., Dec. 15, 1928

DEAR MAMA: I shall spend Christmas on the water and should be home in New York by New Year's Eve. I'll get a Christmas message to you if I have to radio. I've seen a great deal of Rome but I'm half dead with a cold caught in their miserable rain. Better now.   Tom

[Card]

NAPLES

Wed. Dec. 19, 1928[?]

DEAR MAMA:

I'm sailing for New York day after tomorrow (Dec. 21) and should be in N. Y. New Year's Eve. This is Naples—a city of about 1,000,000 people. You see Vesuvius in the distance and part of the Bay of Naples. It is very beautiful but filled with dirty, ragged, noisy, thieving, begging Italians.

Love

TOM

[Card] View of Via Roma, Naples

Dec. 21, 1928

DEAR MAMA: I'm sailing tomorrow. Today I was vaccinated, fumigated, and inspected, with all the other Emigrants. It's Italian (or American) law. They even tried to take my little bit of hair away from me, but I compromised on the back of my neck.

Love,

TOM

NAPOLI DEC 21 1928

LCD JULIA WOLFE

   48 SPRUCE ASHEVILLE NCAR

SAILING VULCANIA TODAY MERRY XMAS

TOM

HARVARD CLUB 27 West 44th Street

Letter undated. Envelope dated June 6, 1929

DEAR MAMA: Thanks for your letter. You say you are expecting me home about June 15—this is a surprise to me as I have not heard of it before. School is over—I finished grading bushels of examination papers last week. It is a tiresome and uninteresting job. I'm glad to be done with it. I have a great deal more time now for myself—Scribners has all the revised and shortened MSS. and are now putting it into type. They tell me they will have the proofs next week—and of course that means more work for me. We have cut out great hunks of the original book— hated to see it go, but it had to. I am now working on some short stories which they asked me to write. Of course, I don't know if they'll like them, but if they do, the advertising will help me out. And I have a new book which I work on when I get time. I find it is necessary for me to be alone a great deal to get work done. I don't like to visit people, or to make trips, or to do anything much besides my work when I am busy at it. It's too bad, of course, but everyone has his own way.

I hope you will not talk too much about my book—I really meant it several months ago when I begged you all not to. I don't think you understand my feelings in the matter very well—I certainly am grateful for the interest you all take—but I know that more things are hurt by too much talk than by too little. I feel that the book is now in Scribners hands, and that it is their place to advertise it, sell it, and to do whatever is necessary to put it forward. I have learned a little patience these last few years— I've had to!—and I know that nothing would be lost by waiting now until announcement of its publication is made. As things stand, I am sure it is known about all over Asheville now—and I think this is a pity. I think this premature advertising has hurt it rather than helped it. I do not like to speak so much about this—but after all, with the exception of one friend, I have been left alone for years now to fight things out by myself—now that I have a chance I want to make the most of it. The book will be out for the Fall season, the story—I think—will come out late in the summer. I got my photographs—some of them were good, and Scribners selected five or six for their own use.—I think Scribners will submit the book to one of the big Book of the Month Clubs, but I do not bank on this—hundreds of books are being published and it would be a miracle if my first book were accepted.

I suppose I shall be in New York most of the summer—I want to be here, naturally, while the book is coming out. May go up to Maine for two or three weeks, and try to find a little shack on the coast, where I can be alone and think of nothing. I'd like to come home to see you all—I don't know whether it is possible to come June 15. Of course, its an expensive trip and I want to stretch my N. Y. U. money through the summer if I can.

I wrote Uncle Henry before going to Europe but I never had an answer. Glad to know he's so happy and has such a fine baby. I am also glad to know that all apparently are in good health. I should like to see Effie and her family, it's been years since I saw her—and I suppose there have been changes in us both. I have several chances to go away this summer—to Maine, and Olin Dows wants me to come up the river to his place at Rhinebeck. But in many ways I have the tastes of an old man—I don't like crowds, I don't like parties and going out, and most of the time *I want to be alone.*

The weather here has been good lately—but we had a cold and rainy spring, and the hot weather is due soon. When it gets hot in New York it's as hot as any where on earth—there are seven million people here, and you *can smell all* of them when the thermometer hits 90.

The prosperity we hear so much about is very uneven—you say the money is in New York, but not all the people in New York, I promise you, have it. I hope business is better with you, and that Asheville is getting on its feet again. I'll write again when I know more about my plans—everything is undecided now.

Love to all,

TOM

HARVARD CLUB 27 West 44th Street

Undated. Date on envelope—July 12, 1929

DEAR MAMA: My proofs have been coming in for over six weeks now—I have had to stay on the job to correct them. My story [1] will be out in the August number of *Scribner's*—the book will be published, I understand, in October. My picture will also be in the back of *Scribners'* for August, along with some announcements about my book [2]—I don't know what they have written about me, but get the August number and read it. I naturally did not feel like coming home while my proofs were coming in—I have had about half of them thus far, but the others should come quicker. When I have finished them, they turn the long galleys into page-proofs—my job will then be over. I may read the page-proof, but they tell me it will not be necessary, since someone at Scribners will do it. It is up to me now to finish some short stories and to get busy on a new novel. All I can do about this one is to hope and pray—the Scribners people have been wonderful, they have worked like dogs on it, and they think it is a fine book. We all hope it will be successful. Please continue to say nothing about it—if any one reads the story and announcements in the August number, and asks when the book will be out, what it's about, and so on, say you don't know, or

[1] An episode from *Look Homeward Angel* called "The Angel on the Porch."

[2] *Look Homeward Angel*, published October 18, 1929.

say nothing. That is always better. Let Scribners do it—they are fine people and good publishers, and they will do more for me than any one else could. By the way—there was a little announcement of my story in *Scribner's Magazine* for July—turn to the back where they have announced the *August* issue—it's only a little bit, but you may be interested.

I am tired and nervous: I have been invited to go to Maine and I am going tomorrow for two weeks. Little place far up on the sea coast, no people around, very quiet. I'm going to think of nothing for two weeks. Scribners will send me more proof there.

I should like to come home for a little visit at end of Aug. or early September. Don't know yet. I'll write you from Maine. I want naturally to do the best I can for myself now—this is an important time for me—and I also want to do the best for every one else.

The N. Y. U. people have appointed me for a new job at $2400—I'd like to get out of it, but perhaps should not take chances till I see how book goes. There's so much sweat and heart-ache, and sometimes so little reward.

We have had terrific heat in New York—great suffering, and many deaths. It gets hot here, but it is not dry—a heavy humid fog comes off the river, and you feel as if you're having a steam bath. It's the worst heat in the world.

I have meant to send you one of the photographs my photog-ra*phess* gave me—would you like one? Then you could see if my nose is the same as ever—I think it is.

I hope you are not mad because I didn't come home June 15th—it was impossible with my work here, and besides you took me by surprise: I never had an idea that you were expecting me, you had said nothing about it before.

Please write me—I am not sure of the Maine address, but as I remember it is care of Mrs. Jessie Benge, C. W. Snow's Cottage, Ocean Point, Maine, but I think you have to write Boothbay Harbor also, as that is the P. O.

I hope this finds you in good health with business improved. I have often thought that your health has grown better instead of worse as you got older—I remember that when I was seven or eight years old and you had just moved to O. K. H. you had two or three years of bad sickness. And as a young woman you did not, I think, have good health.

I am glad to know you are now so well—with all my heart I wish you many more years of health and energy. Few people I know have had so full and active a life as yours.

I do not think I shall ever come home again to live, but we must have faith in and try to love and understand one another. Without that nothing is worth while.

I am sorry none of the family writes me more often. I should like to hear from all of you. Give my love to all and write me when you can.

With Much Love,

TOM

I have been out of town once—over the 4th of July week end —went up to Olin Dows, at his place on the Hudson at Rhinebeck. They have 2000 acres and two houses of 40 rooms each. No one but Olin was there. It is very beautiful country—the great Hudson down below—the Catskills in the distance, and great fields, woods, hills, and farms— But very hot there.

Where I go in Maine will be cold enough for a sweater and blankets. After New York I should like an ice-box.

[*Card*] View of Sea, Ocean Point, Maine

OCEAN POINT, MAINE

July 18, 1929

DEAR MAMA: This is a very beautiful place, but it is wholly unlike Asheville. It is a little place on the wild and rocky Maine coast with a few summer cottages. I hear the sea all day and night—I sleep on the porch of a cottage right in the spruce woods not 25 yards from the water. I fish from a rotten old wharf 100 yards away and pull fish in as fast as I drop the line. A great place to get a rest.

Love,

TOM

OCEAN POINT, ME.

Sunday July 28, 1929

DEAR MAMA: Thanks for your letter which came several days ago. I am leaving here tomorrow morning and may go to Canada for a week or ten days—after that I shall return to New York where I shall probably remain the rest of the summer. The weather here has been splendid—rain only one day, and always cool. At night, several times, we have had to build fires. The coast up here as well as the State of Maine inland is very beautiful—but also very poor. The soil is rocky, it is hard to make things grow, the farmers are giving up the land. This little point of land where I am staying has 75 or 100 cottages—in winter I suppose there are no more than a half dozen people here. A great many summer cottages scattered all along the coast—everyone drives in to Booth Bay, a pretty little village of 4000 of 5000 seven miles from here— You can do shopping there. If

I ever make any money I may buy or build a little place here—
land is cheap—you can buy several good lots on the shore with
spruce trees all around you for the price of a single foot of earth
in Asheville several years ago—good lots are from $250–$500,
I believe. It's a wonderful place for a vacation—no noise except
the ocean, nothing doing, no one has to dress up. You can fish,
swim, sail and loaf to heart's content, and there is always—even
when they're roasting in Boston and New York—a cool breeze
blowing from the ocean.

If I have a chance early in September I may come home for
a few days before school starts. Scribners have been sending
me proofs here, which I have corrected here and sent back to
them. We are getting near the end now—when I finish with the
proofs my job's done. I can only hope for good luck and a
favorable reception after that. I'm anxious to get started on
something else—it is about 3 years since I started the book—of
course time must be counted out for teaching, travelling, and
finding a publisher and correcting the MS. After this, I hope, I
shall not have so much trouble—at least, I have a publisher now.
I once thought I could do a book every year—but that no longer
seems possible—I have to sweat too much blood, it comes too
hard with me, and if my other books are anywhere near as long
as this—I hope they won't be—I have about 3 average-sized books
in one, anyway. But I think I can do good work and finish a
new one every two years—if I keep this up I should have fifteen
or twenty big books done by the time I am 55 or 60 (if I last
that long). This should be enough for me to have my say. But
between now and 50 is the golden time—I hope I can use it
well.

I am glad to know you are well, and have a house full of
people. Don't work too hard and take good care of your health.

I hope all the family is well, and that business has improved. Give my love to all.

TOM

These two weeks up here have done me a lot of good—no longer nervous and getting fat. Slept out of doors whole time.

[Post Card]

MONTREAL, CANADA
Saturday, August 3, 1929

DEAR MAMA: This is a big city of a million or more, and very American in its appearance, as you can see. There is a big French population—about 60% of whole—and street signs, advertisements, etc. are printed in two languages. Beer, ale, and wine in taverns and hotels and restaurants—but you must go to gov't store for stronger stuff. Going on to Quebec—back in 2 or 3 days.

TOM

[Card]

QUEBEC
Tuesday, August 6, 1929

DEAR MAMA: Almost the entire population of this town is French-Canadian and speak no English. I went up to the battle-field where my famous namesake defeated Montcalm—it's to the left of the picture—you can see the beginning of the fortifications.—now a military fort— Very cold grey weather here—starting back to New York tonight— Hope this finds all well—

Love   TOM

HARVARD CLUB
27 West 44th Street
August 13, 1929

DEAR MAMA: Thanks for your letter which I found here at the club today. I came back from Canada last Thursday after a good vacation of over three weeks, most of which I spent in Maine. I went to Canada from Boston, and called up Hilda and Elaine before I went. Hilda and her husband were out of town for the summer at Scituate, a seaside town on the South Shore below Boston, but I talked to her over the phone, and she invited me to come down overnight. This I was unable to do. But Elaine came in from Jamaica to see me, and we talked together most of the afternoon. I tried to find Uncle Henry, but at his old office they told me he had been out of business for a year and lived in Reading. Old Hall, his former partner, talked to me over the phone and insisted on telling me about Henry's marriage, baby, and all, before I told him who I was. I looked up his name in the phone book, but could not find him listed. New England is a very beautiful part of the country, but for the most part very poor—especially in the upper parts—Maine, New Hampshire and Vermont. Wonderful lakes, hills, forests—but the soil is rocky and poor. Canada looks like a rich, magnificent country—naturally—but there are not men enough to till the soil. The population of the whole country is only 8,000,000, and over a million live in Montreal. Saw some wonderful farm country— You could have all the land you want for almost nothing. The railroads own millions of acres and are anxious to develop it. New York is very hot and enervating—it has been a terrible summer. It threatens to rain but doesn't—as a result, the air is sticky and depressing. I was very much interested to know that you had read my story, and that other people had bought the magazine. The story, of course, is only a little section of the book, from which it was taken, but Scribners thought it a good way of announcing the future publication of my book. I can not tell you how fine they have been, how hard they have worked to make the book go, and how much they believe in it. Now, my own work is almost done—I am finishing the last proofs tonight, and there will be very little for me to do hereafter. No one who does not know would believe the amount of work that must be done to publish a book—not only the author's work, of writing and revising it, but all the other work of correcting galley proofs, page proofs, advertising, getting the cover design, etc.— I saw the cover design of my book today—that is to say the paper jacket that covers the real one—and it is very attractive—bright colors, jagged lines, very modern design.

Of course, I am very hopeful and happy. Scribners faith in the book grows, and they think it will be a success. But, of course, we can't tell, and we must not be too sure.

I should like to come home to see you—perhaps at end of this month, or early September. I will let you know in advance. If I come I want only a quiet visit—to see my family and a few friends. I hope you will not work too hard in the house; sorry you have had so many of the family there during summer.

I did not hear from George Mc Coy and suppose he has not written. When I am away from New York the safest address is The Harvard Club. An old schoolmate at Chapel Hill called me up yesterday and I had dinner with him—his name is Jonathan Daniels; he is the youngest son of Josephus Daniels of Raleigh who used to be Sec. of the Navy. He told me he had written a novel—everybody's doing it!—and I suppose he wanted to see if I could take it to a publisher. I have made new friends as a result of the book who have been very kind to me.

Mark Brown's death is a very sad thing. I remember him very well from my boyhood when he lived next to us on Spruce Street.

It is too bad he had to die while comparatively young. I buy an Asheville paper from time to time and see from the social columns that his children—whom I always remember as babies—are now grown up young men and women, going to parties and dances. I am glad to know he will leave them comfortably well off. It is very satisfying to know that you enjoy such good health and keenness of mind—very few people of your years can say as much. I earnestly hope you continue strong and well of mind and body for twenty years more, and believe you will.

Thank you for all the interest you have taken in my book. I hope it will justify all the effort and care that has been spent on it. At any rate, I have made a connection with a fine establishment and fine men—I should have thought all that has happened impossible a year ago and think I am a very lucky fellow. To show my gratitude for their belief in me, I am setting to work on a second book which I shall try to make better than the first.

Please continue to let Scribners give any information about the book. I send my hopes and best wishes for your continued health and happiness.

Love to all,   Tom

I never hear from Fred, and should like to. I have written him but did not get an answer. Suppose he is quite busy; hope he is fully recovered from automobile accident. Got a note from Frank which I shall answer. Hope all are well, and not too hot.

HARVARD CLUB
27 West 44th Street
Tuesday   October 8, 1929

Dear Mama: Thanks very much for your letter. I have been very busy getting started at the University and with my book. The book has been printed already, and copies sent out to reviewers. I am having a copy sent to you in a few days. The book will not be released for sale until Oct. 18th. Of course, I am very much excited about it and hope it has some success. It is very hard for me to get down to work until I see what happens. I am very much up in the air about it, but must settle down and do my work at N. Y. U.

We have had all grades and varieties of weather here since I came back—hot, rainy, and cold—today was a real October day, very bright and quite cold. A friend took me out into the country—leaves turning and very beautiful.

There is a letter in the back of the October *Scribner's* about my story that appeared in August—rather it is a clipping from a newspaper run by Louis Graves at Chapel Hill: he jokes *Scribner's* about saying I came from "a small Southern college"—then he tells where I *did* come from.

My book looks very nice—a good colored paper jacket, with a piece about me on the back, and a well printed, well-bound volume.

Hope this finds you and everyone at home well, and enjoying good health, good business, and good weather.

I will write you more when I am calmer and have more to say.

Love to all,   TOM

HARVARD CLUB
27 West 44th Street
New York   October 17, 1929

DEAR MAMA:

I sent to you the other day an advance copy of my book. I hope it reached you safely.

The book is being published tomorrow—what success it will

have no one can say. It is only one of hundreds of books that are coming out. But we hope for the best.

I hope you will like my book. If you don't, I shall try to write a better one that you do like. I hope it does not seem "modern" to you. All I wanted to do was write as good and interesting a story as possible. Wish me luck and hope for my success. I'll write more in a few days.

With much love,

TOM

If you can get away and pay me a visit this Fall, I shall do all in my power to see that you enjoy yourself.

HARVARD CLUB

27 West 44th Street

New York, November 6, 1929

DEAR MAMA: I have been very busy grading papers and making up work at the University, where I fell behind somewhat after my book came out.

Mabel has written me a couple of letters, and I have also heard from others in Asheville, including George McCoy. I also read the reviews of the book in the Asheville papers. The one in the *Citizen* I thought splendid but it seemed to me the *Times* was unfairly personal. George McCoy in his letter said that the *Times* and some of the Asheville people "read the book from the local angle." This is no way to read a book: it was not written from any "local angle," and none of the reviewers in New York, or any where else besides Asheville, have mentioned any "local angle"! Instead, they have read the book as it should be read—as a writer's creation and vision of life—and they have found it a very honest and moving piece of work. I hope you read the reviews in the *New York Times* and the *New York Herald Tribune.*

I have not lived in Asheville for ten years, but I have always believed that if I ever wrote a book I could expect at least as much kindness and fairness in the town of my birth as I would get from strangers. I am very grateful to all those people, like the people at the *Citizen,* who have judged my work fairly and generously, but I am not grateful to people who try to make of my book a diary of family and town history. In the introduction to the book I stated very plainly that it was made from human experience—as all serious fiction is—but that the book was fiction and represented the writer's own picture of life—that he had taken experience and shaped it into a world of his own making. The *Times* reporter in his review accused me of evading the question "by clever twists of phrases"—there is no evasion there or elsewhere: only a very simple and direct statement of what fiction is.

In short, the characters and scenes in my book are of my own imagining and my own making—they have their roots in human experience, but what life and being they have, I gave to them. There is no scene in my book that is supposed to be literal, and I will not talk to damned fools who ask me if so-and-so in the book is meant to be such and such a person living in Asheville. What the book is about is stated on the very first page, in the opening paragraph: it says that we are born alone—all of us who ever lived or will live—that we live alone, and die alone, and that we are strangers to one another, and never come to know one another. That is not written about people in Asheville—it is written about people everywhere, North, South, East, and West.

Finally, I do not know what any one protests about in **my**

book. The people are like people every where all over the world—
and it seems to me, and to Scribners, and to the people who
have read the book up here that on the whole they are pretty fine
—People: they are not infallible and they make mistakes, but
since I am writing about people and confess that I know very
little about saints and angels, I shall let the reporter on the
Times and any other people who want Gods, rather than men
in their fiction do the job I am unable to do. There is not a
single leading figure in my book who, when faced by a crisis,
does not rise up and show a heroic spirit—they can go over the
book page by page and find this true.

I have only two serious regrets—one, that I did not do a better
piece of work, but I *will* next time; and two, that my book may
have caused pain or distress to any person. But I will also say
that if it has caused pain or distress, they are the result not of
what is really in the book, but of a misunderstanding of the
book's purpose.

I can not write more at present. I am tired from excitement
and from having to do my work at N. Y. U. at the same time. I
will write you more later. My book has had, I understand, the
best reviews any first novel has had in several years, and we are
now hopeful of success. The book is already in its second edition.
I will send you some of the reviews as they come out—I think you
will see what the world in general thinks of the book, and I
don't think you will find anything in them that will cause you
or anyone worry or confusion of the slightest sort. In my future
work, as in this first one, I know you want me to do what I want
to do myself: as good, as honest, and as conscientious work as
I can. If I do that, most people of intelligence will see what
I'm after, and none of us need worry about the opinions of
unfair and unreasonable people.

I send you my best wishes for your health, happiness, and prosperity. Write me when you can.

Your son,

Tom

HARVARD CLUB
27 West 44th Street
New York, Nov 30, 1929

DEAR MAMA: I have been very busy with my book and grading stacks of Freshmen themes, and I have not been able to answer your letter as it should be answered. I will send you a longer letter next week, in which I will speak of certain things you mentioned in your letter. I can only say here, in reference to one point in your letter, that it has never occurred to anyone with whom I have spoken here that Eliza [1] was anything but a very strong, resourceful, and courageous woman, who showed great character and determination in her struggle against the odds of life. That is certainly the way I felt and feel about her, and since I wrote the book my opinion ought to be as good as any one's. Some of the most intelligent people in the country have read the book and think it is a fine thing, and that the leading characters are remarkable people—if this is true I do not think we should be greatly concerned with what spiteful and petty people in small towns think.

I will write you more in a week or so. I send my love, and my wishes for your health and prosperity with this letter. I am tired, but shall get more rest hereafter.

With love,

Tom

[1] Eugene's mother in *Look Homeward Angel*.

1929 DEC 25 AM 12 55

MRS. JULIA E WOLFE

FORWARD 48 SPRUCE ST   ASHEVILLE N CAR—

HEARTIEST WISHES FOR A MERRY CHRISTMAS AND A HAPPY
AND PROSPEROUS NEW YEAR   I HOPE YOU MAY ENJOY MANY
MORE IN HEALTH HAPPINESS AND PROSPERITY WTIH WARMEST
LOVE   WRITING THIS WEEK

TOM

HOTEL BELLEVUE
Beacon Street—Beacon Hill Boston
Friday, Jan 24, 1930

DEAR MAMA: Thanks for your interesting letter which came
a day or two before I left New York. I came up here during
the examination period at the University—I had a few days in
between examinations and I decided to take a little vacation.
I called up Hilda today, and I am having lunch with Elaine tomorrow. Boston is very cold and raw, and the ground is covered
with snow and ice—New York was about the same when I left
it: we have had all kinds of weather this fall from rain and
fog to blizzards and zero. I am delighted to know that you are
in such good health and find so many interesting things to see
and do in Miami. I think you are right about Miami's future—
rich people will go there more and more to get away from all
the cold up here.

I don't know if I told you that I have resigned from the Uni-

versity, and that my resignation takes effect within another
week—at the end of this term. My book is still selling steadily,
and no one knows just how far the sale will go, but Scribners
have very generously advanced me $5000 which they are paying
me in sums of $250 a month (I asked them to do this)—and I
am going to get busy on my new book at once. The English
publisher[1] is also enthusiastic about the book, and thinks it may
have considerable success in England. It comes out there some
time this spring. They have already paid me 100 pounds as an
advance and tell me they will give me more if I get hard up.
So you see, although I am far from rich, I shall have a modest
income to live on until I write a new book. I am very happy, of
course, to be done with teaching—I found it very hard to teach
and write at the same time; and I will now have the chance
really to devote my time to writing.

I asked Scribners to send a copy of the book to the Miami
Herald, as you directed. Thanks for seeing the booksellers there,
and for your interest in the book's success. There have been
so many reviews I can not begin to mention them to you—but
apparently you have seen some of the chief ones—the Times,
the World, the Herald Tribune, the Bookman, the New Republic, the Saturday Review of Literature, Plain Talk, etc.

My next book will deal with different scenes and characters.
I hope and believe it will be a good book, and that its meaning
and purpose will not be misunderstood by some people in Asheville, as the first one was. At any rate, I am still a young fellow
and my life's work is before me: I have only written the first
chapter, and it seems too early to condemn me on the whole.

I hope that you live many years longer in health, happiness,
and mental vigor, and that you see me do work that will represent

[1] William Heinemann, Ltd., of London.

the best in me. I also hope that you will be able to stay in Florida until Spring and that you can dispose of some of your property at a good price.

Enjoy yourself, take an interest in all the life around you and be careful of your health and comfort. I send you my very best wishes for prosperity and good health.

With love,

Tom

(over)

Hilda told me today that she had heard from her father who said that he had a letter from you inviting him and Jenny to spend the winter in one of your houses at Hollywood. But I don't know what he has decided to do; I may go out to Hilda's for dinner to-morrow night and hear more about them all.

ATLANTIC CITY N. J.

April 2nd 1930

DEAR MAMA: I suppose you're back from Miami by this time, and hope you found Asheville warmer than I found Atlantic City. I came here the other day in the engine-cab of the fastest train in the country—The Boardwalk Flyer. Will write you when I get back to New York. Hope this finds you well—

Tom

HARVARD CLUB

27 West 44th Street

Saturday April 26 1930

DEAR MAMA: Just a short letter now to answer your good long

one that I just found here. I am glad you stayed in Miami so long, and sorry you found weather cold and so much work to do when you got back home. Please do not overdo it—I hope Spring has come by the time this letter gets to you: it has been cold and raw in New York for this season, and Spring is very late in coming. I was happy to get such a vigorous and cheerful letter from you—I believe you are much younger and stronger in mind and body than most people twenty years your junior, and with all my heart I wish you long life, health, and prosperity.

I am sorry that my book was any kind of shock to you—I did not want it to be or intend it to be; and I shall try to write other ones which I hope will seem grander and more beautiful to you. I am very sorry to know that anyone in Asheville looks at you with "inquiring looks"; but I should not pay any attention to them—you are a much more remarkable person than any of them, as the world perhaps may someday know.

I do not think the history of the Gant family is over: it seems to me that there is much more to be said, and I propose someday to return to that theme—I hope naturally that added wisdom, maturity, and richness of experience will enable me to handle my theme as it deserves to be handled. Very few critics who have ever written about the book have failed to mention the extraordinary quality of the people in it. I belong to a different generation from that of certain older people who were perhaps shocked by some things in my book, but I really do not think my own generation is worse than theirs: I think in many respects it is much more honest. Every writer who is honest, I think, feels the tragedy of destiny and of much of living, but I hope that I shall never be bitter in what I write, against people. I think some people at home made that mistake about my first book—they thought the author was bitter about people, but he was not: he may have been bitter about the toil, waste, and tragedy of living.

—To talk of other and perhaps more interesting things: I am sailing on the *Volendam* of the Holland American Line on May 10. I am very tired and jumpy over New York and the excitement of these past few months, and my friends are anxious to get me on the boat. It will be a good thing for me, since I need a rest and also get almost frantic at times when people won't leave me alone to work. New York either leaves you alone entirely or tries to eat you up. In the last few months it has tried to eat me up. But I have a little money now—enough to live on modestly while I write a new book—and all I want to do is a good piece of work. I would go away sooner, but I am having quite a siege with the dentist: my teeth—the back ones—are none too good, and I had to have what practically amounted to an operation on the jaw—they hacked, chiseled, ripped, cut, and wrenched to get one out; and they had to sew the wound up later: it has been a long time in healing. I think I am fairly well; I am simply mentally and spiritually tired. I am going to try to write a grand and beautiful book, and I am going to take my time doing it, and let no one rush me into doing cheap and hasty work. I had far rather do one fine thing than a dozen ordinary ones.

Most of the people I have met during this past year I should not care to see again—they were not interested in me as a person, but simply in a new curiosity: something that was being talked of at the moment—but there have been a few fine ones whose friendship I value. You are right about the work of a man's brain and spirit being the worst paid of all work, but I think you are a little unfair to my publishers: they are of course business people, and have got to make their business pay, but I have found them people of high standards and great integrity—they are much fairer people than most publishers, they are an old and honorable firm and their treatment of me on the whole has been generous.

I rejoice that you are still able to travel about and see the world, and take such an interest in everything. You have had a very full and interesting life, and I hope it continues for many more years in full power. I suppose you are right in moving to Miami to live—life there will be warmer and more comfortable than in Asheville—but it does make me a little sad to see the Wolfe family, who have grown up with the town, and lived and died and married there, pass away from it entirely. I hope one of us may remain, or maybe someday return, and live there.

I am proud of my people, proud of my pioneer and mountaineer and Pennsylvania Dutch ancestry,[1] and proud of the place I came from, although I have been told they do not want me back there, and that I am no longer welcome. As I walk through the crowded and noisy streets of this immense city, and look at the dark swarthy faces of Jews, Italians, Greeks, and all the people of the New America that is roaring up around us here, I realize more keenly than ever that I come from the old Americans—the people who settled the country, who fought in its wars, who pushed westward. Two or three weeks ago on my return from Atlantic City I stopped over in Philadelphia, and a friend drove me out into the Pennsylvania Dutch country, where Papa came

---

[1] W. O. Wolfe, Tom's father, was the son of a Holland-Dutch mother, Eleanor Jane (Heikus) Hichus, and a father of English descent. Tom's mother, Julia Elizabeth Westall Wolfe, was chiefly of Scotch-Irish descent, but the name Westall came from an Englishman, her great-grandfather, William Westall, who came to America just after the Revolution.

from. We did not get as far as York Springs, but we did go to Lancaster, a town I have heard him speak of many times. There I saw where half of me came from—it is the richest, fattest farming country you ever looked at, and the Dutch people were out in the great fields behind teams of four big horses abreast. The barns were painted red and were four times as big as the houses and everything was neat as a pin: although I had never been there before it was like something you see in a dream come true, for it was all exactly as he had described it.

One half of me is great fields and mighty barns, and one half of me is the great hills of North Carolina. I will write you again before I go. I send my love, and my hope that this finds you well, strong and happy.

Your son

Tom

HARVARD CLUB
27 West 44th Street
New York, May 6, 1930

DEAR MAMA: Just a line or two more before I sail. I went to see my lawyer [1] today—he is a very fine man: his name is Melville Cane. I talked to him about my literary agent, who has become very demanding and wants part of my earnings, apparently, on everything I ever write. He told me that I had been much more than generous already. Then I made a will [2]—I have not got much except books and manuscripts and some royalties waiting

---

[1] Melville Cane, whose career as a lawyer brought him into particularly close association with writers and publishers.

[2] Tom replaced this will by another in 1937 to a different effect.

at Scribners. In case anything should happen to me, I have left whatever money I may have or that may come in from any royalties or manuscript, to be divided equally between you and my dear friend, Aline Bernstein. She is a very fine and lovely woman, and the best friend I have ever had, and you may depend on her to look after everything with the utmost ability and integrity. I have given Mr. Cane your full name and address, and Mrs. Bernstein also has it: I am going back to Mr. Cane's office tomorrow to sign the document.

Of course it seems foolish for me to make a will when I am still under thirty, and have so little to bequeath, and I hope I shall continue in good health for many years, but one never knows what will happen, and I feel better now that I have done this. I have also instructed Mrs. Bernstein to dispose of my books and few personal belongings as she sees fit, in case of my death, giving to members of my family or to friends whatever they might desire as souvenirs or mementos. I think this takes care of everything; and hope it seems satisfactory to you.

I send everyone again my love and kindest wishes for health, happiness, and success.

I sail Friday at midnight aboard the *Volendam* of the Holland-American line. My address will be care of the Guaranty Trust Co, Paris, Place de la Concorde—the bank on which my Guggenheim letter of credit is issued.

Goodbye again, and good luck and good health. Write me a line when you can.

Your son,

TOM

[*Card*] Panorama of Paris
Paris—May 30, 1930

PARIS,
Thursday May 29, 1930

DEAR MAMA: I hope this finds you and everyone at home well. It has been cold and rainy here—Spring very late—but weather better last day or two. Write me Guaranty Trust Co., Paris.

Love

Tom

[*Card*] Rouen, France: Place et Rue de la République

June 3, 1930.

DEAR MAMA: This is Rouen, where Joan of Arc was burned— it is a good sized flourishing city of over 100,000. The French seem very prosperous and hard at work. I hope this finds you well and business better.

Tom

LONDON.
Nov. 11, 1930

DEAR MAMA: I am sorry not to have written you for so long a time, but I have been hard at work since coming to England and time has gone quickly. I find it very difficult to write letters while I am writing a book—I don't know why—and, I am afraid a great many letters have gone unanswered. Fred has kept me informed of the family news, and I have tried to keep him informed in general of my movements. This seems to be a bad time for everyone and the family apparently is hard hit: things can hardly be worse than they are and I am sure the New Year will bring in some change for the better. I assure you I am willing to do all in my power to help—I don't know how much that will be—but I will do it gladly. Everything will come out right yet: meanwhile we must pull together and keep cheerful. Things in America can not be as bad as they are here in England, for their unemployment situation here is, I'm afraid, a permanent one. There are too many people for so small a country, and there is not enough work to go round. The people have endured hardship, poverty and insufficient food for so long that it has affected their spirit: I think they are in a depressed and despondent state and not capable of making a great effort—I hope I am wrong. In addition, the English climate lives up to its reputation—at this time of year there is so much rain, fog, and dreariness that it is a very hard thing to keep cheerful, even if you have no cause to be depressed. God knows how hard it must be for the thousands of poor wretches who have no shelter for their heads and no money for a meal. There are over 2½ million people out of work in this country—I understand the number at home is 5 million or more—but here the thing has been going on for years: at home we have a great rich country that is not yet fully developed, and it seems to me we ought to have always enough food—in addition, we have a much more bracing climate than these people have. So things could be worse with us.

People in England have been very kind to me this time, I have met some celebrated people and had more invitations than I could use: I am not going out much, and working as much as I can on a new book. I shall probably be here for Christmas this year, but I won't have to spend it alone because I have already had two invitations—I am very grateful of course for this kindness: I have been terribly homesick for America this time and now I want to settle down and live somewhere in my own country. For the first time in my life I have begun to think of getting married and to wonder if there is some nice girl somewhere who would have me: I am weary of all this wandering and loneliness, but first I must try to get this piece of work done and establish myself somehow.

I suppose you will be in Florida when you get this letter. I am sending it off in time to reach you before Christmas—wherever you are I wish you health, happiness, and many years more of a healthy and active life, as well as a pleasant and joyful Christmas. I am not attempting to send anyone Christmas presents—its too hard trying to send them through the customs, but I do not want you to worry over the present hard times, and I assure you that no one in the family will starve as long as I have a penny and anyone needs it. I know that if I am broke I can always get more, so *you must promise* to let me know how things are, and if you are in need of money. Everything will be all right yet, and none of us must suffer useless hardship. Fred tells me that although conditions are very bad everyone in the family has enough food and clothing, and there is no actual physical want— I am happy to think that if he needs help he will let me try to help him, or to help any of you: it gives me great joy and comfort to think that I can, and I have written to my friend Mr. Perkins [1] at Scribners asking him to attend to a little matter which I hope will reach Fred before Christmas altho, because I was rushed here, I was a little late in getting my letter off. Fred has always been very generous to me, and to everyone, and I hope there will never be any false pride between us at any time when we can

---

[1] Maxwell E. Perkins, of the editorial staff of Charles Scribner's Sons, publishers, New York, the original of Foxhall Morton Edwards in *You Can't Go Home Again.*

help each other or the family. I read in a London paper that the Central Bank at Asheville had failed—I hope to God the family did not lose anything, and that all the poor depositors get their money back. Things must be in a terrible condition all over the country—everyone I know has suffered.

Goodbye for the present, Mama, and don't worry: better times for us all are coming in—the main things are to keep alive and happy and healthy. Enjoy yourself there in Florida. Thank God you are there in the sunshine instead of London rain and fog, and have a good Christmas. I hope Fred can spend it with you. I am sending this letter to Asheville because I don't know your Fla. address, but I hope it will be forwarded before Christmas. I hope this finds you happy and healthy: I am well with the exception of a little cold—but I think everybody in London has one at present. I send you again my love and best wishes for Christmas, with hopes for better times for us all.

Tom

[*Christmas card containing message*]

To wish you health and happiness at Christmas and health and prosperity throughout the coming year from Tom

Dear Mama: I hope this as well as the letter I wrote you both get to you before Xmas day. I wish you long life, sound health, happiness and prosperity—as I said before, don't worry—everything is going to come out all right yet. Let me hear.

Tom

LONDON   DEC. 12, 1930

PRINCE GEORGE HOTEL
5th Avenue & 28th Street
New York City
March 9, 1931

DEAR MAMA: I came back a few days ago by the *Europa*, and I have been spending the time looking for a place to live. I have at last found one—a quiet little place in Brooklyn where I will be away from the noise and excitement of New York, and where I am going to work as hard as I can. I have been very homesick and lonely this last year and I was glad to get back to my own country, even though times are bad. People seem to expect a great deal of me in my next book and I am very nervous about it, and also at times I feel very much alone, although there are many people here I could see if I wanted to. Hope and pray for my success—I have had a hard time during the last year, and I am just getting calm and steady again. Everything will be all right with all of us, if we work and hope and keep trying. I shall write you all at greater length when I get settled. My address for the present will be the Harvard Club, or Charles Scribners. I send you my love, and also birthday greetings, even if they are late. I wish you health and many more years of a happy and active life, and I know there are brighter times ahead for all of us, if we have courage to wait and keep on trying. Love and good luck for the present. I will write you soon.

Your son,

TOM

HARVARD CLUB
27 West 44th Street
April 1, 1931

DEAR MAMA: Thanks for your letter and hope you got my telegram. I have been trying to get a story ready for *Scribner's* and was also considerably worried over a friend of mine who was in the hospital—apparently with some sort of collapse. But she is all right now, which is a relief. I sent Mabel a telegram at the same time I sent you one, saying I would come to Wash. but hoped both of you would come here instead. I will send her another telegram and see what she wants to do: of course, I will not miss seeing you, and if you won't come here I'll come to Washington, but I think you should see New York, too; you have never been here, it is the capital of your country, and one of the great cities of the world. I could fix you and Mabel up comfortably in a hotel in Brooklyn heights with a wonderful view of the harbor and the New York skyline, and within 5 minutes by subway of downtown New York and 5 minutes walk of my own apartment. If Fred came he could stay with me at my place —I have an extra bed there. And I'd take care of the expense. Anyway, Mama, I'll see you one place or the other—Wash. or New York—within a few days now, and I'm looking forward to it. If you have time before you leave home write me a line about this—I think you should come to N.Y. if you can—let me hear. I understand you are leaving Sunday—hope this gets to you in time. Meanwhile, love and good luck and best wishes

TOM
40 Verandah Place
Brooklyn, N.Y.

40 Verandah Place
Brooklyn, N.Y.
Monday, June 8, 1931 `

DEAR MAMA: I have often wanted to write to you since you went home, but it has been a busy time with me and I did not get around to it. I got your letter, and have also had letters from Mabel, Fred and Effie. You know more about the Anderson situation than I do; so I won't discuss it except to say that I was glad to help, and hope Effie's family can get off to some sort of new start now. It seems useless to try to save the house—Effie writes me that it would not bring the sum of the mortgage, and there certainly seems to be no hope of her family paying it off. There is some talk here of a revival of business and better times, and I hope it comes soon; from what I hear of Asheville it will take more than a revival to put it on its feet again[1]—it will take a miracle, but sometimes they happen, although I am afraid things are in the soup for a good many years to come.

Mabel writes she is going home for a visit and I know she misses her old life and her friends, but I doubt that there is much to support her and Ralph in Asheville at the present time—these are dark times for everyone, but they will surely grow brighter if we hang on.

I have followed the general course of the bank trials and know that Davis has been sentenced to five years in prison. Have you been going to the trials? Write me about it, and save the newspaper clippings if you can. Davis of course is guilty as hell, but I think we shall live to see the day when he returns and becomes an honored pillar of the Methodist Church again. But I do not think that this generation will live long enough to forget

[1] Asheville's real estate boom had collapsed in 1927, ruining the town's entire financial structure, and reducing most of the well-to-do citizens to poverty. This episode furnished the basis for Tom's story, "Boom Town" which is included in his book, The Hills Beyond.

the effect of his work—it has been ruinous. You used to say it was three generations from shirtsleeves to shirtsleeves—and I suppose that is what has happened to Asheville. When I was a child it was a little sleepy town, then it had its flare of glory, or thought it had, and now I suppose it will go back to its shirtsleeves once again.

I am so glad you enjoyed your visit here. I am sorry you could not stay longer, or see more: I think we did pretty well with the time we had, but I could do more now. I have got everthing settled, and am at peace with everyone, as well as free and heartwhole: I know a very handsome and intelligent young woman now, she is a Ph.D. from Columbia and principal of a school in Westchester county—she earns almost $5000 a year and has a nice little apartment with a beautiful view of the East River. I wish we could have gone to see her when you were here but I did not know her then: she is from Wyoming and grew up on a ranch, her mother was a real pioneer woman and had five sons and two daughters—her younger sister got married a year ago to a boy whose father is vice pres. and will soon be president of the Singer company. She has lots of sense and character, and is very good looking to boot: she has done everything for herself and has made a good job of her life.

I know you will be shocked and surprised to hear that Mrs Dorman,[1] who came down and talked to you here one morning less than two months ago, has been dead and in her grave almost four weeks. Only a short time after you left they noticed a swelling on her stomach and she complained of pain: they took her to a hospital where the doctors found she had cancer. It seems strange that no one had discovered it before. At any rate, she died without much pain only a few weeks after going to the hospital: they kept her drugged all the time, and she died after

[1] Mother of Tom's landlady.

being put to sleep by the hypodermic. She was just about your age, but of course she had never had your health and strength. They took her back to the little town she came from in Maryland, and buried her there.

Mr. Perkins often asks about you, as do my friends Alfred and Cornelia Dashiell.[1] The Dashiells are going abroad on Friday, to Holland, Germany, and Paris, and I have been telling them things I know about these places. I imagine they will be kept busy if they try to do everything I tell them to do. We have had a nice Spring here with considerable rain: there have been some very fine days, and it has not been too hot yet. I intend to stay here and plug away on my book—if it gets too hot I may go off for a few weeks, to Maine or Vermont, but I want to keep at it, as its coming along now. A young lady has offered me the use of a cabin in the Colorado National park—I have never been west and would very much like to see that part of country. When you write me will you please give me the address of the house we lived in in St. Louis. If I ever go there I will look it up. I saw the great air show over New York, I had a grand stand seat as an invited guest on the roof of the Aquarium (where we saw the fishes) and all of the planes—some 600 or more—flew right over us at that point. There were millions of people but to see it, and it was a wonderful sight—they were thick as a flight of birds. The Empire State was opened up with great pomp and ceremony and the tower blazes with light every evening now. I imagine it is the last one of these monsters they will erect for some time.

I live very quietly in Brooklyn, and go to New York every three or four days. I am in good health and spirits. I hope this finds you well and business at home somewhat improved. Write

[1] Alfred Dashiell was managing editor of *Scribner's Magazine* in the years when it published Tom's stories.

and give me the news when you have time. Meanwhile I send you my best wishes for good health and happiness.

Tom

P.S. This morning I got a letter from Fred with a check for $275,[1] returning almost all the money I sent to Effie. I will write him in a few days. I hope he has not misunderstood me, and thinks I am so hard up I need the money badly. I am not: I have not got much money but enough to get along on comfortably for several months at least, and if I work on the book Scribners will keep me going. The other book has been a good property for them, it has not sold in large quantities but it keeps on selling steadily which is remarkable. I have also signed a contract with Swedish publishers and hear it will also be printed in Germany. Perhaps I'll get something out of all this. Who's Who has written me several times for information, so I sent in what there was the other day—hope to make a better showing as time goes on. As I have told you before, if it's a question of food or shelter or the necessities of life I'll chip in as long as I've got chips to chip with, and when I haven't I'll try to get more. Good luck to all.

Tom

[Card]

ORRS ISLAND, MAINE

Aug 7th 1931.

DEAR MAMA: I am staying on this little island which is Casco Bay not far from Portland. It is a quiet place and a good place to get a vacation. I shall be here a week or ten days. Hope this finds you well—

Tom

[1] Tom had sent his sister money to help save her home in Anderson, S. C. from seizure for taxes and mortgage.

HARVARD CLUB
27 West 44th Street
N.Y.
Sept 21, 1931

DEAR MAMA: Thanks for your letter—I have wanted to answer sooner, but the summer here has been so hot that my effort to get some work done has been about all I could do. As I imagined we had one more siege of it after I wrote Fred: about a week or ten days of the hottest weather of the summer. We have had several cool days and nights now, but the pavements and buildings are not yet cooled off—and in the subways the air is foul and stinking. When you see how people suffer here in summer you wonder how they stand it and why they keep on—but most of them would rather live here than anywhere on earth. The autumn here is usually fine—October a good month: I won't be sorry to see it come.

I suppose you have read of the closing of the London Stock Exchange, and that the Bank of England has stopped the gold standard—conditions in England are very serious, as I know. (Last winter I saw half naked wretches sitting on park benches at three in the morning in a freezing rain and sleet: often I saw a man and a woman huddled together with their arms around each other for warmth, and with sodden newspapers, rags, or anything they could find over their shoulders.)

The trouble in England will affect the whole world, and we may soon be in as serious a condition ourselves—and perhaps we will not meet it as well as they have. No one seems to be doing anything about it, everyone is standing around with his mouth open as if he expected the gates of heaven to open the next moment and rain milk and honey all over him. People talk about "the pendulum swinging backward" and "conditions are bound to change"— This is foolish talk: conditions are not *bound* to change unless something is done to change them, and at present it seems that any change will be for the worse. The business men who boasted of their knowledge and wisdom two years ago are a set of foolish little boys—they know nothing, are as ignorant as you or I about conditions, and some of them now admit it.— It is no good talking now of the panic of 1907, or 1893, and of how things got better later—the present situation can't be compared with that. For the first time in history we have far too much rather than too little: and machinery can produce faster than we can consume. Our enormous wheat & cotton crops amount to nothing unless people have money to buy them—and we are glutted, literally starving in the midst of plenty, unable to market at a profit what we produce.

This system of over-production will not improve, will get worse, unless something is done to control it—I think we are at the end of a period: it may be that the whole Capitalistic system is finished—if so, I think we should welcome some other one that is not so stupid and wasteful. I do not believe we can go through another year like the last one without violence and bloodshed, for our people are, and have always been, violent and lawless, and this is even more true now with the vast foreign populations in cities like New York and Chicago. You have lived through one kind of world; you may live to see the beginning of another one.

As for me, I have lived in a little town and in a big city and I have seen calamity strike in both places—I have seen how little the wise men knew, I know how wrong and foolish their system was and I am ready for anything that is better and that will make men happier, and I think that should be the attitude of any decent person.

If you can buy food cheaply now and feel like preserving it, let me know and I'll send the money. I need little and am hard at work: if I work hard and get things done, nothing else matters—but I must have peace of mind and be free from worry for the next six or eight months.

If you are ever in need of anything, let me know at once and I'll send you money. If you need, say, $50 a month to live on, I'll send it to you—I'd like to send more, but if you have your house you might be able to manage on that. Anyway, I'll see to it that you are never in want of any necessity, and you need have no worry on that score.

I'd like to help Fred more, but at present I'm not able—but in a pinch would do what I could. Of course, I won't listen to anything Frank writes me again—I'm pulling and hoping that Mabel comes through on her rooming house.

My book—the first one—will probably be sold to Grosset and Dunlap (I believe that's the firm) about New Year's for their Dollar Reprints. If that happens, I stand to get a few hundred dollars out of it, and the English publisher is going to bring out a 5-shilling edition—so I may get a little more. I can't hear anything about the Swedish translation, although I've finally got *part*—not all—of my advance of $100 from my agent. Two of the movies—Fox and someone else—have written me about rights to the second book but alas! I don't think I shall ever write anything the movies would find suitable—although I'd like to get the money.

I may move out of my present place in October—and go to Brooklyn Heights—that is the section above the harbor—there are hundreds of places empty there, and I think rents will drop after Oct. 1—they have come *way* down already. I have told Marjorie Dorman I will not continue to pay $65 a mo. for that place—of course light and gas is thrown in—and what is called "maid service"—Marjorie Dorman is in many respects good hearted and likable. I have almost completely cut out drinking, by the way—I don't take a drink once a week, and feel no desire for it. I'll give B'klyn and quiet living credit for that.

However, I like liquor and think it is a blessing instead of a curse: it becomes a curse only when people abuse it—and that is true of anything—food, tobacco, or even coca cola. I'd like to see beer come back—a big stein of it for five cents: I think we'd all be better off—but, of course, as long as they prefer to sneak around the corner and pay 50 cents for a drink of near-poison, there's not much hope.

I never see any Asheville people, and am sorry for it—there are many people in Asheville I'd like to see, and I should hate them to think I was bitter or angry and wanted to see no more of the whole lot. It so happens that the few A. people here in New York who have tried to see me are just the ones I am anxious to avoid—I will not mention names, but I had to speak plainly and insultingly to my chief botherer a few days ago—one who suddenly discovered a year or so back that we were always great friends in Asheville—she accused me, of course, of turning my nose up at old friends and said Bruce Webb [1] had told her I had done the same to him: it is quite true I did my best to avoid Webb when he was here in N.Y.—he was trying to sell me life insurance and even went to Scribners to try to get them to insure me—but as you know I had no more than a speaking acquaintance with him at home, and of course, the things Mabel tells me his father said to her after my book came out were neither friendly nor decent; why should I see any of these people, and

---

[1] Son of the owner of the Asheville *Citizen* and Asheville *Times*, who had been an undergraduate of the University of North Carolina with Tom.

what do I owe them? Inasmuch as the young woman I mention tries to fill out her dull mean little life with gossip about people she could never know or understand, and might even try slander and lies now—please correct any impression that I dislike Asheville people if occasion arises, but *say nothing*, unless it does. Then state the truth, which is just what I have told you and what you know, and we have nothing to fear: the decent people will know the truth, and as for the others, I care not a curse what they think or believe.

I have nothing to fear, anyway, as long as I work: there are perhaps three people in the world who know or understand what I am like. I have these, and I am happy in their friendship. But my feelings toward life are honest and friendly, and I do not insult or curse people who have some honest and friendly feeling for me.— As for cheap, slanderous, cheating and canting swine— I see no reason why I should not tell them plainly what they are.

This is about all the news for the present—I don't come to Manhattan often, but am here now, and saw Mr. Perkins an hour ago: he is well and has not suffered so much this year from his annual dose of hay fever. He sends his regards to you.

All is well with me as long as I can work: when that goes wrong life goes wrong. I'll be delighted to see you and take care of you any time you want to come up: just write and let me know. I had thought I'd write Fred a letter also, now, but this is so long I'll wait a day or two. Tell him I got his letter with the very full and accurate information about the Wolfes in and near York Springs: I thank him for answering so quickly and so fully—I may go there for a day or two in October and if I do his letter will be of the greatest value to me: think I'll look up Aunt Mary,[1] Gil's wife, first of all, since she seems to be the last

[1] Mrs. Gilbert Wolfe, of York Springs, Penn.

of the old crowd, and could probably inform me about the younger ones.

I hope this finds you and Fred and everyone well. I did not mean in my letter that I was in want myself and could not help anyone else: I'm glad to help in any case of need, but I do want to make it plain that I'm by no means rolling in money, that I have to watch my step—and I therefore thought it a very mean and ugly trick for X to get money from me if he only wanted it to go on a spree—if he really needed it for the family, and it went to their support, I have no complaint to make.

Good bye for the present. Write when you have time. I think we're in for very bad times, but if we hold on, we'll live through to something better, I believe. Wishing you good health and happiness,

Your son,

TOM

HARVARD CLUB
27 West 44th Street
Oct. 12, 1931

DEAR MAMA: I just want to write you a note to tell you your package arrived in good condition a few days ago, and to thank you and Fred for your splendid and generous gift. I can truthfully say you could not have picked out anything I needed more than socks, handkerchiefs, and ties. I was reduced to two pairs of unmatched socks with holes in the toes, and two neckties, each embroidered with the steak and gravy of the past three years. I am very grateful for these fine and useful things. I know that buying so many of each must have represented quite a sum for you now, and I hope you did nothing to pinch you. I appreciate the thought and spirit of the gift as much as the thing itself, and I would feel just the same if you had sent only a pocket handkerchief. But I was badly in need of just the things you sent, and I am using them now.

This is all for the present—I haven't much news, save that I have been much depressed by the news of the sudden and terrible death of a man [1] I knew at Harvard, who was one of my best friends there. Olin Dows, another friend, went up and attended the police investigation and the story he told me is a pretty bad and messy one—we all believe now he died a natural death but a good many ugly things came to light in the investigation. It's a sad but very interesting story, and I shall tell you about it some time.

I will close now, thanking you and Fred again for your fine and useful gift, and wishing you both long life, health, happiness, and a return to better times and better future.

Your son,

Tom

HARVARD CLUB
27 West 44th Street
Thurs., Nov. 5, 1931

DEAR MAMA: Just want to write you a note to let you know that I have moved from my old place in Brooklyn and to give you my new address. I am now living at *111 Columbia Heights, Brooklyn*— My phone number is the same as before, Main 4-0189. Please send any mail to the above address. My new place costs no more than the old one, and is superior to it in every way. First,

---

[1] Kenneth Raesbeck was found dead in a graveyard at Westport, Conn. with marks of violence upon him.

I am living on Brooklyn Hts. the nicest part of town—and convenient to subway, restaurants and stores—all within 2 minutes walk. I have an entire floor—two big sunny rooms, a big fine kitchen, a good bath room. If you come up for a visit will have lots of room for you. This is all for this time—remember new address. I have had bad cold but now better. Hope this finds all well and happy. They say here that business is picking up.

Love to all—

Tom

HARVARD CLUB
27 West 44th Street
Dec. 4, 1931

Dear Mama: Thanks for your interesting letter and for your fruit cake, which arrived in good condition a few days ago. I have had several pieces of the cake, and have given some to some of my friends, and every one pronounces it delicious—as good as they ever tasted. The little bottle of wine in the cake was also intact and greatly appreciated.

As you already know, I went down to Washington Thanksgiving Day and returned the day after. I used an excursion ticket and should have come back Thanksgiving night, but I was so tired and besides wanted to talk to Mabel, that I stayed over and came back in regular way next day. Even so I saved a few dollars, since the excursion round trip was less than half the regular one-way fare. I had some slight hope of seeing you and Fred there, but as I had heard nothing definite didn't believe you would be. Mabel, I thought, looked well, and Ralph better than I hoped to find him. She has both her apartments pretty well rented and told me she made about $75 a month over rent—also that Ralph would begin to get $150 a month disability insurance, soon. If they get this they should make out all right.— I think Mabel has felt the strain of these last few months, and is somewhat over-wrought, but I believe she is going to be all right now. If people get control of themselves they can probably get control of every-thing else—this is the important thing. I talked to Ralph and he talked sensibly and hopefully and seemed to be confident things would turn out all right.

I am working hard and desperately—it's do or die now—and there can be no rest or let up for me now until I finish. I want to ask you not to say anything to any one about my work—Mabel showed me an article in one of the Asheville papers in which you were quoted—I am sure you did not say the things they printed —but the article was misleading and embarrassing and at the present time I want to be free of this kind of thing! I will finish my book when I finish it; it will be published when a publisher takes it—and when that will be, or what it's about is at present no one's business but my own.

I am glad you enjoyed your Thanksgiving Day, and hope you will have many more, and that we all have more to be thankful for next year. People are pretty depressed here and I suppose it's just as bad, or worse, in smaller places. I'd like to see you all but I'm afraid I can't do much travelling or visiting until I finish the job I'm on. If you get as far as Washington—you or Fred, or both of you—I hope you will come the rest of the way and spend a day or two here in N. Y. I could probably take care of you all in my place, and if not I'd put you up at the St. George— we went up on the roof there—which is only two minutes walk. Take good care of your health, keep warm, and have plenty to eat. If you need any money let me know and I'll get it for you, meanwhile I send you best wishes for health and happiness.

Your son Tom

When I was in Washington Ralph and Mabel drove me over Potomoc to Arlington—the cemetery and Lee's old home. It was the first time I'd set foot in the South in 2 years—since I don't consider Maryland South, although the Marylanders do. Arlington is a beautiful place and Lee's house one of the finest I've ever seen. Did you ever go there? If not, you should do it next time. It's well worth a visit.

B BROOKLYN NY FEB 15 1932
MRS JULIA E WOLFE, CARE MRS R H WHEATON

THE GRAMERCY 825 VERMONT NORTHWEST WASHINGTON DC BEST WISHES FOR HAPPY BIRTHDAY AND FOR MANY MORE YEARS OF HEALTHY ACTIVE LIFE HOPE AND BELIEVE ANOTHER YEAR WILL FIND US ALL IN BETTER AND HAPPIER CIRCUMSTANCES LET ME KNOW IF YOU NEED ANYTHING AND ENJOY YOUR VISIT HOPE ALL ARE WELL I AM ALL RIGHT NOW WORKING LOVE

TOM

III COLUMBIA HEIGHTS
Brooklyn, New York
May 29, 1932

DEAR MAMA: This is Sunday and the first day I have taken off from work in several weeks, and I am accordingly taking the opportunity it gives me to write you. Tomorrow here is also a holiday—Memorial Day, I believe—at any rate, it is a Civil War day which I can't remember in the South, I don't think ours comes at the same time. All New York, therefore, is enjoying a long holiday week-end. Scribners closed Friday night until

Tuesday morning. I have had two invitations to visit people in the country this week end but I have taken neither, preferring to rest alone at home and to get ready for the great grind of hard work that is before me these next 3 months.

I have finished another long story[1] for Scribner's—I got through with my work on the proofs Friday afternoon: as usual it was too long and I had to revise and shorten it. Even so, it is about 35,000 words, the longest piece they have ever published in a single issue: even now it is a complete short novel, as long as many novels which are printed, and as you will see when you read it, I have only begun to use the material at my disposal— I could easily have written ten times as much, and someday I will—when my long book is finished.

Perkins is enthusiastic about it. He says it is a great story, the true stuff of life, and one of the best things I ever did. If this is so, as I told you in my last letter, I can thank you, because I have used many of the stories you have told me, together with others of my own: the story is told completely in the words of one person, a woman, who starts out to tell her son about a single incident and in the course of telling it brings in memories, stories, and recollections that cover a period of seventy years. In the telling the story weaves back and forth like a web and for that reason I have called it *The Web of Earth*. The story is about everything that goes to make up life—the happiness, the sorrow, the joy, the pain, the triumph and the suffering—it tells about everything—but you need feel no alarm or nervousness: it is "on the side of the angels," it has been written to the glory of mankind, and not to their shame, it says that life, even with its grief and pain, is good, and that people, even with all their faults,

---

[1] *The Web of Earth* published in *Scribner's Magazine* July 1932, and in the volume *From Death to Morning* in 1935.

mistakes, and errors, are all right. As for the person who tells
the story, everything that is written is written as an honorable
tribute to her courage, strength, and character. Perkins says the
story shows that a life without toil, sorrow, and hardship mixed
in with the good and prosperous times would be a life that was
worthless, dull, and uninteresting—that only a life which has
everything in it—the good times, the bad times, grief as well as
happiness—is rich and worth living.

I have told you all this because I think the curiosity seekers
and gossips may call you up and try to pump you as they have
before, and because I want you to know that you have nothing
to worry about: the fair and intelligent people will see at once
what the story is about, and as for the others—those who want
to know if Bill Smith is really Tom Jones, and if such and such
a thing really happened—I don't think you need bother very much
about them: if they pester you with questions I think you might
tell them that I have not the slightest interest in printing local
gossip or digging up old scandals, that if I had and wanted to deal
in material of that sort the result would be a far different one. I
think you might say that, as you understand it, your son is interested in putting down a part of his picture of life as he sees it,
and to do it as sincerely and honestly as he can—that the web of
life—its web of fortune, misfortune, joy and grief, is the same
everywhere, but that the writer, naturally, must use the material
he has seen and knows in showing this. But I don't think you
need say anything, if you don't want to; the story is all right, and
everyone in it is all right, and every honest, decent, and sensible
reader will understand this. It will be out in the July number of
Scribner's which appears about June 18.

Fred wrote me he might come to N. Y. on a week-end excursion—I was expecting him but he didn't come; he wrote later say-

ing he was hard-up and didn't want to borrow the money from Gibson.[1] I was sorry about this, if I had known I would gladly have advanced the money for the trip and I hope he manages to come up later. I enjoyed your long and interesting letter. I am glad to know you are well and hope this finds you in the best of health and spirits. I am well but pretty tired—when I finish my book I'll take a rest. Goodbye, Mama, for this time— Write when you can—let me know if you need anything.

Love,

Tom

101 COLUMBIA HEIGHTS [2]
Brooklyn, N. Y.
August 9, 1932

DEAR MAMA:

I got your telegram late last night. Thanks for your promptness in answering me. You saved me from being swindled out of $15 or $20 by a very clever rascal. I know you will be curious to know the story so I'm going to tell you all I know of it, although there are still several very mysterious facts which I do not understand.

About three o'clock yesterday afternoon, my phone rang and a man spoke to me over the wire who said that he was Walter Brown of Asheville. I had not the faintest idea who Walter Brown was but I knew there were hundreds of Browns at home and I ran over the list of my acquaintance—Sanford Brown, Caney Brown, Latt Brown, etc.,—and failed completely to place this Walter Brown. However, he said that he was a friend of my

[1] Sloane Gibson, a manufacturer of ice cream in High Point, N. C., with whom Fred was associated.
[2] Tom lived here from the Fall of 1932 to the Fall of 1933.

family and that he knew you and that he had seen you and that you had given him my address and phone number here in Brooklyn and asked him to come to see me. Of course I said, "How do you do, Mr. Brown. How long will you be in town and how is everyone at home?" just as if I did know him because I thought he might really be someone I had met and I did not want to offend him if he was a friend of the family's. He said that he was in town only for the day and was leaving at midnight and seeing a way out of the difficulty, I said that was a great pity because if he were staying longer I should be glad to see him and find out about the folks at home. He then asked if he could not see me anyway for a few moments saying he was most anxious to talk to me and that he would take only a little of my time. I thought he was probably another bore who had written a book or a story and wanted me to take it to Scribners, so I planned to get out of it saying I would be busy all afternoon and had been invited out to dinner at seven o'clock. He then asked if he could see me for a few minutes at six thirty and I told him to come on.

At six-thirty, yesterday afternoon, my bell rang, I released the catch, and in a moment a strapping young buck nigger between the ages of thirty and thirty-five came bounding up my steps, walked into my room and said that he was Walter Brown. You could have knocked me over with a feather when I saw this distinguished gentleman of color and of course I thought it was a pretty fresh way for an Asheville darky to act—to call me up and announce himself as a friend of the family and to give no indication of his race or color before he came. He made himself at home in my most comfortable chair and lit a cigarette and still I said nothing to him because I thought if he had really known you all and had come the whole way out to Brooklyn to see me simply because he knew my family and you had asked him to look me up, I was not going to offend him no matter what his race or color was. I then asked about you and how you were and when he had seen you last. To my great surprise, he said it had been over a year since he had seen you or since he had been in Asheville. Still trying to place him, I asked some more questions about Asheville and how he came to know you and he said that his mother was a woman named Amelia Brown who had cooked for you and further that this same Amelia Brown had worked for Mabel in Washington within the last two years. He further said that his mother, Amelia Brown, had died in Washington about five months ago and had left an estate which, he said, was worth from three to four thousand dollars, although it was "all tied up" at present.

He further said that Amelia Brown had named you and Mabel as executors of this estate because of the great respect and confidence she had for you. Now, Mamma, the amazing thing about this rascal's story is this: He seemed to be so completely familiar with the facts about the family's life that I was practically convinced he was telling me the truth and even now I cannot understand where he managed to get all this information. He inquired repeatedly about Mr. and Mrs. Wheaton and he asked how they were and I told him, of course, that they had suffered like everyone else from the Asheville boom and had lost their home. He then said, very quickly, "But they're still living at the Gramercy,[1] aren't they?"—which proved conclusively that he knew they were living in Washington. He spoke of you, repeatedly, and even referred to you as Miss Julia and asked how Fred was and how he was getting along. You can imagine by the time he got through with all this, I no longer had much

---

[1] At this time Tom's sister, Mabel Wheaton, was managing a rooming house in Washington called The Gramercy.

doubt about anything he said. I was pretty well convinced that the facts were as he had stated them—that his mother had worked for you and that he was an Asheville darky. He had few of the characteristics of speech and manner of a Southern negro, he was what people in the South call an "educated nigger," and still curious to know how he got this way, I asked him what he did and how long he had lived in the North. He said he was a musician and that he had been educated at the New England Conservatory of Music and since I had heard him refer, not only to his mother but to his sister who shared with him in this estate of which you and Mabel were supposed to be executors, it somehow occurred to me all at once that this educated coon was the brother of Myrtis, the little girl that Mabel had working for her at Asheville. So I said to him, "Have you got a sister named Myrtis?"—and immediately, without the slightest hesitation he grinned and said, "That's right. You've got it now. Myrtis is my sister." Of course I suppose I put the words in his mouth but he was so slick an article that there was not the slightest clumsiness or hesitation in his answer. After this, I was sure I had him placed and I was really somewhat touched to think that he thought so much of the family that he had come to see me.

I then asked him what he was doing and if things had gone well with him. He looked very sad and he said that things had gone very badly with him during the last year or two. He then paused and after a moment quietly remarked that he had been released from Sing Sing Prison the day before. I asked him then what he had done that he should be imprisoned for it and he answered that a year and four months ago he had been driving a car across Columbus Circle, New York City, and had run over a man who had died from his injuries nine days later. Brown said that the car he was driving was not his own although he had a car which another negro had stolen and driven away down South. Brown said he had no driver's license at the time this accident occurred and that although the accident was not his fault and the man he had injured absolved him of blame in a written statement just before he died, he had been sentenced, nevertheless, to serve a term of from two and one-half to five years at Sing Sing Prison. He said the sentence had been commuted and that he had been paroled the day before on good behavior after having served one year and four months. At the time the accident occurred, Brown said, he was doing very well in his profession as a musician. He said that he was the leader of a negro orchestra and had made quite a reputation for himself as a player of negro spirituals and hymns and other kinds of negro music. When the accident occurred he said he was on his way to fulfill an engagement at the home of a wealthy woman in Tuxedo Park, New York, for which he was to receive $125. Further, he claims that he had thirteen hundred dollars in the bank at the time of his arrest and that when he was brought into court a Jewish lawyer named Rosenberg had approached him and had offered to defend him for $300. Brown claims this Rosenberg then produced a check, gave Brown a fountain pen and asked him to fill the check out for $300 but that the clerk of the court yelled at them saying that they were in a court room and that if they had business to transact, they must do it elsewhere. Rosenberg said, "At least he has time to sign his name. I'll fill it in, myself." And Brown said that he had foolishly done this, signing his name to a blank check which this shyster lawyer had later filled in for the full amount of Brown's deposit in the bank. Brown was sentenced to serve a term in Sing Sing and he claims that his parole came not only as a result of his good behavior while in prison but because a well-known hotel owner in California—

he told me the man's name—had wired and offered him a good job out there at $60 a week as an orchestra director if he could succeed in obtaining his release. He then had the effrontery to claim that he had written you from prison and explained the circumstances to you and his lack of funds and that you had managed to get fifteen or twenty dollars in interest or rent out of his mother's estate and had added five or ten dollars of your own and had sent him $25.

This sum, added to the five dollars the prison authorities give each prisoner on his release and the small sum of money which he had earned in prison—he told me each prisoner was paid a cent and a half a day for his labor—gave him a sum of $45. He said it was imperative for him to go to California immediately because his job there began next week and he said the bus fare which was the cheapest way of travelling was $55. He further had the gall to state that he had called you up on the long distance telephone yesterday morning and had explained the situation to you and that you had told him you had sent him all that you were able to send but that he should come and see me and tell me the story and that you had given him my address and telephone number.

Well, Mamma, the whole story sounded pretty convincing. I suppose his lies were so stupendous that I did not see how he could possibly have made them up and I think I should have given him the money then and there if I had had it but fortunately I did not have enough in my pocket to give him what he said he needed and the Scribners' office was closed for the day. Further, a remnant of caution prompted me to wait until I had telegraphed you to find out if the facts were as he had stated them and I told him straight out that this was what I was going to do and that if I helped him at all I could not help him anyway until the next morning when the Scribners' office would be open. Of course I suppose he knew his goose was cooked when I told him I was going to telegraph you and he said that if he could possibly get away last night it would be very important to him and would get him to his job one day sooner. But I wrote the telegram which I sent to you before him and read it to him and asked him if he thought it was a fair statement of the facts and he said that he did. He then began to jingle a few coins around in his pocket and said that he had only 45¢ to live on until the next day. I then asked him what had become of the $45 or so which he had got from you and from the prison authorities and he had an answer for this, too. He said that he was so anxious to get away from New York and to get out West where his job was waiting for him and so afraid that his money would get away from him that he had invested almost every penny of it as a deposit on the ticket and that if I wished to confirm this I could call up the bus company and they would tell me that he had told the truth. In the face of this smooth story I still had wit enough left to ask him why, if this man out West thought so highly of his ability and was so eager to employ him that he had even written to the prison authorities to aid in getting him his parole, he had not also sent along money enough to pay his fare across the country. Well, the smooth and persuasive Mr. Brown had an answer for this too. He said that he had telegraphed his employer in California explaining his difficulty and asking for money and that he had received an answer from this man's secretary who said that the man was away on a few weeks' fishing trip in the State of Washington and could not be reached or communicated with. He said the man would not return before next Monday and that until that time he could expect no help from him. I then asked him if he had any letters which this man had written to him or his papers of parole from the prison and he said that all of these were in the keeping of the prison authorities. It sounded pretty good and everything had the ring of truth, even to the stories he told me of his life in prison. I asked him a good many questions about the food and the housing and the rules of regulations of prison life and he told me all about it,—and I have no doubt he spoke from personal experience. Anyway, before he left, I gave him a dollar which, added to the 45¢ which he said he had, I knew would keep him for the night and buy his supper. He said that he had taken a room in town and was paying 50¢ a day for it. Well, he went away and I sent you the telegram and you know the rest. Of course, when I got the answer you and Fred sent me last night, I thought that was the end of Brown and that I should hear no more from him. He had promised to call me at ten o'clock this morning but ten o'clock came and passed and he did not call. To my immense surprise, however, he did call me shortly after twelve o'clock today and I then told him that I had heard from you and that you said you did not know him and had never heard of him. I told him I did not know who he was but to keep away from my place and that if he attempted to see me again, I would turn him over to the authorities. I suppose he called me this morning on the thousand to one chance that I had not heard from you and that I would be fool enough to fall for his swindle.

Now, here's the final episode of this amazing story: At one o'clock today my friend Fritz Dashiell whom you know, called me up. He has just returned from a trip to Colorado where he made a speech to the summer school of the State University out there. I began to tell him the remarkable story of Mr. Brown and before I had talked a minute he began to laugh and said, "Go on, but I'll tell you the rest of the story when you get through." Then, when I had finished he told me that a man, and we think undoubtedly this same man, approached old Mr. Bridges[1] who was formerly editor of *Scribner's Magazine*, just a week or so ago with this same story save that he had changed the details as to family, etc., and Mr. Bridges had been so taken in that he had given him $5.00. In its general outline, the story he told Mr. Bridges was the same as the story he told me. He went to see Mr. Bridges at the University Club where he lives and he told Bridges that he had formerly been in the employ of no less a personage than Woodrow Wilson who was in Mr. Bridges' class at Princeton and was one of Bridges' closest friends. So you see Mr. Brown doesn't blink at anything and when he starts to tell a lie, he can tell it high, wide and fancy. He spoke to Bridges in such a touching manner of Woodrow Wilson's children, in particular speaking of the respect and affection he felt for Miss Margaret who is now, I believe, the wife of William Gibbs McAdoo, that old man Bridges broke down and wept. Further, Doctor Brown was on his way West to California again where a job was waiting for him, as usual—and where do you suppose? Why, in the home of Mr. McAdoo, of course, and of Miss Margaret and all he needed was $5 to make up his fare and the only reason he couldn't get it from his old friend, McAdoo, was because McAdoo was away on a speaking trip, or a hunting trip, or a vacation and couldn't be reached! So Bridges gave him the $5.

Well, I thought you'd like to hear the story because it seems to me to be a good one and although it cost me $1.90 in telegrams and donations to Mr. Brown, I think it is worth it and it could have been a great deal worse. Of course the thing that still mystifies me and Fritz Dashiell and all of us is where this fellow

[1] Robert Bridges, editor of *Scribner's Magazine* from 1914 to 1930.

gets hold of all this amazing information about the friends and
lives and families of different people. I do not yet understand
how he could have known about you and Mabel and Fred and
Asheville and spoken about you all in such a way that I could
have sworn he had been born in Asheville and known us all, all
his life. Some of us think there may be a kind of big criminal
information bureau up in Harlem which is the big black section
of New York City and where niggers from all over the country
have assembled. We think that this fellow may be a member of
such an organization and if he is, of course he would be able
through negroes living in Harlem who have come there from
all over the South, to get the stories and facts about people everywhere. But if there is any truth in what he says, if anything I
have told you wakens any memory in you and if you think you
can spot this darky as someone who really did live in Asheville
once, I wish you would let me know. The strange part about
it all is that he is willing to work so hard and to concoct so
smooth a story when he apparently gets so little out of it. All he
asked me for was $7 which, he said, would just complete the
amount he needed for bus fare, the $15 was my own suggestion
because I knew the man would have to eat during the week it
would take him to get across the continent. And all he asked
Mr. Bridges for was $5. Thus he got only one dollar from me
and five dollars from Mr. Bridges. And I should say he did at
least a hundred dollars' worth of hard work in collecting all this
information about us and in concocting a story so smooth that we
were both ready to swallow it down, almost without question.

Well that's the whole story now, and I think you now know as
much about it as I do. If you have anything further to contribute,
please let me know.

I have meant to write you for some time but I have written

you a longer letter about this episode than I intended so I will defer until another time some other things I wanted to tell you about.

I was very happy about getting or rather sharing in the *Scribner's* prize.[1] It was a totally unexpected windfall to me since, at the time I wrote the story I did not even know that *Scribner's Magazine* was holding a contest. The award, therefore, was almost wholly unexpected and it was certainly welcome because I had begun to worry about money and this makes the immediate future considerably brighter and more secure. For your own benefit, if you do not understand this already, I should like to tell you that I did not get $5,000 as the Asheville papers stated, but $2,500. The three judges voted a tie between my story and another man's, or rather the final result came out in an exact tie and of course *Scribner's* could not afford to give both of us $5,000 each but there is a very curious, and it seems to me, very foolish ruling in the United States Post Office which says that a prize offered in a magazine contest must be awarded to one person and that if there is a tie the full amount must be awarded to each of the contestants in the tie. The post office apparently made this ruling because of the practice of several cheap and unscrupulous magazines which would announce a prize for the best story in a contest and then divide the prize among a hundred different contestants, thereby securing a great deal of manuscript for next to nothing. Of course there was no question of anything of this sort in the *Scribner's* contest. It is an honorable and high-grade publication and everyone knows it, but the post office is inflexible in its ruling and might even have power to stop

[1] *Scribner's Magazine* had offered a prize of five thousand dollars for the best long story submitted within a certain period. The judges could not decide between *A Portrait of Bascom Hawke* by Tom and *The Big Short Trip* by John Herrmann. The award was therefore divided.

the whole national circulation of the magazine by holding up
the issue in the New York post office. Fritz was afraid of this
and while he told me he thought *Scribner's* could undoubtedly
win out in the end, an issue might be delayed for several days
or even a week and he therefore met the situation by stating the
award ambiguously. He simply said that the prize had been
awarded to me and to Herrmann without stating the amount
that either of us got. For your own information, the amount was
$2,500 and I consider this perfectly fair but I am not yet exactly
rolling in wealth inasmuch as I owe part of this sum to Scribners
already and must go as carefully and easily as I can on what is
left until I complete something else which may bring me a little
money. I have gone ahead with my work this summer, although
I have lost some time recently because of a stroke of ill luck which
forced me to move from my place at 111 Columbia Heights to
my present address which you will please note, 101 Columbia
Heights. My 'phone number remains the same, and by the way,
another curious element in Professor Brown's story was that you
had given him my address and when I asked him what address
you had given him, he said "101 Columbia Heights." I told him
this was impossible since I had moved here only a week ago and
had not yet informed you of the change and he immediately corrected himself and said that 111 was the address he had.

I had to get out of the other place where you stayed in the
spring because the Clarks who were my landlords had not been
able to make the house go. But Clark gave me no warning of all
this until about four days before the first of August so I had to
drop everything I was doing and spend three or four days sweating around in the sun until I found this place. I am now living in
a small apartment house for the first time in my life. I have two
very nice rooms, a bath, and a kitchen, and although the place

is not as big as the place I had before, it is cleaner and more modern and more private. The owners put in an electric icebox for me and the rent is $15 a month lower than it was at the other place. In addition, the place is cool and I have a very nice view of New York Harbor and of the skyscrapers, which I shall take pleasure in showing to you if you come up here to visit me. If I don't write you very often, sometimes, it is because I've got to press on to finish now and will have very little time for anything else, but as I have told you, if you need anything, I want you to let me know instantly, and if I can help you, I will do it.

I hope this finds you all well and happy. Please write me and give me the news when you have time.

With love to all.

Tom

1932 DEC 21 AM 7 31

CFA 14 46 NL B BROOKLYN NY 20

MRS JULIA E WOLFE

  48 SPRUCE ST ASHEVILLE NCAR

HOPE YOU WILL GO TO WASHINGTON XMAS IF YOU FEEL LIKE MAKING TRIP IF YOU NEED MORE MONEY LET ME KNOW HAVE NOT BEEN WELL BUT ALL RIGHT NOW AM SENDING FIFTEEN NOW BUT IF YOU NEED ME FOR TRIP WIRE AT ONCE AM WRITING LOVE

Tom

101 COLUMBIA HEIGHTS
Brooklyn, N. Y.
Jan 15, 1933

(I have delayed sending this till Sunday, Jan 15):

DEAR MAMA: Your good long letter came this morning, and I want to answer at once and give you what news there is. Fred has already been here and returned to Philadelphia: he came up Saturday and was here with me until Monday afternoon. He also called me up from Philadelphia tonight, and I told him I had a letter from you and that you are well. He is starting out in a day or so with Richter [1]—his employer—to look over his territory and get acquainted with it. I hope he is able to make the job pay—I know something of the country he will work—it is one of the finest fattest farming districts in the whole country, and the farmers certainly look thrifty and prosperous—but of course most of them are Penn. Dutch and they have the reputation of being very close, and holding on hard to every dollar. But he may be able to crack their shell and get some business from them. Anyway it's worth giving a try. I was glad to see him again and I think he enjoyed his visit here. I had plenty of room here in the apartment to take care of him but unfortunately had no extra bed or mattress where he could sleep. So we found a room with a bath at a hotel next door, and which cost him $2.00 a day—the next time he comes I hope to have a couch or something for him to sleep in here—of course, all I have myself is a cot, and the two of us would never have got on that. We had a good bright day Sunday, and walked and rode the subways all over town. We went to the roof of his hotel where there was a fine view of New York and all the harbor, we walked across the Brooklyn Bridge,

[1] He was sales manager of the district in which Fred was then employed in selling farm machinery.

we took the subway to Columbia University and looked around the University, St. Lukes Hospital, and went all through the Cathedral of St. John the Divine—not yet finished but an enormous church. Then we walked to Riverside Drive, got a good look at the new Geo. Washington Bridge, rode downtown to the bright lights of Broadway again, saw a movie, then ate, saw Radio City, walked up 5th Ave, across the Columbus Circle, back through Central Park, down Park Avenue, and went through the great new Waldorf Astoria hotel; then walked to Grand Central Station which Fred had never seen, explored that pretty thoroughly, and then took subway back to Brooklyn, arriving home at half past twelve at night. It was a pretty full day and I was tired. On Monday, we had breakfast in my place, checked out of his hotel, went to town and met all the people at Scribners, and went to lunch with Max Perkins—same place you went. Then we went back to Grand Central where Fred had checked his suit case, rode Shuttle to Times Square, and went to Pennsylvania Station where he got a train for Phil. at 2:30.

We managed to see a good deal in two days time—he said tonight when he called that he might come up again this next week end. He is going out on trip with Richter tomorrow or next day but expects to be back in Phil. by Saturday. I can give you the news about myself in a hurry. I worked hard all through the summer until late October when I just gave out completely— had never been so fagged out mentally, physically, and every other way. I got on a boat and went to Bermuda, which was a bad thing to do because the place is terribly expensive, and I did not like it—spent a lot of money and got no rest. Came back on boat to Boston with a chest cold that got pretty serious—got so I couldn't talk—but went out to visit a friend at Andover Mass.

where I slept and rested for four days and got on my feet again. Since then I have been coming back slowly and have done considerable work— Am now trying to finish a story which will bring me in some money, maybe, and then go back and finish my book. I'm almost broke but guess I'll be all right if I can only keep my health and energy. I have been hounded and driven crazy the past three years by letters and fool questions about books, stories, writings, or just plain damned impudent curiosity —but if I get some peace of mind and quiet everything will be all right,—I don't know if I told you I also went to York Springs [1] for two or three days at beginning of October— Stayed with Aunt Mary (Gil's wife) and her son Edgar (they all call him Jim). They were mighty nice to me and wanted me to stay longer— Jim is a gay fellow about my age, is Justice of the Peace in the village, and has the job of distributing one of the Harrisburg papers through all the county between Harrisburg and Gettysburg. I went with him on his rounds and saw the country—also the little house where Papa's mother [2] & Augusta [3] lived, place where they all lived, etc. Met several people who knew and remembered Papa. A very strange thing happened while I was there: Jim and I were going to visit our cousin, Charles Wolfe, who was Geo. Wolfe's son, but of course a much older man than either of us—66. He was said to be a wealthy and prosperous man and lived in Dellsburg, a town about 8 miles from York Springs. Well, he died very suddenly a day or two after I got there—one of his sons came early one morning with the news—

[1] The native town of Tom's father about eight miles from Gettysburg, Penn. Here it was, as is recorded in *Of Time and the River* that W. O. Gant, whose original was Tom's father, stood by the roadside with his brother as Confederate troops marched by toward Gettysburg. Tom's father often told of this incident, and of later hearing the thunder of artillery.

[2] Eleanor Jane Heickus.

[3] Mrs. Augusta Wolfe Martin.

Jim and I went over and saw the body and he looked so much like Papa it was startling. The same long lean look, the same thin long nose, grey mustache, grey hair—I'd have known him for one of Papa's people if no one had ever told me who he was. Also went over and saw his wife, his sisters, and two or three of his children the day I left—on way to Harrisburg— Aunt Mary, Jim and his wife were with me. Aunt Mary is quite old now— 76 or 78, I think—but quite spry— Her son, the Charley Wolfe who was at Norfolk in p.o., and later in Colorado, died out in the Philippines a few months ago of tuberculosis and she is quite broken up about it. Everyone remembered you and Papa and spoke about you— Charley Wolfe's wife asked about you and said she and Charley were intending to come to Asheville to see you all— His death was sudden and unexpected—we knew he had been sick in bed but considered nothing serious—nurse told me he was getting much better and had just been shaved by a barber about six o'clock in evening. Doctor thought he'd be up and out in day or so. Nurse left room for few minutes, when she came back she found him unconscious and struggling for breath. In five minutes he was dead—don't know what the trouble was, he had a "fallen stomach," they said, and had not been in very good health for several years. Supposed to be a rich man, and owns several farms.— Aunt Mary wanted to hear all about you and I know if you ever went there she and Jim would be delighted to see you. She has two or three other sons and a daughter Esther—all married, I think—went to see the one who lives in Harrisburg—Harry—he is now a grey haired man a mechanic in shops of Reading Railroad with grown daughter. Emory, I believe, is a teacher in Pittsburgh and makes six or seven thousand dollars a year. In spite of this, Jim is left to support his mother—although he is not so well off as the others.—Your fruit cake arrived in good shape and I find it delicious—still have most of it, as I have been down with a bad cold and didn't feel much like eating. Conditions here are very bad and have shown no signs of improvement. Everyone is waiting to see what Roosevelt and his crowd will do—if they can do anything—but meanwhile just marking time. There have not been any riots or serious disturbances yet and there is a great effort being made to collect money and see that the unemployed get food and shelter. In spite of this I am afraid there is great suffering and hardship. No one knows what the future will bring, but everyone hopes for better times. We have had one or two spells of cold weather and one big snow but the winter has not been very severe. Fred and I saw the great new buildings of Radio City—very wonderful to look at, but who is going to rent them? I understand that there are sixty floors in Empire State without a rented office in them. Yet I went out a day or two before Christmas to buy a shirt and found stores like Macy's and Saks packed and jammed with people. I suppose there is still a great deal of money and wealth which some people have, as well as all the poverty and hardship which other people have. But I don't think we can go through another year like the last without serious trouble. Let's hope that this will not happen.— I am glad you enjoyed your Christmas—Fred told me he bought good turkey and that you had a big dinner. I was well taken care of— spent Christmas Eve in country with friends, where I telephoned you, and came back Christmas day to have dinner with Mr. Wheelock[1] and his family in the city. Also spent New Year's in country with Dashiell and his family. I am glad to hear you are coming to Wash. for inauguration and will look forward to seeing

[1] John Hall Wheelock, the poet, and a member of the editorial staff of Charles Scribner's Sons.

you about that time. It has been twenty years since I saw Wilson inaugurated with you, and in that time a great deal has happened to all of us. I hope the next twenty will be happier, more prosperous ones for us all, and for this coming year I wish you all good health and happiness it is possible to have.— It is now late and I will end this letter, sending you my love and my best hopes for your good health. If there is anything you need, or that I can do let me know at once. Write when you can. With love

Your Son,

Tom

Wed., Jan. 11, 1933

P.S. I am using pencil because I have no pen and ink in place— I am very sorry to hear that Uncle Will[1] has lost everything. I hope enough is realized when his affairs are wound up to give him something to live on the rest of his life. Fred tells me Uncle Jim[2] still is solvent and in good shape, but that very few people in Asheville are. It is hard to see what Asheville is going to do. It seems that they did enough damage in two or three years to ruin the town for fifty years to come— Our people were flying too high and forgetting how to tell the truth—everything bluff and brag and blow—this is what the whole country was doing and we're paying through the nose for it right now.

[1] William Harrison Westall, dealer in building material and real estate operator in Asheville, N. C., born 1863. At one time paid the largest tax of any citizen in Asheville.

[2] James Manassas Westall, named for his uncle and the Battle of Manassas in which the uncle was killed in 1861.

101 COLUMBIA HEIGHTS
Brooklyn, N. Y.
February 27, 1933.

DEAR MAMA:

I got your card the other day and was glad to hear you are in Washington this week. I am working as hard as I can trying to finish up another long section of my book, which incidentally I also hope to sell to *Scribner's Magazine*, and my present intention is to work hard up thru Friday and then try to get down to Washington Friday night or Saturday morning in time for the inauguration. I think I shall be able to do this but if I am not I shall certainly get down over the week-end or within a few days thereafter.

I have my back right up against the wall at the present time and have almost no money, so it is up to me now to get the book done, not only for the sake of earning some money but for the sake of getting back my hope and belief and self-confidence again, without which everything will be lost for me. I believe and Perkins believes that I now have it, for I came back here shortly after the first of the year, and after I made a little trip down to Baltimore and Washington with Mr. Perkins, plunged into work and did more work in one month than I had ever done before in my life in a similar period of time. Perkins says that I have the whole book in a nutshell, a very big nutshell it is true, for he already has over 100,000 words, and that if I can go ahead now and let nothing interfere with me until I finish we will have a fine book, and will bring it out next autumn. I also got down to my last ten dollars but *Scribner's* have bought two long stories out of the book and will probably buy another, all three of which they propose to run in successive numbers, the first beginning, I believe, in the May number.

What I am trying to tell you is this; that I have been in a very desperate condition but everything will probably be all right yet, if I simply go ahead and do my work now. A great part of this trouble has been my own fault but I have honestly tried to do the best I could and had a good deal to put up with these last three years. We also believe here, I mean the people at Scribners and myself, that all the sweating and working and writing I have done the last three years will not be lost but that it will fit into this book and the other books which are to follow. But, I do want to say also that I have been badgered, tormented, and almost driven mad at times by fool questions, fool letters from fool people, the tantrums of crazy women, and about ten million words of advice, criticism and instructions how to write my next book from people who know nothing about it. Therefore, I beg and plead of all of you that if I come to Washington, you will follow my earnest wishes in this one thing, and not to talk, mention or speak about books, stories or what I intend to do, or regale me with stories about what butchers, bakers, doctors, preachers or Government clerks or anyone else in Asheville has said, or will say or is saying about me. Let's forget about it for a day or two, I beg of you, and I am making this plea so strong because I do not think you understand the kind of strain a writer works under when he is trying to get a big piece of work done, and how necessary it is that he have peace and quiet, and be able to forget about it once in a while. Anyone who has never tried it, of course, thinks that writing is the easiest and laziest kind of work in the world, whereas it is really so much more exhausting, nerve racking and vitality consuming than any other kind of work I have ever seen or heard of that there is no comparison whatever.

Now Mama, I have said all this simply in order to let you

know exactly how things stand and to tell you that I think things will still be all right, and that after all these months of desperate effort and confusion I have seemed to begin to unravel the knot and to have found the way to get started, which Perkins now thinks is where the trouble was, and the whole river now seems to be flowing, and I know that none of you are going to misunderstand me or take offense because I have spoken plainly of what is really a desperate and critical situation, and have asked you all to have kindness and tolerance and understanding enough now to help me all you can, because I have never believed that any one of you would like to see me fail and make a tragic mess out of my life when the great and golden opportunity still remains for me to make a fine and good success, and to get the kind of happiness and satisfaction from my work that I must have. That is the reason I have spoken to you plainly and because I am coming down to see you and am looking forward to it so much.

I have been working ten, twelve and fourteen hours a day here for several weeks and that is the reason I let your birthday go by the other day without writing to you. I must confess to you that I cannot remember the exact date of your own birthday or of any member of the family, or of any one for that matter, but that simply means that I have no kind of memory for birthdays. I do know that yours falls in between Lincoln's and Washington's birthday, which is more than I remember about anyone else's, and even though your birthday is passed, I want to send you now my warmest congratulations on having lived such a long, active and interesting life, and on having reached your present age in such fine health, and with all your faculties as keen and alert as they ever were. I do not suppose one person in ten thousand can say as much as this, and certainly I do not know of any other person your age who can. I also believe that you will go on for many years longer enjoying good health and with your interest and pleasure in life unimpaired.

This is all that I can write you now, because I must get started on the day's work, but I shall let you know by post card or telegram when I am coming—in time for the inauguration, if possible, but if not, as soon thereafter as I can. In any case, I hope you have a fine day for the inauguration and get a good seat or place in the crowd to see it from. I think that today, when exactly twenty years have passed, I could take you to almost the exact spot where we stood twenty years ago and saw Woodrow Wilson ride past to his inauguration with President Taft. That street in which we stood was either A or B Street; I believe it has been cleared away and the houses torn down, but I think I could take you to the place again and not miss it by many feet. I also remember many things about that day when I was barely twelve years old, and I wonder if you remember them. I was standing in front of you at the very edge of the curb wedged against the rope, and almost afraid to breathe or move, because there was a very disagreeable and bad-tempered Yankee and his wife right behind me, who kept saying all the time—

"Well we may get to see some of this inauguration if this little boy here will only stand still for a few minutes"—or—

"This is the most fidgety and restless little boy I ever saw in my whole life. I wish he would try to keep quiet just for a minute," etc. I do not suppose you noticed it or paid any attention to it, but I have never forgotten it. I was in agony about it at the time and all the time the troops and the great men kept marching past I was afraid to take a long breath for fear of disturbing this bad-tempered man and his wife, and I believe that is the main reason why ever since I have always had a great deal of sympathy for fidgety boys and would not say anything to them under almost any circumstances.

Well Mama, this is all that I have time for at the present time and I hope this letter finds you in the best of health and spirits, and Mabel and Ralph as well.

Meanwhile, until I see you, I send you all my love and my best wishes for your good health and happiness.   TOM

                                    101 COLUMBIA HEIGHTS
                                    Brooklyn, N. Y.
                                    March 2, 1933.

DEAR MAMA:

Thanks for your letter which came this morning. I am going to try to get a train or bus or some other means of transportation tomorrow night so that I can get down to Washington in time for the Inauguration Saturday morning. I am trying to finish another long section of the book today or tomorrow and would like to have this off my mind before I leave, but, if I do not finish it I will probably try to come on anyway.

Scribner's have so far taken two long stories out of the book and they want a third, which they propose to publish in successive numbers beginning with the May issue. They are enthusiastic about the stories and say they are different from anything else that has ever been done, and so on, but they get very cautious when money is mentioned, and are paying me very little for them. They gave me $250 for the first one, and I am afraid that is all they are going to offer me for the second one which they have taken, but for which they have not yet set a price. I am getting a little tired of being told what a famous author I am and how everyone is waiting to see my next production, and then having to worry from week to week where the rent is coming from.

I have become so attached and got so much in the habit of thinking only of *Scribner's* that it never occurred to me that I might send a story to any one else, and since I know very little about the publishing world and do not mix up with the literary life I hardly know how to begin. But I am meeting an agent tomorrow, a well-known firm, which is considered the best not only in this country but also abroad, and I am going to try to find out if some of these stories which I have written will bring me in more money than I have been getting. If an agent can do this for me he will be well worth the commission he charges.

The second story which *Scribner's* have taken, but for which they have not set a price, but for which I am sure they are going to give me only $250 is 30,000 words long, which is to say, about one-half the length of an average size book, and it is also one of the best things I ever wrote. Now, I am not sneering at the $250 but I know that five such stories as that a year would be considered a big year's work by almost any other writer in America, for the story is really the length of a short novel, and I do not see yet how it is possible for me to live, pay the expense of a stenographer, which unfortunately I must do at the present time since I have never learned to type, and all the other expenses, unless I get paid more for these stories.

Meanwhile, of course, the thing that is desperately important is getting the big book done and I ought not to worry so much about expenses as I do and also I have no time to take my stuff around to different people to see if I can sell it and get more money than I have heretofore been paid. Well, enough of this for the present.

I am glad you had the trip to York Springs and saw Aunt Mary and Jim and his wife and also had the chance of going over the field of Gettysburg with Fred. I have been across the battle field myself but it was in a hired car driven by some country boy up there who had been taught a little speech to say and annoyed me so much by getting it all wrong. I have read so much about that battle that I now understand pretty well what happened and I would much rather go with Fred or someone I know than in a hired car. In summer, in autumn and I imagine also in spring, it is a very beautiful spot for it seemed to be especially created by God or the devil for a battle field, and I am sorry that you could not have seen it on some such season as that when it looked as it must have looked on those hot days in July when the battle was fought. I was very glad and interested to know that so many of your own kinsmen were in that battle and in the other battles of the War and, of course, several of Papa's people, as you know, including his older brother George and George Lentz's father were on the Union side in the war. So we seem to have been represented on every side there was.

I hope I will be in Washington in time to be with you for the inauguration parade, but in view of the tremendous crowds which I understand will be there, and the fact that you have come so far to see it I think that if you can get a seat for $2 or $3 which will enable you to see it, it will be a good investment and well worth your while, and I will cheerfully contribute the necessary funds.

This is all for the present as I must now go to work. Take care of yourself and see to it that you get a good view of the parade if I am not there in time to see it with you. If nothing unforeseen occurs I shall get there to spend the day at any rate, before the week is over.

Tom

BROOKLYN, N. Y.

March 29, 1933.

DEAR MAMA:

Thanks for your letter and glad to hear that you reached home safely and found everything all right.

We have had a pretty raw and windy month of March but it is now ending and there are a few signs of spring about. I have been very hard at work since I left you but intend to do even more, if possible, this spring. I imagine you will be getting some warm weather before long now as the season is a little more advanced at home than it is here, but you should be prepared for sudden changes which may still be ahead of you for several weeks.

I have had two or three letters from Fred and he seems to be in pretty good spirits, although he says there is not much business as yet. I do not know what he has decided to do about going South to work for the man in Spartanburg or to stay on in his present job with Richter but I think that he is going to stay on for a while to see if business does get better.

People seem to be much more hopeful here although there has been little improvement in business as yet. I understand the breweries are looking forward to prosperous times and are spending great sums of money on new equipment and taking on thousands of men. They think that they will have beer here early in April and they are trying now to keep it as far as possible out of the hands of the politicians and grafters and run it on an honest basis. I do not suppose you will have beer in North Carolina yet since that is one of the States which is supposed to be on the dry side, although Bob Reynold's election sounded pretty wet.

My book[1] came out in Germany the beginning of March ac-

<hr />

[1] *Look Homeward, Angel.*

cording to a letter I had from the publisher but since then I have heard nothing more from him and I do not know if this trouble which they are having there now has hurt its sale or not. I hope not. I am having another meeting with the literary agent I spoke to you about and will see him on Saturday and perhaps give him some pieces I have written in an effort to get some money. He thinks he can sell them and can get more money than *Scribner's* have been paying me and if he can I will let him have them.

I have been well but getting pretty tired the last week or two since I have kept going at a pretty steady clip for the last two months or more, with the exception of those few days I took off to go to Washington.

There is not much news that I can give you at present. The first of my three stories will be out in the May number which comes out late in April, I believe, and if anyone at home asks you tell them not to be excited because there is nothing in it about Asheville or any of the people there.

I hope this letter finds you well and not in want of anything that you need. If you do need anything I want you to let me know at once and I will get it for you if I can.

Do you have anywhere at home a picture of Papa's father and mother made at some time in their younger days?

With love and best wishes for your health and happiness

Your son,

TOM

101 COLUMBIA HEIGHTS
Brooklyn, N. Y.
April 21, 1933.

DEAR MAMA:

Thanks for your long letter and for the flowers which were remarkably fresh when they got here in spite of their long trip.

I am sorry you did not get to go to Washington for Easter and were disappointed in your plans. I know that they were expecting you because Fred wrote me a card from Harrisburg and said you probably would be there. I did not go to Washington myself although I intended to but guessed you were not there because I thought if you were they would let me know; in that case I should have gone on down.

I have done nothing and have been able to do nothing for the last week but rest and I am just getting back to work today. I did not go to Washington because I was too tired to go and felt that I would do better simply to stay at home and try to get some sleep, since I have not been able to sleep well for some time. I feel much better now and wish I could take a few days more but they are pushing me at Scribners and I have got to get back to it.

I turned in an additional 600 pages of typed manuscript a week ago, practically all of which I had done since I saw you at Washington and that in addition to what they had before makes almost 1000 typed pages which they have in their safe at Scribners. This means that I have the first two parts or about one-half of the completed manuscript of the four-part book, or series of books, on which I have been working for two or three years. We hope and expect to get these first two parts in publishable shape by autumn and then if I am still alive and can keep going to get the next two parts finished as soon thereafter as possible. When I say parts, I mean that each part is a very long book in itself and that the whole four parts would be one of the longest books anyone ever wrote. Perkins seems very hopeful and even enthusiastic. As for myself, I know that if I can keep myself going at the terrific rate I have been going for the last three or four months I can get the first two parts revised and in some sort of decent shape this summer.

Of course, when I let down this way and am fagged out I get depressed and down in the mouth but I think when I get to work again I will be all right. Yes, I did take some pieces to the new agent I spoke to you about and he has been pushing me to bring him some stuff and told me he would have no difficulty in selling one of the pieces I brought to him, but I am so beset and pressed on all sides that I do not see how I can take the time off to do any work on them even though I need the money badly.

Today I must get back to work on the proofs and make revisions on the story which is coming out in *Scribner's Magazine* next month, the June issue,[1] which will only be the second story of the three I promised them. As for the third story we have not even decided yet what we shall use and this means a great deal more work, and this is also on my mind as I promised to give them three stories.

Everyone, of course, including the editors of magazines, is out to do the best he can for himself and I am afraid most people do not care very much how you get along or spend much time worrying about your own welfare and best interests. I cannot do any more than I have done for the last three months because I have simply worked until I dropped, and I have done that day after day, and I do not think anyone can do much more than that. Now I am prepared to try it again for three or four months longer and hope that something will come of it as some kind of reward for all this trouble and unhappiness. I have no money left and what they have been paying me for these stories just about keeps me going until I can write a new one, but I do not know yet what I am going to do when I get so fagged out that I cannot write any new ones or cannot sell them. All I know how to do at the present time is to keep going as long as I can.

I am sorry to think that you are alone there at home but very

[1] "The Web of Earth."

glad to know that you are in such good health. I know what being alone is like and how hard it must be for anyone who has always been used to having lots of people around him. I have been alone a great deal in my life, more than anyone I know, and in fact have spent most of my time alone since my sixteenth year. It has been very hard at times but it is something you get used to as you go on, although I think you never lose hope that some day you will get out of it.

I had always thought that I might some day return to Asheville or to that part of the country where I was born and which I know the best but I am afraid that Asheville itself has fixed it so that is no longer possible. I have gotten over the disappointment and pain I felt because of the way they treated my book and the things they said about me at that time and I never spent much time worrying about the threats of people who would write me an anonymous letter. The thing I cannot and will not endure is the ugly, prying curiosity of people into your life and for that reason I won't come back. It took me fifteen years of being alone to make a life for myself and now that life is my own, for better or worse, or whether I ever have any great success or not, and no outsider is going to violate it. The privacy and obscurity of my own life is something I will defend with all I have and I will not allow people to thrust themselves into my life and claim to be my friends, as some people have done these past three years, when they have never been my friends and know nothing about me. My intention had always been to go home and see the few people that I know and who had been my friends and start to live among them again as any decent person has a right to do but I will not be poked and pryed at by a mob of people I have never known and whose only interest in you is to dig out some scrap of gossip or pretend to have some affectionate or friendly interest in you because you got your name in the paper once or twice. I dislike the whole booster-boom-town-country club whoop-it-up kind of spirit because the whole thing is a lie and there is not a single decent and honest human value in it and everybody knows it, and the friendship of such people cannot be depended upon any more than their assertions that a piece of real estate is worth ten times more than what it is really worth, or that the town has twice as many people as it really has. As you say, no one can ever change the hills and valleys of North Carolina and that is the thing I miss and also the people I knew there who were my friends. As for the rest of it, the country-clubs, the real estate men, the booms, the people trying to pretend to be something they are not, you can find that anywhere. I do not miss it and do not have to go home to find it.

Fred has not written me what his plans are concerning his present job. I gather from what he said that he intended to hold on a while longer and see if business will not improve, so that he can make it pay. I suppose, as you say, that he missed seeing his girl and may want to go back into that part of the country where he can be nearer to her and see her more often. Of course he should know best what to do.

As bad as conditions are up here I doubt that they are as bad as they are at home, and he might be able to do something here if he holds on. Of course, everybody is so much in doubt about the future and about all we have to travel on at present is hope, but we all hope things are going to improve now and some people say they really are already.

I agree with you that it seems hard to see any immediate hope for Asheville. They invested their whole lives in a toy balloon and when the balloon burst there was nothing left, not even the wind they pumped into it. I hope a little wisdom has been left as a kind of dividend for all their grief and loss but even of this no one can be sure, for people have a way of being taken in by the same illusion a second time even when it dropped to nothing but ruin the first time. As scattered and bankrupt as we all are in the family, we still seem to be in much better shape than many other people I have heard about, and most of us, thank heaven, still have our health and some kind of employment, and I hope that things will be better for us.

I have heard nothing further from the German edition except what I told you when I was in Washington. Mr. Wheelock at Scribners wrote me this morning, saying that he had received a review of the German edition of the book, which came from a newspaper in Zurich, Switzerland, which praises the book very highly. This must mean, of course, that the book has really been published but I have heard nothing from them now in almost two months and I do not know whether all the trouble they have been having in Germany has had anything to do with it or not. I hope not, because it would mean a good deal to me now to make something out of the German edition.

We have had a great deal of rain in the last month and spring has seemed late in coming. Today is a very fine, bright sunny day, still a little chilly, but the leaves and flowers have not burst out yet, you can see them coming everywhere, and I think it will only need a few warm days to make them all come jumping out. I suppose it is almost full spring in Asheville by this time but we are later here.

This is all for this time. I have made no marriages, performed no other entangling alliances since I saw you and do not see how in the present state of my finances it would be possible, and may be it is a good thing for all concerned that I am not so bur-dened at present.

I am glad to know you are well and think you will feel even better and in better spirits now that spring is here, and people can get around better to visit one another.

I shall let you know what I am doing and how my work is going and what the prospects are. Let me hear from you when you can.

Meanwhile, with love and best wishes for your health,

Your son,

TOM

101 COLUMBIA HEIGHTS
Brooklyn, N. Y.
May 14, 1933.

DEAR MAMA:

I want to write you a few lines just to wish you health and happiness today and for many days hereafter. I understand that this is Mother's Day and while I think it is a good idea to set aside a day for mothers, it seems to me to be a much better one to hope that every day will be a good day not only for you but for all the rest of us and for so many of our friends who have lost their wealth, their hope and their belief in life during the last three or four years. So, I hope that from now on all of us will have better days and for you in particular I wish a long life and good health and full activity for many years to come.

I went down to Pennsylvania for a few days last week and came back Monday. Fred and I stayed together at Gettysburg and drove over a great deal of the surrounding country. We saw Aunt Mary and Jim and Dorothy once or twice and they all spoke to me about your visit. We had bad rainy weather most of the time. The country was beautiful and has the finest and richest looking farms I have ever seen. Fred's back is giving him a great deal of trouble but the trouble seems to increase with wet weather and I think he is going to be all right as soon as the warm days come.

This is all that I can write you at present as I am busy again today on the last of three stories which I sold *Scribner's* and which has to be revised and shortened a great deal before it can go into the magazine.

I send you again my warmest wishes for your health and happiness and success in all you do.

Your son,   TOM

101 COLUMBIA HEIGHTS
Brooklyn, N. Y.
July 3, 1933.

DEAR MAMA:

I haven't had a chance to write you for sometime because of the stories I had to do for *Scribner's* which required a great deal of cutting and revision before we could get them into the space given to us and because of the long book and a good many business worries. Now I have got some of the immediate troubles settled but still have a great deal of work on the book before me and have promised to stay here until I can give them the whole manuscript.

If I do that we will be in a good position because we will have about three books ready and another coming. They have already planned to bring out a special edition of a short book early in the autumn and a long book later on, and a book of stories after that. Much remains to be done, but I think I see the way out of the woods now and we are all hoping for the best.

I am still hard up but if I can get these books published I may come out yet.

We have had some terribly hot, sticky weather so far this summer but today there has been a sudden change and it is very cool. I know we will get plenty of hot weather later on and I dread it, since the heat here is very sticky and enervating and it is hard to do your best work under such conditions.

I cannot write you much more now but I do want to get this note off to you on the eve of the Fourth of July to wish you health and happiness and to hope that the next year will be a much better year for all of us and that we can see each other before much more time has passed.

I saw Roy Dock the other day and had lunch with him and told him that if I could get away later on in the summer or autumn I might come down to Asheville or Balsam for a week or two. I should like to go to a little place like Balsam because it would be quiet and cool and I think a better place to rest than Asheville but I see no immediate prospect of going to either place. I told Roy to go to see you if he got the chance and he said that he would. He is going to leave New York for good now and make his home hereafter in Balsam and in Florida and I think he intends to go into the fruit business down there on his own hook.

This is all for the present. I send you my love and best wishes and hope you will let me know if you need anything.

Please don't say anything to any one about what I told you of my work.

Tom

101 COLUMBIA HEIGHTS
Brooklyn, N. Y.
July 12, 1933.

DEAR MAMA:

Just a line to acknowledge your post card and the box of apples which arrived this morning. I have just opened up the box and the apples seem to have come through in first rate condition. I do not know how long it has been since I last saw June Apples but it seems to have been a long, long time. I do not think they have them very much up here, or one doesn't see them often in the markets. I am almost tempted to keep them as a souvenir of old times but I know they would not keep, and besides I know you intended for me to eat them.

I won't write much more now because I just wanted to let you know that the apples came in good condition. I will write you at greater length later.

I got a very fine letter—in fact it was one long chant of praise —from a writer named Percy MacKaye, who is spending the summer in Arden. I have known his work for a long time because he has been writing books and plays for many, many years and is well-known. I was very happy to get his letter which was about my train story in *Scribner's*. It was one of the best letters I ever had from anyone.

Also got a card from Fred a day or two ago saying he had just come back from High Point and had not time to go to Asheville but had talked to you over the phone and that you were well. He had also stopped over to see Mabel on his way back. I am delighted to know that you are well and that times seem to be a little better than they were. Thanks for your kind offer of help but I don't need it at present and hope if all goes well to be in better condition later on.

The weather has been cooler lately and I hope some of the worst is over. I wish I could get away for a week or two to go to some place in the mountains like Balsam but I don't know whether this will be possible until later on in the fall.

This is all that I will write at present. Thanks again for the box of apples. I send my best wishes for your health and happiness and hope you will let me know at once if there is anything that I can do for you.

TOM

101 COLUMBIA HEIGHTS
Brooklyn, N. Y.
August 3, 1933.

DEAR MAMA:

Thanks for your letter which came this morning. I stayed with Mabel in Washington almost a week which was longer than I had intended but thought I would stay away until the weather got cooler, but when I got back here I got into the worst heat-wave they have ever known here. Today for the first time in almost a week we are getting relief but for five hot days it was intolerable. The mercury hit 100 one day and was almost that bad on two or three other days. In addition the humidity, which is really what makes this heat up here intolerable, was very bad. There have been a great number of deaths and prostrations. People here find it hard to understand why a southerner, like myself, should mind this New York weather. I suppose they think we are used to frying and stewing the whole summer through at home. When I tell them that never in my childhood did I know such weather as we have here in New York in the summer time they can hardly believe it. But, western North

Carolina really has about the coolest and most agreeable summer climate of any place I have seen in this country.

Mabel seemed very well, looked better and seemed to be in better health than I have seen her for a long time. Of course she has a tough problem on her hands with many of her roomers, not only with those who try to beat their rent, but with all the cranks, freaks and half-cracked people of which there are a great number in Washington. I think she is making out very well, all things considered, and if better times come back I believe she has a chance to go on to some better kind of success. Fred drove me down to Washington from Gettysburg and stayed with us for a day or two before he went back. He seems well but I think rather unsettled and disturbed in his mind about his future plans. I hope that all goes well with him and that he comes to a decision about his life that will bring him a little security, peace and happiness for I think he needs it.

Yes if I ever get through the work I am doing now and am able to get anything from it I hope to get out of New York and make some such change as you have mentioned. Perhaps settle somewhere in the country, although just where I do not know yet. I like the mountains and hills at home as well as anything I have yet seen but there are many things about life in a place like Asheville that I do not like. I mean real estate, booster-stuff, the pretense and show, the country clubs and social activities and the idle gossiping people prying into one's affairs.

It seems to me that life at home has changed a great deal since I was a child and that a great deal of the old simple unpretending spirit of people has changed. I do not think that it is a change for the better and the new life is one I do not care to live. I should have come home to see you this summer if I could have seen you and the few people I still know and whom I have always considered my friends but I do not want to answer ten thousand questions from people that I do not know. I am too tired to be bothered in this way and if I go anywhere I want to go where I can be left alone and get a little rest. I have thought of going to Balsam, where Roy Dock lives, and renting a cabin there, but if such a simple and natural move as that has to be gossiped about and explained in Asheville I don't want to do it. I have been so pestered and annoyed in the last two or three years by letters, questions, and the prying curiosity of strangers that I have become almost a fanatic on the question of a man's right to his own privacy and the freedom of his individual life from intrusion. In other words I think I have as much right to live in my own way, to make my own friends and to come and go as I please as any butcher or baker has. Many people, however, seem to think that because you write stories and books that get printed, your whole life becomes a piece of public property. I do not think so and will fight against it as long as I have life left in me.

No I don't know what will be the outcome of these great changes which are now taking place in our life. We are either sheep being led to the slaughter or sheep being led to the green pastures. At any rate most of us are more hopeful than we have been in a long time, even if we do not know very well where we are going. I think people are glad to know that some decisive action is being taken at last and hail it with relief after the apathy and stagnation of the last administration. Some things I think definitely have been good. I think that the repeal of the 18th Amendment will be a great accomplishment although it will be many many years before we can hope to wipe out entirely the crime, gangsterism and vicious corruption that prohibition caused.

I am glad that you and Mabel are planning to go to the Chicago Exposition. I think you are wise in waiting until September or October as the weather will be pleasant then and you can enjoy your trip without fear of sweltering in a heat wave. I had an offer from a New York newspaper sometime ago to fly out there and back free of charge in one of the big new passenger planes which have recently been put in service but I turned it down because I had already arranged to meet Fred in Pennsylvania. I wish I had the chance again. You can leave here at two o'clock in the afternoon and be out there by sunset. I understand these latest model planes cover the whole thousand miles in about six hours. In ten years time I feel sure that traveling in this way will be a commonplace occurrence to all of us.

Thanks for the clipping about Mr. MacKaye. He continues to write me very fine letters and has invited me to come and stay with him out on the Beale Plantation if I come home this summer and has also invited me to go along with them on a trip they are making soon to Marion, Virginia, where there is to be a great gathering of mountaineers who will sing their old songs and play their pieces. However, I doubt if I shall get to see him this summer, but have hopes of meeting him when he comes to New York. He has written me four or five letters now, also has written Scribners about me and I sincerely appreciate his generous interest and praise for my work.

There is not much news; at present I am trying to go along with my work again after the trip to Washington and keep at it although the hot weather slows me down. Autumn and spring are the seasons that I like the best. I feel well and think I am in good health, and I am glad to know that all goes well with you. It is certainly good to hear that you suffer from no lack of good fresh food and vegetables. I am in no danger at all of starving but

I do get very tired sometimes of the dead, warmed-over, steamed-up food that one gets in restaurants and cafeterias.

This is all for the present. Let me hear from you when you have time to write and let me know if there is anything that I can do for you.

Meanwhile, with best wishes for your health and happiness,

Your son   TOM

MONTPELIER VERMONT
Wed., Sept 13, 1933

DEAR MAMA: I want to write you a few lines before I get back to Brooklyn and will write you a longer letter from there. A friend of mine,[1] who is a writer and lives in Connecticut, invited me out for the week end last Sat. and I persuaded him to come along with me to Vermont for a few days vacation. We have been driving around up here for two or three days now and are staying in Montpelier, which is the state capital, tonight. This is one of the most beautiful states I have ever seen. There is a range of mountains—the Green mtns.—that runs the whole length of the state from north to south and between the range of these mountains there are some of the greenest and most beautiful valleys I have ever seen. We have done considerable tramping around on country roads also, eating at farmhouses, and going wherever we wanted to go, and I feel better than I have felt in months. It is such a relief to get away from all the confusion, noise, and fatigue of the city into all this peace and beauty. The weather has been fine and clear, but the nights are already cold up here and we had a big frost two nights ago—I'll

[1] Robert Raynolds, the author of several novels, one of which he dedicated to Tom.

write you when I get back about going to Chicago, I am delighted that you are making the trip and want you to see it but don't know whether I'll be able to meet you or not. I have so much work to do when I get back, and I got away up here because I was exhausted and could go no further—had an attack of ptomaine poisoning and sheer nervous fatigue—cramps in stomach and unable to hold food—so had to get away. But am feeling much better now. The thought of my work is on my mind all the time, and now I've got to get back to it, so can't tell about Chicago. But will write definitely when I get back in two or three days. Meanwhile, with love and best wishes for your health and happiness—

Your son,   TOM

101 COLUMBIA HEIGHTS
Brooklyn, N. Y.
Tues., Sept. 26, 1933

DEAR MAMA: Just a few lines to you now which I will try to get off to you before you leave for Chicago. I have been looking for a new place to live—cheaper and *bigger* than place I've got—and will have to move *somewhere* this week or pay another month's rent *here* which I don't want to do. Haven't definitely decided on place yet although have seen many but will let you know next address as soon as I have one. Meanwhile, suppose this address will do, as will leave forwarding address wherever I go. About the grapes, I know you want me to tell you the truth about it, and the truth is that when I got back home from Vermont I found the package against my door, and could smell it fifty feet away. The grapes, I am sorry to say, were reduced almost to a mass of rotting pulp, there were a few good ones and I picked out as many as I could, enough to get the taste and flavor of home again, but the rest I had to throw away as the little bugs began to swarm around them.

Now about Chicago. Mama, I don't know and don't believe I can make it. First I've got to move and *Scribner's* have bought another story which is not ready yet and must be ready for the Christmas issue—*i.e.* the issue that comes out about Nov. 20 which is to say I must have it ready by *mid*-October! I wish you'd let me know where you and Mabel can be found in Chicago— then, if I could get away I might come and meet you. Please let me know—I'm so glad you can make the trip and wish you'd tell me if you need some money—could get it and be delighted to let you have it. Enjoy yourself, and get a comfortable place to stay in, take things easy and don't try to overdo it, see a little at a time, and if it's a question of staying a day or two longer, do so. As I say, if a chance of making the trip appears, I may come on.

I want you or Mabel to do something for me right away—I want you to write me a post card or a letter and give me the exact dates of Ben's birth and death. The reason I ask this is that Scribners are going to publish my story *No Door*[1] in book form and if they agree, and I think they will, I want to dedicate the book to Ben. The dedication would read—"For Benjamin Harrison Wolfe—Oct ? 189—(?)—Oct ? 1918, and then something I've written myself. I can't remember these dates—so please let me have them *exactly*. This is all for present. Let me know at once if you need anything. I don't think I can come to Chicago but if I can will wire you. Meanwhile good health and a happy trip and take things easy.

Love,

Toм

[1] Later published in the volume of short stories, *From Death to Morning.*

DEAR MAMMA:

I do not know whether you will be home or not when this letter gets there. I would have written you to Chicago, but during the past week I have been moving and now I cannot find the post card which you sent me with your address. That is the reason I did not write you out there.

Mabel's card told me that Dietz was there with you and I am awfully glad you took him along. I wish I could have met you, but I saw no way of leaving here with moving and the necessity of getting two stories done, which *Scribner's* have taken, but which need a tremendous lot of work done on them in a short time.

I suppose you will write me and tell me about the Fair and how it compares with St. Louis in 1904. I gathered from Mabel's card that the weather was fine and that you all were enjoying the trip. I hope that was the case and that you did not tire yourself out, but took things slowly. I hope you got my special delivery which I sent to Asheville a day or two before your departure. I suppose if you did not get it before you left, there was some one at home to forward it on to you in New Albany or Chicago.

The weather here just now is very fine. It is one of the times of the year I like best and I hope now I can get some good work done.

Please write me when you can and tell me about your trip and if there is anything you need that I can do for you. Meanwhile, with love and best wishes for you in everything you do.

Your son,

TOM

P.S. My new address is: 5 Montague Terrace, Brooklyn, N. Y.

5 MONTAGUE TERRACE
Brooklyn, N. Y.
Oct. 30, 1933.

Mrs. Julia E. Wolfe
48 Spruce Street
Asheville, N. C.

DEAR MAMA:

Thanks for your letter and for sending me the dates I asked you for. Are you going to Washington any time soon and will you let me know when you are going? I think Fred told me in one of his letters that you might come up this week. Mabel has asked me to come down but I thought I might wait until I knew you would also be there, because it may be hard for me to make several trips this fall. I am trying to get another piece finished which I hope *Scribner's* will take and I hope to be finished with it this week.

There is not much news to give you since I moved into this new place because I have not done much but keep at my work since I came here. It is a very nice roomy kind of place and if you ever came up here to visit me, there would be plenty of room for you although I would have to get a couch or cot for you to sleep on.

I see Mr. Perkins from time to time and he always asks to be remembered to you. He and his family have moved into town this year and are living here in a house his wife owns and I have been to see them three or four times.

I have wanted to go down to spend a week-end with Fred in Pennsylvania, but will not leave here until I get through with this piece of work I am doing. He writes me that he may come up for the week-end about November 5th, if I can not go down there.

The weather has been real autumn recently, although nothing

very cold yet. I don't doubt that you found it colder at home than you did in Chicago. I think it can get just as cold in Asheville as it does here and some of the coldest weather I remember was at home. I heard the other day that there were already indications of improvement in business down South and I hope this is true. I don't think we can say as much here. Of course, I can not say for certain, but the general impression seems to be that things in New York have picked up very little, if at all, but people are still hopeful that there will be an improvement after the city election here and after the repeal of prohibition. Last winter was a pretty dark and desperate one for many people in this city. Some people say this one is going to be worse, but I hope things may really be on the up-grade now and that such a winter as last one doesn't happen again. I don't know whether conditions are really worse in New York than in other places or not. Some people seem to think they may be better, but I think one gets a worse impression of suffering and hardship here because among such a great population, there are so many in want, and one sees more of it.

Please let me know how you are and if there is anything you need; also, if you intend going to Washington before Thanksgiving.

I think this is all I have to tell you at the present time. I hope this finds you recovered from your cold, and I send my wishes, as always, for your good health and happiness.

Your son

Tom

5 MONTAGUE TERRACE
Brooklyn, N. Y.
November 23, 1933.

Mrs. Julia E. Wolfe
48 Spruce Street
Asheville, N. C.

DEAR MAMA:

A postcard from Mabel this morning informed me that Mr. Salmer [1] died Sunday and that you were with him when he died. I know what a sad thing this must be for you and that you have lost a good friend. All of us I know feel sad about it because we all liked him. I never knew or suspected that he had tuberculosis, but this must have been the trouble because Fred wrote me a few days ago that he was ill and you were afraid that this was what was wrong with him, and now Mabel writes that he had a hemorrhage right in front of you and died before the doctor could get there, but she said he died without pain and we are all glad of that. Please write and tell me about it when you get a chance and let me know if there is anything I can do for you.

I have heard that you were going up to see Mabel around Thanksgiving and I hope you will come up to see us all as soon as you feel you can leave home. This is all for the present.

I am working right ahead and have sold two more stories to *Scribner's*, which was a God-send for me as I was very hard up, and I also have hopes now of selling some of my manuscript to other magazines, which may perhaps pay more than *Scribner's*. Anyway, I can always manage to get some money for you if you need it, so I hope you will never hesitate to let me know.

Mr. Perkins asks about you often and I know he would like to see you again.

[1] Theodore Salmer was a roomer in Mrs. Wolfe's rooming house The Old Kentucky Home, from 1922 to 1933.

With love and best wishes for your health and hoping you will let me hear from you soon and tell me if you want anything,

Your son,

TOM

P. S. I have been thinking of going down to Washington to see Mabel if I can get away some week-end, but I have waited until I heard from you some definite news about your plans, because of course I should like to go to Washington when you are there.

If you are coming up soon, I wonder if it would be too much trouble for you to bring along with you the old album we used to have in the parlor, together with any pictures you may have of Papa as a young man or of any other members of his family. Please let me know what time you expect to go to Washington.

5 MONTAGUE TERRACE
Brooklyn, N. Y.
Dec 15th 1933.

(The first part of this letter is missing)

I have been pretty busy for some time and managed to sell two stories to *Scribner's* and have one in the hands of an agent who thinks he is going to sell it somewhere, although so far there has been no result. I think we'll all pull out of the woods some day and that I will get something out of all the work I have done the last three or four years. Last night, about half-past eleven o'clock, I took Mr. Perkins over 500,000 words of manuscript, which represents the closest approach to a complete draft, however rough, that he has ever had of my new book. God knows a lot of it is still fragmentary and broken up, but at any rate he can now look at it and get an idea of what the whole book will be like and give me an opinion on it.

It has been a terrific job. Time after time I have been down in the black pit of despair, but in spite of the rough, unfinished form in which I have given Mr. Perkins the manuscript and the tremendous amount of work that still remains to be done, I do feel now wonderfully hopeful about it and believe that if he will say the word and tell me to go ahead, I think it within my grasp to do another piece of work of which I can be proud. If it ever gets published it will be a far longer book than *Look Homeward, Angel* and I know it will have some of the best writing I ever did in it, because the three long pieces which were published in *Scribner's Magazine* last summer—and these pieces were highly praised—will be included, and I know that I have other stuff in the book that is just as good.

This is about all for the present. There is not much news to give you. I can realize from your letter how depressing things must look in Asheville. They look bad enough here, although Mr. Perkins and some other people I know seem to believe that they are really better than they were a year ago. I hope they are right, although the signs of improvement are not very evident to me yet.

I agree with you that I don't see what Asheville is going to do. The real damage there of course was done seven or eight years ago, although it took most of them years to realize the extent of their loss. It is a pretty gloomy prospect for the people now living there to face.

Let me know if you will be in Washington in time for Christmas. I think you ought to come if you can. And if you do, we must all try to get together and have a good Christmas. Please let me know at once if you need anything and have money to make the trip on.

Meanwhile, with love and best wishes for your health,

Your son

TOM

Brooklyn, N. Y.
January 30, 1934

DEAR MAMA:

I've meant to write you for some time, but had little chance since I came back from Washington. Perkins now has the manuscript of my book.[1] We are working on it together two or three hours every day, and meanwhile I am going ahead re-writing, putting in missing scenes and so on. There is no doubt now but that we will get through, although how long the book will be we don't dare think. I am very happy about it, and feel that I can do any amount of work on the manuscript now that I know the biggest part of the job is done.

I have not bought any new clothes yet, but I did buy an overcoat, so don't worry about my keeping warm. I'll get some clothes, too, if I ever get a chance to get out and order them. I hope you are keeping warm at home. We are having another cold spell here. The temperature went down to about zero this morning. The night I left you in Washington was the coldest I've ever felt. There was no heat in the train whatever, and the passengers walked up and down the aisle most of the night stamping their feet to keep warm. I got back to Brooklyn at daybreak just as the mercury fell to three below zero, and three below on Brooklyn Heights with that wind off the Harbor going through you like a knife is cold enough, and that's what made me buy the over-coat.

I still have some of your fruit cake. It seems to me this last one was especially good, one of the best you ever made. I'll be sorry when it's gone.

Now I've got to end this letter because there's work to do, but I hope this finds you well and happy. Please let me know if

[1] *Of Time and the River.*

there's anything you need and how you are. If I can get through this big piece of work which has given me so much trouble, I'll look forward to seeing you probably in the Spring. Write when you can, and let me know the news. Meanwhile, with love and best wishes for your health and happiness.

Always,

Tom

5 MONTAGUE TERRACE
Brooklyn, N. Y.
February 13, 1934

Dear Mama:

I want to get this letter off to you even if it's only a short one to wish you a happy birthday and many more years of a healthy and vigorous life.

You told me one time how I came home from school many years ago and told you I had just learned that two great Americans, Lincoln and Washington, had their birthday in February, and then you told me that three great Americans had their birthday in February, and when I looked puzzled you said that you were the third. You have already lived longer than either of the other two, and had as full and eventful a life as any one I know. Everything has happened to you that life can bring, the good as well as the bad, sorrow and happiness altogether, and now I hope that the remainder of your life will be just as interesting as the first part of it except that you may miss all the trouble and know only the joy.

It seems hard to believe that your life goes back all the way to before the Civil War, and that you've lived through half the nation's history. Even the years that I've lived seem crowded and exciting enough, but you have seen and known many things that I have not.

Finally, I hope that this year is going to mark a big improvement in all our fortunes, not only in our own lives, but in the lives of people everywhere who have suffered and lost so much these past few years.

As for myself, I am looking forward to the year with hope and confidence because this year I shall complete another big piece of work, and hope to get from it some reward for all the sweat and heartbreak that has gone into it. I don't know that I shall, but at any rate we can all hope that I do.

This is all for the present. We have had a terribly cold winter here, and I am afraid the suffering of many people has been intense. The mercury fell to about fifteen degrees below zero here a week ago, which is the coldest weather, I think, I've ever experienced either in New York or any where else. I know you must have had some of it in Asheville, but I hope it was much less severe.

I hope this letter finds you in good health and spirits. If you need anything please let me know at once. Meanwhile I send you again my warmest wishes for a happy birthday and for many more years of health and happiness.

Your son,   Tom

5 MONTAGUE TERRACE
Brooklyn, N. Y.
March 8, 1934

DEAR MAMA:

I am very much worried about the news in your postal card that you have been down sick with fever and a bad cold. I hope by the time this letter gets to you, you will have completely recovered and will not take any more chances with cold weather and insufficient heat. If you are unable to keep warm in the house and another cold spell comes, I think you ought to go immediately to a hotel or some place where you'll be assured of warmth and comfort, and I will cheerfully and immediately pay the bill if you will do this because in the long run it's so much easier and better and cheaper to stay well than to get sick.

It has been a terrible winter. I had hoped we were through with the worst of it because the last few days have been very mild and almost Spring like, but even as I write this letter to you the snow has begun to fall fast over Brooklyn Heights, and as I look out across New York Harbor from my window, the whole harbor and the great buildings of Manhattan have been blotted out.

The month of February was, I think, the coldest and stormiest month I've ever experienced. The temperature fell below zero time and again, the lowest mark being fifteen degrees below zero. But fifteen below zero in New York is far worse than fifteen degrees below in any other place I know about. The climate here is damp and humid, and this, when combined either with intense cold or intense heat such as we get here in the summer, causes great suffering.

I have sometimes thought during the last year that if I ever make a little money again I may buy a farm or a few acres of ground in some such place as Yancey County where all your folks came from, or up in Vermont which I visited last autumn. Vermont is one of the most beautiful places on earth, and you could get a farm there cheap, but people talk about the coldness of the winters. I am sure, however, that you would not mind the cold up there as you do in New York because although the temperature gets much lower, the air is dry and one does not feel it as much.

I do not think I've ever known another winter equal to this one for sustained cold weather. The bad part of it really began the night I left you and Fred at the station in Washington a few days after Christmas. That night coming up to New York in the day coach is about the coldest I ever lived through. There was no heat whatever in the train, and the passengers stood up and stamped their feet along the aisles to keep from freezing.

I got back to Brooklyn here toward daybreak when the temperature was four below. A wind that cut like a razor blade was blowing off the harbor, and that experience was enough to make me go and buy an overcoat. I had nothing, as you know, but the old raincoat I was wearing in Washington.

Since that time, we've had an unending succession of storms and zero weather. The streets have just during the last day or two become free from the snow and ice of the last big storm. The snow had drifted up in some places over here on Brooklyn Heights three or four feet deep, and after that, cold weather came and froze it hard. I am afraid this winter has brought great suffering to many people. It's unfortunate that it had to come when so many people are out of work and have no money for food or fuel.

I was talking to an old Italian woman last night who cleans up at the *Scribner's* offices when the business day is over. She lives in a tenement in the Italian section on the upper East side of New York. She told me that for more than four years her husband, her son, and her son-in-law have not been able to find any work, and this old woman must keep the whole crowd going including her daughter and her daughter's two children on what she can earn as scrub woman at *Scribner's*. All of these people live together in a little four or five roomed tenement flat on the East side. The place is unheated save for such heat as they can provide for themselves, and she told me times have been so hard they haven't always been able to keep warm.

Of course there are families worse off than this, but I think this is a typical example of what poor people in New York have gone through this winter and in the last few years.

I have gone on steadily with my work, and all of a sudden, after going through a very depressing time, things have got much better with me. I have sold several stories, one to the *American Mercury*, and although they paid me very little for all the work I put into it, I was glad to get even what I got, and now the agent that sold it believes he can sell several others. My English publisher, when he was in New York a few weeks ago, told me he would send me a contract and deposit an advance to my account at Charles Scribner's when he got back to England. I have heard nothing further from this as yet, but I suppose he'll keep his word. In addition, Scribners yesterday sold the rights to *Look Homeward, Angel*[1] to a publishing house that brings out a collection of classics and the best known modern books, and which is known as the *Modern Library*. We got an advance of five hundred dollars which, according to my contract, I must share fifty-fifty with Scribners. This also holds true for any royalties the book may make in the *Modern Library* edition. Of course, the *Modern Library* edition sells for only a dollar, and the royalty is only ten percent, so that Scribners and I will get only ten cents a copy, or five cents apiece on each copy sold. But Perkins thought it was a wise move to make for several reasons. First, because the *Modern Library* is a collection of famous works of famous writers, and he thinks the prestige of having the book

[1] Charles Scribner's Sons did not surrender the rights to the book, which has been selling in their regular edition steadily ever since publication. They merely authorized the publication of an edition in the Modern Library published by Random House, and the book is still published in that Library.

printed in this edition will be valuable. Also, although the royalty is much smaller, the chance of having a considerable sale now is much greater in this low priced edition. Another thing that should help us is that the people who buy the *Modern Library* books are likely to be people of higher intelligence and education than the average reading public, and Perkins feels this will be a very valuable audience to have, particularly since my new book will be ready about September, so on the whole it was probably a wise move.

I have also signed an agreement on Perkins' advice with a play writer who is making a dramatization of *Look Homeward, Angel.* According to the terms of the agreement he is to make a suitable dramatization within three months, and to find a producer and a theatrical production within eighteen months. I share all royalties, whether from the stage production or movie and radio rights, etc., on a fifty-fifty basis with the dramatist. This means that I am prevented by the agreement from selling the book rights to *Look Homeward, Angel* to the moving pictures if I have an offer, but must first give the dramatist the chance to sell the dramatic rights to the movies. Of course if this happened, I'd have to share the moving picture rights with him fifty-fifty, but Perkins advised me to sign the agreement on the grounds that a bird in the hand is worth two in the bush, and that the movies pay much more for a dramatization that has had a New York production than they pay for the rights of a book.

Finally, I had another letter from Germany the other day in which the German publisher informed me that I have a small sum of money coming to me as additional royalties from Germany. Like most of the other profits I have been telling you about, it has not arrived yet. But things look much more cheerful than they did two months ago. I think there's no doubt that we'll finish the big job now and that the thing will be ready for pub-

lication in the autumn. That, of course, is the most important
thing of all. I thought you'd be glad to hear of these various
things, and now we can hope that they will bring me some success and profit.

This is all for the present. Please write and let me know as
soon as you can how you are and if you have completely recovered from the cold and fever. Don't take any more chances with
cold weather and a cold house, but go where you can keep warm
until warm weather comes again.

I forgot to tell you that on the strength of these various trans-
actions and sales I went out and bought a new suit of clothes
the other day. I had to go out to dinner with Perkins and his
wife and another lady, and I had really got to the point where I
felt disgraced every time I appeared in public. I had nothing left
that would hold together except that brown tweed coat and a
pair of trousers which had once, I suppose, been dark grey but
which were now turning green. The whole thing was coming
apart at the seams, and I never knew from one moment to the
next when it would be divided into fragments like Jacob's coat of
many colors that you read of in the Bible. I had to buy the first
suit that would come anywhere near fitting me. It is not a very
good fit, but they promised to remedy the worst defects and to
make whatever alterations they could if I brought it back to them.
Anyway, I don't feel quite so naked as I did before.

I got a letter from Fred this morning in which he said he might
be up here about the sixteenth. I hope he comes. He says the
winter has been terrible in Pennsylvania, and that business has
been very poor, and I suppose it has been. It must be very hard
to persuade people to buy farm machinery in such weather as
we've had.

This is all for the present. Please let me know how you are
as soon as possible. Get everything you need to keep you warm

and comfortable. Let me know at once if you want anything, and I will send it to you.

Meanwhile, love and best wishes for good health and happiness.

Your son,

TOM

P. S. I forgot to tell you that *The Web of Earth* is coming out towards the end of this month in book form. It will have the leading position in a book of stories[1] which Alfred Dashiell of *Scribner's Magazine*, whom you know, is editing. As the book contains short stories by many famous people, I am quite excited about it. It is hard for me to think of it as a short story because it is almost the length of a whole book, and will be much longer than any other story in the volume. Perkins tells me that Scribners wants to bring out some of my stories next winter or Spring after the big book comes out, and, of course, when this comes out *The Web of Earth, Portrait of Bascom Hawke,* and others will be included.

I won't get much out of the use of the story in Dashiell's book —forty or fifty dollars, perhaps,—but again it is probably a good thing to do because it will bring the story to the notice of the book reading public and should also help the big book when it comes out.

Brooklyn, N. Y.
March 31, 1934

DEAR MAMA:

Thanks for your card. Because the weather is still so uncertain I think you are perhaps wise in deciding not to go to Washington

---

[1] *Editor's Choice,* an anthology of stories published in 1934 by Henry Holt & Co., New York.

for Easter although I know we would all like to see you. During the last few days here there have been evidences of spring. Yesterday was really a beautiful day, but my experience with April in New York has been that anything can happen from sunshine to blizzards. There is really not much spring up this way until the end of April. Down home spring is in full swing by that time. Anyway, I am relieved and happy to know that winter is over at last and that you won't have to be exposed to any more cold weather.

I took several days off from work and spent most of the time sleeping. I am back at work now and feel better for the rest. Fred was up here a week or two ago on Sunday. We went out and had dinner at the Dashiell's. I had already accepted the invitation to go out before Fred came so I took him along with me. Fritz Dashiell is just recovering from an operation for appendicitis but there were no complications and he has made a quick recovery. Later in the afternoon we came back to New York and had supper with the Perkins family. Fred took a train back about ten-thirty, and wrote later to tell me that he got back to Harrisburg in time to get a good night's sleep. I hope he enjoyed himself while here and will come back when he feels like it.

This is all for the present. I want to see you when this long grind of work is finally over, and I do not have to worry about it any more. For the present I want to send you all my best wishes for good health and a happy Easter and better times for all of us. I hope this finds you well and completely recovered from your attack of Flu.

Your son,

Tom

5 MONTAGUE TERRACE
Brooklyn, N. Y.
April 5, 1934

DEAR MAMA:

Just a note to thank you for the flowers which arrived this morning. I am happy to say they came through in fine condition and were almost as fresh as if they'd just come out of the ground. The young lady who types for me arranged them in glasses full of water and they have not only brightened up the room, they have also brought back to me many memories of home and springtime there. We shall have no such flowers as these up here for several weeks. The weather is still uncertain as it always is here in April, cold and wet one day and perhaps bright the next. I am so glad to know that spring has come at home and that you will not have to bother with cold weather from now on.

Altogether, this has been a very exciting day for me. Just before your flowers came, I got a telephone call from the literary agent who has some stories of mine and has already sold one to *The American Mercury*. He tells me that *The American Mercury* people have called up and want to serialize my book in the *Mercury*. This is, I think, an almost unheard of thing for them to do, and, of course, I am pretty excited about it. The only trouble is that the book is of such immense length that I don't see how they could possibly get through with the serialization in less than two or three years, and, of course, they could not print anything that long, and in addition I could not wait that long for Scribners are going to try to publish the book in October. As you may know, if a book is serialized in a magazine, you must wait until the last installment has appeared before the book can be published.

I called up Mr. Perkins and told him the news and the agent

is going to talk to him today. As I suspected, Mr. Perkins did not like the idea. I think he feels first of all that the book is too long for serialization and that we could not wait so long a time, and I think he also feels that Scribners have stood by me and ought to have first call upon my work. I think he is right because he certainly has been the best friend I ever had and has worked for my success and stood by me in the most wonderful and un-selfish way. I am convinced that his first and strongest wish has been to see me do a fine piece of work, and that any thought of profit which might come to Scribners as a result of it has been secondary. But the *Mercury* is one of the highest grade maga-zines in the country and it is, of course, very wonderful to know they thought enough of my work to make such a proposal. At this moment I don't see how it could be done, but I do think there are parts and chapters in the book which they might pub-lish. They were very enthusiastic about a story called "Boom Town" which they are going to publish in the May issue, and they may have heard that this story is really a chapter out of the book.

This is all for the present. Please do not say anything about this because since nothing has been done about it, I should not want it to be talked about. I hope this finds you well and that all the bad weather at home is over. Goodbye for the present. Let me know if you want anything and take care of yourself. With love and thanks again for the flowers,

Your son,

Том

Brooklyn, N. Y.
April 18, 1934

DEAR MAMA:

Thanks for your nice letter. We are having a spell of fine spring weather here in New York and I hope it will last, also that you are getting your share of it at home. It is a welcome relief after the bitter winter we have gone through, but I read in the New York paper the other day that one of the New York baseball teams which was playing an exhibition game in Asheville got snowed out in the ninth inning, and I remember going home for Christmas several years ago when the weather in Asheville was bitter cold and worse than anything they had in New York.

I called up Mr. Dashiell to find out when his book was going to be published. As you surmised, it is delayed because of his recent appendicitis operation and also because of some publication difficulties which he now tells me have been cleared up. The book should be out the early part of May and I will send you a copy myself when it is published. Dashiell also called me up this morning with a very exciting proposal which I am tempted to accept. The Summer School at the University of Colorado has written him asking him if he will recommend the services of a novelist who can give a one week course of lectures this summer. They offer to pay $350 for it, which would cover the expenses of the trip with some to spare. I know that I shall be pretty tired by that time. I have been told that Colorado is a beautiful state and that Boulder, where the University is situated, is a very pretty place. I have always wanted to see something of the West and if I accept this offer I would get a little much needed rest and change; if I have a big job of revising and cutting ahead of me as I know I shall have, a trip of this sort might come in at just the right time.

I am having dinner tonight with the editor of *The American Mercury* and I hope that something will come out of this also. They are quite enthusiastic about a story called *Boom Town* which should be out in a few days in the May number, and my agent informs me that he is also anxious to publish some more of my work if it is suitable for magazine publication. The *Boom Town* piece, like practically everything else I have written in the last four years, is a chapter out of this enormous book. If people at home think they find some reference to themselves and to Asheville in this story, I hope they will feel this time that both my head and my heart are in the right place and that I have written as one of them and as one who has felt sincere regret and sympathy for the misfortune and loss that many people he has known all his life have suffered. At any rate there is not an atom of bitterness or scorn in this story, and I imagine that many people who are still suffering from the mad real estate speculation of a few years ago will agree with what I say and would even speak more strongly about it than I have. I think that one reason the *Mercury* may like the story is because it tells what happened not only in Asheville but everywhere throughout the country during those years of frenzied gambling and speculation. As for the characters who appear in the story, I have tried to picture them as the good people I know them to be, and I don't think that there can be any doubt this time of my intention.

I don't know whether I told you that the rights to *Bascom Hawke* have also been bought from Scribners for publication in another anthology which will come out, I think, in the fall. We did not get much—$100—and, of course, I must split this with Scribners, but from another point of view we thought it a good thing to do. This kind of publication in book form is of course more permanent than magazine publication and helps to sustain interest in your work, and also should help create an audience for your future work.

This is all for the present. I feel pretty tired mentally but otherwise all right. I hope this finds you well, completely recovered from your attack of flu and enjoying some fine spring weather. Fred wrote me that he did not like the idea of your spending another winter alone in Asheville and thinks that next winter you should go to Florida or spend the winter with one of us in a place where you can be warm and comfortable and have someone to look after you if you catch cold. I think he is right about this, and by next winter I hope to be in a position not only to visit you or have you visit me if you feel like it but also to help in a more material way. It is unfortunate that all our family should be so scattered as it now is, but of course unavoidable circumstances and the hard times of the last four years are responsible for that. I have an idea that Fred will eventually return South if he finds work he can do there, and of course for his own sake I want him to find happiness and be near the people he cares for most.

I want you to know that I can now help you if you need help of any kind and I earnestly request you to let me know instantly if you ever need anything or if any situation arises where you need my help.

I know you are happy to see spring and good weather come back again. I wish I could be there to enjoy it with you. I know how much you enjoy being out of doors and working in the earth and I imagine that spring at home will be at its best just about this time.

Goodbye and good luck for the present. Please let me hear

from you soon and let me know if there is anything you want and need. With love and best wishes,

Your son,

Tom

I forgot to tell you that I have another story, a very short one in *Scribner's Magazine* which is out today. I will send you a copy and also a copy of the *Mercury* when it comes out.

5 MONTAGUE TERRACE
Brooklyn, N. Y.
July 19, 1934

Dear Mamma:

I have just got time for a few lines before I start to work. I wrote Fred a long letter the other day anyway, and I suppose he will tell you any news he thinks might interest you.

I bought an Asheville paper last night and was very sorry to read in its news of the death of Uncle Jim's wife. I suppose you went to the funeral, and if you think it advisable, I am going to ask you if you will call up Uncle Jim, or Jack,[1] or some other member of the family, and tell them how sorry I was to hear about Aunt Minnie's death and extend my sympathy to them. I am asking you to do this for me only because I know you will be able to judge whether or not it is the proper thing to do. As you know, I have not seen any of their family for several years and I have heard that they did not like some things in my book, and I should therefore not want to write them if my letter would be embarrassing or unwelcome to them. I did not know Aunt Minnie very well, but I always thought of her as a fine woman

---

[1] James M. Westall and his son, of Asheville, Tom's maternal uncle and cousin.

and a good wife and mother, and since I feel nothing but respect and sympathy for the whole family, I should like you to tell them so—if you think it advisable; if not, please say nothing about it.

This is all for the present. I will write you more when I have time for it. We have had a very hot summer here, but I have not noticed it so much because I have kept at work.

Mabel wrote me a post-card on her way to Asheville, and I suppose she will be there when this letter arrives.

I hope this finds you all in good health and enjoying the summer and being together again. Also I hope to see you in the autumn, when my work is done.

Meanwhile, until I hear from you, with love and best wishes to all.

Your son,

Tom

BROOKLYN, N. Y.
August 31, 1934

Dear Mama:

I was glad to get your letter. As I have not heard from you in some time, I was beginning to get a little worried. I know you have had a very busy summer at home with all the family visiting you and having to look after the house. I am glad you got to see all of them and hope it didn't put too much of a tax on your strength.

I have also had a very busy summer, although I have gone nowhere. I haven't been out of town since May, and have stayed right here working. I am pretty tired from the accumulation of work for two or three years, but my spirits are much better now than they have been in a long time. The end is now in sight. The proofs of my book have begun to come in and we already have about half of it in type. I have worked on it for so long that it is very hard for me to let it go now. I keep wanting to put in something else, but Mr. Perkins feels that we are now almost ready and that the book is already so long—over 400,000 words—and he is doing all he can to prevent me from making it any longer. He too is very tired—he has had no vacation in two or three years and I'm afraid that is largely my fault. He has been meeting me almost every night for months and working with me on the manuscript, and since he has the duties of a great publishing house on his shoulders all day long, you can understand that it is pretty much of a strain on his energy, but we both feel good now about the book. We have finally come through and Mr. Perkins says he thinks it is better than the other one, and I hope that both of us, Mr. Perkins especially, will be able to take a vacation soon.

Sometimes I feel that I would like to go on and work and work on the book until I was entirely satisfied with it, no matter how many more years it took or how long it would be, but I think this is not fair either to Perkins and Scribners or to myself. Perkins wants me to go on to finish up other books. They already have a book of stories[1] which can be got ready in a very short time, and he has the manuscript of another long novel[2] to follow this, really the second part of this one, and I have at home here the manuscript of a third long novel[3] which will be the

---

[1] *From Death to Morning.*

[2] This refers to Books IV through VII of *The Web and the Rock* which mainly record the love story of Esther Jack and George Webber. In the original plan this was to have been part of *Of Time and the River* and was to continue the story, begun at the end of that novel, of Esther and Eugene. But Tom at that time was unable to master some of the problems presented by this material, and so it was decided to end the book as it now stands.

[3] Probably Tom meant a projected novel of which he had written fragments, which was to have been called *The Hills Beyond Pentland.* Parts of this material were used in the first half of *The Web and the Rock*, in *You Can't Go Home Again* and in *The Hills Beyond*, all published by Harper & Brothers, New York.

third part of this one, so you see I have really done lots of work these last four years and we now hope to show the public something of the results of it. Of course, we hope—and we can do no more than hope in these hard times—to have some success, not only in critical approval, but in money, to reward us for all this time and work.

I don't know when the book will be out—there is still a great deal of cutting to be done, and all the proof has got to be gone over word for word, but I should like if possible to get through with my part of it by October. I think I could do this if I were not tired. I manage to put in a good day's work every day now, but when I have my full energy and feel good, there is almost no limit to what I can do, but of course you know that when you are very tired you can get just so far and no farther. You go at a kind of steady dog-trot day after day. If I keep going at the dog-trot it may take longer. If I can get away for a week in September and then get back I'd be able to get going at full steam again.

We have had one break of good luck this summer. July was a terribly hot month, but August here has been delightfully cool almost every day, and the last two or three days the temperature got down in the 50's—it has been like autumn. However, we generally get one hot spell in September before the summer is finally over, and I suppose that will happen this year too.

It will be wonderful to get this book job done and not have to think about it any more. I should like to go away somewhere for two months when it is over and see new places and some interesting things and forget all about writing for that time. I don't think I'd be able to forget about it for a much longer time than that. It has become so much a part of my life now that it is in my blood. There are hundreds of things that I want to say, and I will never live long enough to say them all, and of course

I have got to come back here to finish up the remaining books of this series on which I have been working for several years.

Publishing is a very mysterious business. It is hard to predict what kind of sale or reception a book will have, and advertising seems to do very little good. For example, Scribners published about a month ago a book called *So Red the Rose*, which was written by a man [1] who had written eight or ten other books and had never had much sale on any of them. From the first day the sales on this new book started to boom, and it has kept going ever since and it is now a best-seller all over the country. So you see it is a very strange business and it is very hard for us to know what will happen, but we are hoping to have good luck with this one, and regardless of what happens, it is a great relief just to get it done, to get it out of my system, to be able to forget about it and go on to other things.

This is all for the present. I can't think of any other news to give you right now. I thought you would be interested in hearing about my work and glad to know that I am near the end of it. I hope this finds you well and completely recovered from your cold.

We will get together soon, I'm sure, either this fall or by Christmas, and have a good visit when we don't have something hanging over our heads to worry us. I will let you know later how things are coming along, and perhaps then we can make plans for a visit. I may come home or you might come up here or we might go to Washington. Anyway, we will get together and just forget about work and worry for awhile.

I'm glad that Fred gets up to see you every week or two. It is

[1] A remarkably successful novel by Stark Young, published in 1934. All of his earlier books had had satisfactory and long continued sales, but small ones as compared to this.

good to know that he is near you, where you can see each other often.

Please don't say anything to anyone about what I have told you about the book. Gossip, as you know, has a way of flying and growing by leaps and bounds, and I should prefer to have any announcement concerning the book or anything I publish come from the publisher.

Please take care of yourself. Don't over-work—there is no need for it now, and nothing can be gained by it. Don't bother very much about the roomers—if they pay you no more than you say they are paying it's not worth your while to slave for them, and as I've told you before, if you need anything, please let me know, and I am sure that I can always manage to get it for you. I do hope that I will get something out of all this work I have done, not only in order to get a little more security for myself, but also to feel that I might be of a little help to other people that I know who need it, but even now I can always get enough to tide you over your present needs or any emergency that might arise, so please let me know if you need any.

Goodbye for the present. Write me soon and tell me the news, and meanwhile, take care of yourself.

With love, your son

TOM

P.S. Sometime when you are not busy, I wish you would jot down at your leisure a memorandum for me concerning the different branches of your family. I don't mean the present ones so much, because I think I'm fairly well acquainted with that, but the older branches of your father's and your grandfather's time and even before that if you know anything about it. I would just like, for example, to get a list of the twenty children or more that your grandfather had by his two marriages and what happened to them and where they settled and what parts of the country they moved to, and so forth. You told me a great deal about it one time and it got so complicated that I couldn't carry it around in my head.

I'm asking you to do this because some day after I get through with these books that I'm working on now, I may wind the whole thing up with a book which will try to tell through the hundreds of members of one family the whole story of America. I don't know whether it can be done. It may be too vast an undertaking, but I keep thinking about it and if I tell how one family like your own, for instance, going back a hundred and fifty years or more to pioneer and Colonial days and with all their settling in various places, pushing Westward, marrying into other families everywhere, etc., finally weaving a kind of great web, it really would have the whole history of the country in it. For example, your own father [1] and Uncle Bacchus [2] and other of your relatives who were in the Civil War on the Southern side and Papa's brother, George, [3] and his sister's husband, Lentz, [4] and others in that group in Pennsylvania who fought on the Northern side, and the rest of you who stayed at home or what you did, what your lives were like during that time—the whole story of the Civil War could be told in the lives of those people.

All I would like you to do if you get the chance and it's not too big a tax on you, is just to jot down a memorandum of the

[1] Thomas Carey Westall, of Buncombe County, N. C.

[2] Bacchus Westall, Tom's great-uncle, in whom Tom was always deeply interested. He first appears as a character in *Of Time and the River* as one of the Confederate soldiers seen by W. O. Gant, the portrait of W. O. Wolfe, when on the march to Gettysburg.

[3] George Wolfe, of York Springs, Penn.

[4] George Lentz, husband of Sarah Ellen Wolfe.

names of all these people and the different branches of your family; if you have time, put down any notes that you may remember about them which I wouldn't know.

I suppose you understand by now that one reason that I have always tried to write about the things I know myself is that no man could possibly have anything better than that to write about, and because if you explore your own back-yard carefully enough and compare it with all the other things you find out, you may some day find out what the whole earth is like.

And now good-bye for the present. Let me hear from you when you can.

[*Post Card*]

CHICAGO,
Tues., Sept. 25, 1934

DEAR MAMA: I've done what all the rest of you have done and came to see the Fair. Been here about three days—got low rate $27.25 round trip ticket from New York and sat up all the way out. Like Chicago—and am getting the first real vacation I've had in long time—I wrote you a letter the other night but didn't finish—will write before leaving— Am writing this from great new post office which is to be opened in day or two by Farley and others—

Love,   TOM

NEW YORK
Wednesday Oct 17, 1934

DEAR MAMA: I hope you'll be able to read this scrawl—I have no typist at present and have to write you in the only way I know— First of all I want to thank you for your beautiful and *useful* birthday presents. I can't get socks around here big enough to fit me and I was down to my last pair and that was more *hole* than *sock*. I don't know where you got those you sent me but they are perfect—big enough and also long enough—those I had been wearing ended about the ankles—these come way up. Also, I want to thank you for the beautiful necktie—I only had two, and they were worn to a frazzle—you couldn't have sent me anything I needed more. I am glad to say the grapes arrived in much better shape than last year—I am following your suggestion and adding water to them and will now try my hand at wine-making.— I had a wonderful trip to Chicago—saw the sights, looked up some old friends, went to the Fair, stopped off in Ohio and Pittsburgh on my way back and have done very little since I came back. I feel very much rested and eager to get to work again. Perkins says the book is finished and doesn't want me to do any more to it—but I have been with it so long I hate to give it up. There are still some scenes to be revised—it is very long— way over 1000 pages in book form—but the big job is over and now I can only wait and hope for the best,—of course, there are several books to follow and I must begin to work on them but I have done a big job the last few years and I hope we get something out of it. Mr. Dashiell's book, by the way,—the one that has *The Web of Earth* story in it—is just off the press—he has promised to give me a copy and I'll send you one as soon as possible. Perkins saw a copy and says my story comes first and takes up the first 110 pages in the book—The Modern Library edition of *Look Homeward, Angel* is also on the market now. I have some copies here they sent me and I'll send you one of those. I don't know when the big book will come out—it's a big job of printing and correcting, as you know—but from what they say I judge it will be about the first of the year or shortly thereafter. The publishing business goes by seasons—there are two big seasons, the Fall and the Spring—in between come the *dead* times and a publisher tries to avoid bringing a book out then, if he can. For the Fall season any time between August and October is good, but after that until the first of the year and after is bad— The Spring season begins after the first of the year and goes on to April—so I suppose my book will come out during that time. But please don't say anything about it to anyone—the publishers ought to do it, any announcement should come from them— In spite of my long vacation, I may take another this week end—a friend of the Perkins family—a lady from Virginia [1] wants me to come down and spend the week end at her place. The place is about 40 miles from Washington—if I went she would drive over and meet me in Washington—Perkins wants me to go—he says it is the most beautiful place he ever saw—an old plantation two or three hundred years old—and the home is beautiful— If I go, I'll stop by to see Mabel, but I haven't made up my mind yet what I'm going to do. This is all for the present —I feel rested and much better and hope this finds you in good health and happy. Let me know at once if there is anything you need and write me soon. Meanwhile, with love and best wishes to all,

Your son

Toм

[1] Miss Elizabeth Lemmon, of Middleburg, Virgina, who was deeply interested in Tom's writings from the beginning.

Mrs. Julia E. Wolfe
48 Spruce Street
Asheville, N. C.

5 MONTAGUE TERRACE
Brooklyn, New York
November 18, 1934

DEAR MAMMA:

I want to write you a few lines today while I have the chance, because I am going to be pretty busy now for some time to come. I have had a good vacation—almost too good, in fact—for I have found it very hard to get back to work again. Now all of the book has been set in type, but I have done almost nothing as yet to correct the proofs, and this must be done right away before they can put the book into pages.

Yes, I did make the trip to Virginia and had a fine visit in one of the most beautiful old plantation houses you ever saw. Stopped off and saw Mabel for a few hours on the way back through Washington and was glad to see that she seemed to be in good health and spirits. She spoke about coming up here with Virginia[1] over the week-end, but I have heard nothing from her since. Fred mentions in his last letter that she and Virginia have some plan of coming up here over Thanksgiving, and I hope they do, because nothing would delight me better. We could either have Thanksgiving dinner all alone or I am sure some of my friends would be delighted to have us dine with them if they knew she was coming.

Am sorry to hear about your cold and hope you are all over it by now. It is pretty hard to keep from having colds when you are living in a house that can't be thoroughly heated. I know Mabel wants you to come up to Washington, and later on in the Winter when the weather gets cold, I think we will all be glad

[1] Virginia and Fredericka Gambrell were daughters of Tom's oldest sister.

if you would escape the cold weather and go to Florida, and although we are not very prosperous, I am sure we could arrange for you to make the trip without difficulty.

The weather here, so far, has been remarkably good. There have been a few raw days and just a little touch of cold weather, but nothing to amount to anything yet, and today is a very fine and mild one. I feel very well myself. My rest has helped me a whole lot, except that I feel very sleepy and lazy and very much worried because of the long vacation I have taken and all the work that has piled up and that has to be done. Now, however, I intend to see if I can't work with renewed energy and strength. I was pretty tired when I knocked off, and really did need a rest.

There seems to be a more hopeful feeling around since the last election, although I really don't know how much conditions have actually improved. People, though, seem to be putting their faith whole-heartedly in Roosevelt and his Administration, and, of course, like all of us, I hope we don't get disappointed.

Please let me hear from you as soon as you can and let me know what your plans are about coming North and so on. Also let me know if you need anything.

Although I have work and manuscript on hand to keep me busy for several years, it looks as if we have almost conquered the first, and I hope, the greatest obstacle.

There is very little more to tell you at present. Mr. Dashiell's book, by the way, which has *The Web of Earth* story in it is off the press and has had several good reviews in the New York papers. I have intended several times to send you a copy, but will take care of it next week. All of the reviews that I have seen have mentioned my story, and two of them—the *New York Sun* and the *New York Times*—gave it a very enthusiastic notice. I will see that you get a copy in the next day or two.

Meanwhile, I hope this finds you well and happy, and not lacking for anything.

Write me when you can.

With much love,

Your son,

Tom

P. S.

One night, a week ago, while I was walking with a friend from North Carolina, on Broadway, I had a great surprise. Three girls rushed across the street toward me and in a moment we were all shaking hands, although it took me a minute or two to recognize them. They were Margaret Roberts, Patricia Pattison and a Miss Parker, who told me she was Heywood Parker's girl. They are apparently all living together here in New York, and they gave me their address. Margaret and Patricia have grown up to be good-looking and attractive young women, and they seemed glad to see me, as, of course, I hope they were, and they gave me their address and asked me to call them up. It gave me a strange feeling to see these kids, whom I remember as babes in arms when I first went to the Roberts school, now grown up into young women of mature and marriageable age. I kept thinking all the time that it couldn't be true, that there must be some mistake, and that surely none of these girls could be over fourteen or fifteen years of age, but a little swift calculation after I left them convinced me that they must all be in their twenties. I was eleven years old the Autumn I started in at Roberts School, and Margaret must have been about two years old then—which would mean that she is twenty-five or twenty-six now. It seems scarcely possible, but there you are. They all looked like intelligent, attractive girls, and I hope they get lots of success and happiness from life.

Got a letter from Fred only yesterday. I have not written him in some time, but tell him I will write him soon. And now, goodbye for the present.

CHARLES SCRIBNER'S SONS
PUBLISHERS
597 Fifth Avenue, New York
Dec. 31, 1934

DEAR MAMA:

I want to write you a few lines to wish you and all a happy New Year, and tell you that I am expecting you here in a few days. The ride up on the train was wonderfully comfortable. There were not many people travelling. The coaches have reclining backs that you can sleep in, and there is also a lunch counter on the train where you can get sandwiches and coffee. When you get to Jersey City you will find the buses waiting beside the train. All you have to do is get into the one marked Brooklyn. They will take care of your baggage, stow it away behind, and you will have a comfortable seat. You will get to the B & O office on Joralemon Street in Brooklyn about 7:20 or 7:30, and I will be waiting there to meet you.

The janitor and his wife in my house are going to fix my place up tomorrow, clean it all up, and put in a couch for you, so everything will be ready when you come. I think you will have a very comfortable and easy trip. Please let me know if possible by postcard what day you are arriving.

Meanwhile, with love to all, and best wishes again for a happy New Year,—Mr. Perkins also sends his New Year's greeting to all of you.

Your son,

TOM

January 14, 1935

DEAR MAMMA:

I got your card and I hope you made the trip back home safely and that this finds you well. I am very sorry to hear that you took sick after getting back to Washington. You certainly seemed perfectly well here and I think you may have taken cold on your way down on the train. Please take care of yourself now that you are back in Asheville and cannot depend on comfortable heat in the house. I wish you would get ready and start off to Florida as soon as possible. I think you ought to go immediately and stay until spring. I probably shall not go away until next month. Everything so far as I am concerned is finished for the book. They won't let me do anything more to it and it is now all set in page print so that I can't make any more changes even if I wanted to. Mr. Perkins is going down to Key West this week to visit Mr. Hemingway and will be gone I think between two and three weeks. Whatever I do I won't go away until he comes back and I hope to hear from you before I go. I don't think I shall stay away long, there is too much for me to do and I'll have to get started on it sometime soon. They want to bring out a book of stories next fall and although they already have enough stories to make a very long book I want to write some new ones that I have in mind and get some money for them if possible by selling them to magazines.

Physically, I feel pretty good and rested up. The main reason I want to get away is because I have stayed here and worked on this book so long and got into a kind of groove and now that the book has been taken away from me I am fiddling around at loose ends and not getting much done. I think if I break it by getting away somewhere I will be able to get going again. Of course I've got to do that because there is so much work ahead that remains to be finished. I am glad if you enjoyed your visit up here and if I am back here in the spring and living here I hope you will come again. Please let me know as soon as you can how you are and what your plans are. Also, if you need anything, and how much, I will get it for you. This is all for the present. I hope this finds you well and in good spirits.

With love and best wishes, your son,

TOM

BROOKLYN, N. Y.
February 1, 1935

DEAR MAMMA:

I have just written Fred and I want to get a short letter off to you before you go away. Fred tells me you are leaving for Florida February third. I don't know whether you'll get this letter before you leave or not but I hope so. I'm very glad to know you are going and I hope you will stay until the warm weather comes. New York is still covered with snow and ice as a result of the big blizzard we had the other day and the weather has been very cold since. I know it must have been cold at home, too, and I have thought about you and wished you had already gone to Florida. Mr. Perkins went down to Key West about a week ago to visit Mr. Hemingway. We all hoped he would stay and get a good rest for he has had no vacation for three or four years but I understand that he has telegraphed that he will be back next Monday.

I am going away and before I go I wish you would please let me know if you need anything and how much. I am signing a new contract with Scribners for a book of stories and I also hope to make arrangements with them to write some pieces about the places I go to on my trip. If I can do this I may be able to take the trip without it costing anything. I told you I was going to Denmark but that country sounds too cold and icy after all the snow and blizzard of this past week or two and at present it looks as if I may get passage on a freighter which goes to the Mediterranean and stops off at various ports in Spain, France, Italy, Greece and Egypt. I think I can do this at a pretty low cost, more cheaply in fact than I could keep on living here in New York. The trip will be a very interesting one and I should see many new and interesting places. I want to get started on a new piece of work and it looks as if I may have to get out of Brooklyn before I do. I have been here so long and have been tied to this book so long that I've got to make some sort of change now and start again. The book will be out on March the eighth and I will send you an advance copy before I go away. Of course we are all hoping and praying for success. That's all I can do now and I know Scribners will do all in their power to make it go. At any rate, the job is done now, it's all over so far as I am concerned and beyond hoping that it is well received by the critics and the public and that I manage to pay my debts and that Scribners get some reward for all their pains and labor there is nothing I can do except to begin thinking of a new piece of work and trying to get started on it as soon as possible.

This is all for the present. I hope to hear from you soon, and earnestly hope you will let me know what you need and in what way I can help you. Please take care of yourself, and be sure to get comfortable quarters and good accommodations wherever you go. You ought not to come back home before warm weather and if you will only stay down there I am sure I will be able to send you whatever funds you need. I will write you again at greater length before I go away. I am trying to get some stories ready with the hope that my agent will be able to market them so I'll write nothing further at present. Meanwhile, I am sending my love, best wishes for health and happiness and a good trip.

Your son,

TOM

Undated

DEAR MAMA: Please excuse me for not having written you sooner. For three weeks I have been driven at a frantic pace—hundreds of books to autograph, people coming for interviews, the telephone ringing all day long—and moving out of Brooklyn, getting ready to go to Europe, and a thousand other things— I knew you would understand—or rather *guess* that this was the situation—and excuse me for my failure to write. Mama, I am sailing for Europe tomorrow morning on the Ile de France— I am terribly tired and glad to get away—but people here have been wonderfully good and kind to me— I can't tell you much about the book—please don't think "I'm counting chickens before they're hatched"—the whole thing may be a failure and a "flop"—it is useless to predict before the book comes out but the truth of the matter is that *it looks good*— They have had *three* editions already —a total of 20,000 copies—and the advance orders already amount to 13,000—or almost as many as *Look Homeward, Angel* sold all told. We don't know what reviewers will say but we have seen one or two advance reviews—and they were wonderful— Of course the others may be very bad— This is all I can tell you now—please say nothing about it—let others say it and say nothing yourself—but *pray* for me! If you need money write or wire Max Perkins at Scribners—he will send it to you. *Please* stay in Florida— I will be abroad about two months and when I come back I will be ready to *go* again—the last few weeks, the excitement, the phone calls, interviews, etc., have worn me out. I'm just waiting to get on boat and flop in a bunk.

—I believe, I hope, I pray that good fortune is ahead—*don't worry!* The book is all right—and what Max calls "the great jam" is broken—there are *three* more to follow—*two* of them almost ready— Goodbye for the present, love and health and good luck to you, don't hope too soon—but it looks as if *finally, finally* everything is going to be all right— I've got to get away for a month or so, I'm worn out.

—John Terry[1] is here with me as I write this and sends his love—says to tell you he'll send you Mrs. Macaulay's address— She's in Miami now— Stay there until Spring comes—and wire Perkins if you need money— I'll write you as soon as I land in France. Meanwhile, love and best wishes for health and success.

Tom

ST. GEORGE'S COURT,
26 HANOVER SQUARE, W. I.
Telephone Mayfair 4015/6.
Thursday, March 28, 1935

DEAR MAMA: I've wanted to write you a dozen times but this is the first time since I left home that I've written any letters or felt like it—am just beginning to recover from all the strain and tension of last few months and to eat and sleep regularly again— The last few weeks in New York were frantic—what with final proofs on book, interviews, packing up and getting furniture and MSS stored, getting ready to go away, and being pestered by every kind of bore, fool, FRESH and crack-pot you can think of—I was just about all in when I got in the boat and don't

[1] John S. Terry, editor of this volume, was one of Tom's closest friends from their undergraduate days at the University of North Carolina.

think I could have stood it much longer— Did you get a long
letter I sent to Miami General Delivery by Air Mail just a few
hours before I sailed— Also sent Fred a telegram—and tried to
reach Mabel over long distance—Woman who answered it
said Mabel was either asleep or had gone out with dog—but
hope she delivered message and told her I had phoned—as you
know I sailed from New York on the *Ile de France*—we had a
fairly rough crossing—a big ship but rocked, rolled and pitched
so I got little sleep—but wasn't sick— Landed at Havre six days
later and then was in Paris for a little more than two weeks—
But couldn't rest or get quiet in Paris—it seemed that all the
nervous strain and tension of last few months accumulated and
broke there—I walked the Streets all night long and worried
my head off thinking about my book and how it was going and
what kind of reception it would have— Finally got cable and a
letter from Mr. Perkins which put me somewhat more at ease—
but still couldn't sleep— I came over to England Sunday and
already feel much better— People here have been very kind to
me—my publisher, Frere Reeves, was waiting for me with his
car when the Channel boat got to Folkestone—and he took me immediately to his home in the country which was only fifteen or
twenty miles away—a beautiful place in Kent overlooking the
marshes— His wife, a fine girl, was waiting for us—we went
for a walk in the country—and already I began to feel better—
Came back and had a fine dinner—sat around fire and talked—
and about ten o'clock started the drive up to London—70 miles
away— I was dog tired when I got here—but felt quieter than
in weeks—went to a hotel for the night and slept like a top.
Now I am living for a week or two in a little "service flat" which
Pat (Frere's wife) found for me—they bring me a good breakfast
every morning and look after me in every way— I am beginning

to eat and sleep regularly for first time in months or years—and I ought to be ready for hard work when I come back— Everyone has been fine to me here—Frere and his wife, other old friends I used to know here, I am not lonely and am beginning to "come back"—to get my energy and vitality back again— Mr Hugh Walpole, the English novelist has been very kind and generous to me—he had me to lunch, with Frere and Pat, at his flat in Picadilly yesterday—a wonderful place full of priceless books (all first editions) manuscripts and paintings, sculpture etc—and he has asked me to come to lunch again on Saturday— I appreciate the kindness of all these people more than I can say—they have certainly *not* treated me like a stranger—Frere's house (Heinemann) intend, I understand, to publish my three long books waiting to follow this one—one of which is completely finished—and the other two almost completed—save for the final draught— I've done no writing save make notes on this trip so far but already my fingers are itching to get at it again— This is all for the present— I've seen some interesting things but will have to wait to tell you about them— Tell others I'll write soon— I hope this finds you in good health and enjoying life— It should be Spring in Asheville when this gets there— Please take care of yourself and let publishers know if you need anything— Meanwhile, much love—

Your son—

TOM

ST. GEORGE'S COURT
26, Hanover Square
W.1

(Tom's mother was unable to find the first and last part of this letter. It seems to be one of the first letters written after he

arrived in England in 1935. This page evidently begins with a
reference to his English publishers.)

back here in June—and for their sake as well as for my own I
hope they get some adequate reward for all their effort—and of
course that goes doubly for Scribners, and most of all for Max
Perkins, who has been as true and good a friend as any man
could have— He has stood by me for years and believed in me
and now, I hope and pray to God that my book will get a reception and have a success that will be worthy of Mr. Perkins'
friendship— I have had no mail from America except two cables
from Max and a letter from him—and these indicated that the
book was being well received— But I have seen or read nothing
else—they are not sending me any mail but holding it until I
come back—they want me to try to get a rest and "forget about
it" for a time while I'm away—and I think this is a good idea if
I can succeed in doing so—I do hope that I may pay my debt to
Scribners and get a little money from this book—to get a little
security and freedom from worry while I go on writing—and also
to help some of you who may need help— Mama, if you need
anything please write to Mr. Perkins, as I told you— They are not
sending my mail on, but of course if you or any member of the
family want to get in touch with me you can do so instantly
through Perkins—I'd give you an address now if I could, but I
don't know where I'm going to be— I'll be here only two weeks
—and then I may go to Denmark, to Berlin, even to Russia— So
Perkins is the best address— I'll be home in May and hope to see
you then— It has been a long hard pull this book—but if it will
only "get over" it looks as if the jam is broken—

[*Post Card*]

LONDON
Saturday, April 13, 1935

DEAR MAMA:

I have got to go to Berlin next week to see my German publisher and may even go to Russia but will be back home in May—
Hope to see you soon— Am beginning to feel better, more rested,
and have bought some new clothes.

TOM

[*Card*] View of Marine Parade and Beach, Yarmouth, England.
Norwich, England, April 27, 1935.

April 27th 1935

DEAR MAMA: This place is a fishing town and summer resort on
the coast of Norfolk in the eastern part of England— A great
many of the Pilgrim fathers including Abe Lincoln's ancestors
came from this part of Eng.

Love,

TOM

[*Post Card*] View of Hyacinth Field

AMSTERDAM,
May 3, 1935

DEAR MAMA: I know you like flowers—that's why I picked out
this card for you— Coming up to Amsterdam on the train yesterday the earth burst into colors such as I have never seen before— Hundreds of acres as far as eyes could reach of flowers—
just as if the earth had been painted all different colors— Am

going on to Berlin tomorrow— Will write from there. Hope you are well.

Love—

TOM

[Post Card]

AMSTERDAM, HOLLAND

DEAR MAMA: This is a very busy, clean, and thrifty little country, as you have heard. I have never seen so many canals in my life—not even in Venice—the country is full of them and they use them in the cities in place of streets. Hope you are well. Will write.

Love,

TOM

HOTEL AMZOO
Berlin W. 15
Kurfürstendamm 25
Thursday, May 17, 1935

DEAR MAMA: Have just time for a few lines to say hello and briefly give you the news. After leaving London, I went to Cambridge and to Norfolk county for a week or so, then to Holland for about a week (where the flowers are the most beautiful you ever saw) then stopped off, on way to Berlin, at old city of Hanover in Germany, and have been here in Berlin a little more than a week. They have really almost killed me with kindness here, the American ambassador and his wife (Mr and Mrs Dodd), their son and daughter,[1] my publisher here, and many German people have taken me around, had me to parties, din-

---

[1] William Dodd, Jr., and Martha Dodd, author of *Through Embassy Eyes* in which Tom figures.

ners, theatres, etc until I'm "just worn out with it and am croak-
ing" like a bull frog with a deep chest cold which I find hard to
shake off. Berlin is a very magnificent, well laid-out and prosperous looking town with wonderful parks and buildings but Spring
is very late and cold here—although the flowers and trees are all
out. I have many things to tell you about my trip—so much in
fact that I will have to wait until I see you or can write you all
about it at greater length— I must see my publisher today to
sign contract for new book and get some money from him if I
can— His contract is not as good as the first—600 marks advance
instead of 1000 and 7½% royalties instead of 10%; but he says
times are hard. American money is much depreciated, and the
publishing business in Germany so bad at present, and the expense of publishing my book so great that this is best he can do
—so it looks as if I'll have to take it. It's better to get something
than nothing—it's almost impossible to get money *out* of Germany
today, against the law here to take or send it out—the publisher
says there is a way, of sending me my royalties but it's so complicated and uncertain that if I can get 600 marks today I'll take
it and try to spend it here— This is all for present— Hope this
finds you well and in good spirits— Write to Perkins if you need
anything.

With love—

TOM

[Post Card]

COPENHAGEN,
June 16, 1935

DEAR MAMA: I am here in Copenhagen—a beautiful city—and
intend to sail for home Bremen (Germany) next week— Hated
to leave Berlin, they were so friendly and kind—will tell you all
about it soon—

TOM

[*Post Card*]

COPENHAGEN,
June 18, 1935

DEAR MAMA: This is another view of Copenhagen—a very beautiful and gay city and the people very friendly— Expect to be home in another two weeks—

TOM

[*Post Card*]

HAMBURG,
Wed. June 26, 1935

DEAR MAMA: I am sailing for America from Bremen—2 hours from here—on the S.S. *Bremen*—which sails Friday morning— less than 2 days from now— Arrived here this morning from Copenhagen—had been without sleep over 24 hrs. I was dog tired and still am— This is a big city—the 2d in Germany—but have not seen much of it yet— Have had a wonderful trip— much to think and write about— Will get back N.Y. July 4—

TOM

NEW YORK, NEW YORK
July 8, 1935

Mrs. Julia E. Wolfe
48 Spruce Street
Asheville, North Carolina

DEAR MAMA:

I got back here the Fourth of July on the *Bremen* and have been kept pretty busy ever since reading the enormous number of letters that have accumulated during the four months I was away. I am working here at Scribners today with a young lady who is going to help me to answer them. I can just write you this note now to let you know that I am back home again, but I will write you a long letter in a few days and tell you all the news and about my plans.

I have got to go to Colorado towards the end of the month to give a lecture [1] at a writers' conference at the University there. They will pay $250 which will cover my expenses and give me a chance to see a part of the country I want very much to see. I haven't time to give much other news now except to say that I am wonderfully happy about the success I seem to have had and very, very grateful to all my friends here at Scribners who have made it possible. It makes me want to do more to justify their belief, and I know that now with a little money and free from the worry and self-doubt that bothered me so much these last four or five years, I shall do far better next time than I have ever done before.

I found several postcards from Mabel, saying she is coming to Asheville and wants to know if I can come with her. I am going to write her as soon as possible.

If it is possible, I may come home for a few days on my way to Colorado, and if that cannot be arranged, I will come back by Asheville on my return.

I had a wonderful trip, which I will tell you about later, but it is also very good to be back home again.

If you need anything, let me know at once. I am staying at a hotel here from which I shall probably move in a day or two, but you can reach me here at Scribners.

Good-by for the present.

With much love and best wishes to all,   TOM

[1] This lecture, delivered at the Writers' Conference, Boulder, Colorado, was later developed into the book, *The Story of a Novel*, published in 1936, by Charles Scribner's Sons, New York.

NEW YORK CENTRAL LINES—En Route
Between Buffalo and Chicago—
Saturday night.
[Envelope dated 7/28/35]

DEAR MAMA: I'm on my way West to Colorado—will arrive there Monday morning. I've been terribly busy in N. Y. answering letters and preparing my lecture and just managed to get off at the last moment.— I'm looking forward to my Western trip and intend to go the whole way to the Pacific coast—New Mexico, Arizona, California the Northwest and back through Salt Lake, etc.— I intend to stop off in St. Louis on my way back to see house we lived in—will you please send me the correct address at once, it's most important. My address until August 8th will be Writers' Conference, Boulder, Colorado, care of Mr. Edward Davison. Please write me there. I am looking forward to seeing the West with the greatest interest. Will be back in N. Y. beginning of September and will then get to work with all my might. There is much news to tell you, but can't here because of the motion of the train. Will write from Col. Love to all, let me or Perkins know if you need anything, and please don't forget to send me the St. Louis address and any other information about St. L. you remember—

Love,   TOM

[Card]

GREELEY, COLO
July 30th 1935

DEAR MAMA: Have been here in Greeley just a day but like the West and the people very much.

[Card]

GRAND CANYON, ARIZ.
Wed., August 2, 1935
DEAR MAMA: I am here at the Grand Canyon today on my way to California— This post card cannot begin to do justice to this wonderful sight and I have no words to tell you about it here— will write later—

TOM

[Card]

SANTA FE, N. MEXICO
Aug. 26th, 1935
DEAR MAMA: I have meant to write sooner but what between lectures in Colorado and the wonderful hospitality people have showed me everywhere I have had no time— This is a wonderful country, 7500 feet up, and great mountains and deserts all around.

TOM

[Card]

TENNESSEE, COLO.
Sept. 10, 1935.
DEAR MAMA: I am writing you this on the train in Colorado— coming back East by way of the Denver and Rio Grande railroad— Going through the Rockies now and in a few hours will go through Royal Gorge—a beautiful trip.

TOM

[*Card*]

SAN FRANCISCO, CALIF.

Sept. 11, 1935

DEAR MAMA: I am on my way back home today after a wonderful trip in which I have seen and learned very interesting things about our country— Will stop off at Salt Lake and St. Louis for a few hours— Writing later—

TOM

NB 1121   12 BDAY—NEWYORK NY   1936 FEB 17 PM 6 31
MRS JULIA E WOLFE
       SENATE HOTEL   139 NORTH EAST   2 AVE MIAMI FLO
ALL MY LOVE AND WISHES FOR MANY MORE HAPPY BIRTHDAYS
AM WRITING

TOM

865 FIRST AVENUE
New York, N. Y.
March 15, 1936

DEAR MAMA:

I wanted to write to you for some time, and especially to get a letter to you in time for your birthday, to wish you a happy birthday, and all good health and success this coming year, but I have been down with a touch of the "flu" for the last week, and although I now feel better it seems to be a slow business getting over it. I kept right on working because of the work that had to be done, and I did not go to bed, but I suppose I might have been better off if I had.

I had dinner with the Perkinses Saturday night and told them I thought I was all right again, but Mrs. Perkins took my temperature and found I had two degrees of fever, so I probably had more than that a day or two before. I understand there's been an epidemic everywhere this winter, so I suppose I was due to get my share of it.

I had a wonderful trip through the South and was everywhere received with the greatest cordiality and kindness. But I didn't get much rest, and I was pretty tired when I went down there. The people in New Orleans never seemed to go to bed at all and they overwhelmed me with well-meant and much appreciated hospitality, but I finally had to get out of town just to get rid of some of the people. I went up to Biloxi, Miss., on the Gulf coast, for a day or two, then up to Atlanta, where more friends were waiting for me, then up to Southern Pines, N. C., to visit my friend James Boyd,[1] then to Raleigh and Chapel Hill, where I saw dozens of my old teachers and school mates again, then up to Warrenton, N.C., to stay with my friend Bill Polk, who is mayor of the town, then directly back to New York. It was a good trip, but I stayed away longer than I intended and had to get back here and get to work again. I had hoped to come to Asheville, had planned to come up from Atlanta, which is not far away, but when I telephoned from Atlanta I gathered there was some confusion about my coming and, since my visit did not seem to be convenient, I thought I'd better go on to see some of the people who had been expecting me.

However, if I can finish a big piece of work this spring I do

---

[1] The author of *Drums, Marching On,* etc., published by Charles Scribner's Sons, New York.

plan to return later on, in the latter part of April or early in May. I have heard from friends in Asheville that they would be glad to see me and would be able to put me up, so there ought not to be any difficulty about that.

My troubles with the lawyers and law suits still continue. It has been a hard two years but I begin now to see that the whole business is a highly organized racket—the idea being to get as much out of the victim as the victim will pay rather than go to the expense of going to court and suffering the additional cost of time, worry and money which a court trial involves.

The libel case out in Brooklyn, which is another attempt to get money, started out a month before Christmas with the people suing for $125,000 and has now come to the place where they are down to $1500. It's the same old business all over again, except that this time I don't have to bear it entirely alone. But of course I'm defending it in conjunction with Scribners, who are also named as parties in the suit. Scribners, however, felt it so important to act strongly here, because of its possible effect on the future, that they got the best libel lawyer in the country. I have seen the gentleman's offices, and I'm afraid his fees are in proportion to his reputation. Shall we pay these people $1500— God knows where my share of it is coming from; all the work I do nowadays, everything I sell, seems to go largely towards paying lawyers fees, income tax or something of this sort—or shall we take it into court where, as I understand it, there is no question of our legal rights, where we can win, but where we must also pay a terribly expensive, dollar-a-second, high-pressure legal expert, and his assistants, for their services.

The final thing is a boy in New Jersey [1] who has my manu-

[1] Tom had turned over several of his manuscripts for sale to an agent. Disputes followed which led to a law suit successfully brought by Tom for the recovery of the manuscripts.

scripts, which I have been trying to recover for the last year, and which apparently he has been selling, or offering for sale. As you know, I brought suit against him last summer and the court issued an injunction which as I understand it prevents him from selling any of my manuscripts I mentioned. Apparently, he managed to get hold of other manuscripts also, how and in what way I do not know, except that I did not give them to him. And I suppose he has been free to sell these. At any rate he has apparently been steadily reduced to a more desperate situation, and from his original wild letters in which he demanded that I actually give up to him all the manuscript that I'd ever written, of whatever sort, and the instant payment of $2000 as commission, etc., he has written my attorneys in New Jersey one wild letter after another, finally coming down to a demand for $500, for which he will graciously be pleased to return my own manuscript to me. I told my lawyer before going South that the whole proposal was preposterous and that I should not have to pay one penny for the return of my manuscripts. With this my New York lawyer was in utter agreement and said there was no other course for me but to take it into court. This was the way I left it when I went South after Christmas. While I was South, however, in New Orleans, I got another long letter from my lawyer, Mr. Mitchell,[1] here in New York, who told me that the boy had now apparently resorted to threats in a letter which he was apparently mad enough to send to my New Jersey attorneys—you see, I had to get a completely new set of attorneys out there, since the boy lives in New Jersey and my New York lawyer has no license to practice there. This not only complicates matters but adds to my expense—but the boy had threatened if we did not settle for the sum he demanded, namely $500, and

---

[1] Cornelius von Erden Mitchell, of Mitchell & Van Winkle, New York.

pressed the case against him further, he would do these things: (1) go to North Carolina and stir up libel suits against me; (2) go to Brooklyn and join forces with the people suing me for libel there; (3) make public what he described as 'salacious material', which he claimed to have found in a manuscript in his possession, in an effort to damage me. He further said, according to the contents of a letter communicated to me by Mr. Mitchell, that he was willing to go to jail if necessary, but that he would do these things. The result of it was that my New Jersey attorneys, who were apparently reputable people, but also, I'm afraid, not the people to handle a case of this sort—I did not pick them, by the way, Mr. Mitchell did—these people instead of acting promptly and vigorously, upon receipt of this highly improper letter, which has now become a matter for action at the district attorney's office, were thrown, if you please, in a state of panic. The boy or his attorney apparently sent them a copy of the alleged salacious material, which was taken from my notebooks, and which, if they had been a little better informed, they would have seen was in no respect worse, or as bad, as many things which have appeared in books of modern writers, in those of Hemingway, Faulkner, or even in my own—instead of acting promptly as they should have done on receipt of this letter, they frantically sent a messenger to Mr. Mitchell, who wrote me and told me that I'd better return from my holiday at once. I did blow up then and wrote him a pretty strong letter in which I said that it was an outrage that I should have to endure any more of this sort of thing, which has hounded my life for two years now, that I should have to yield to this kind of threat, that the honest man is allowed to be victimized by every racket of this sort that comes along. I think this letter finally spurred them into action. At any rate, I succeeded in having a conference with a member of my New Jersey firm the other day, the first time I'd ever succeeded in talking with one of them, and they admitted to me all of these things: first of all, there was no longer, if there had ever been, any question of the legal aspects of the case or of my rights; that there was no question now of my being able to recover all of the manuscript that was left and to get a judgement against the boy for those which he had improperly sold; and finally, they admitted that he had written them a letter containing these threats and that he could now be held legally accountable for it. I asked them then why did we delay in taking the proper decisive action. Their answer was that if I took the case to court and had them represent me it would cost me an additional $500, and that although they were certain to recover the manuscripts that were left, they didn't know how much was left, or what the value of what was left would be, and finally, that although we could get a judgement against the boy for those he had sold there would be almost no chance of collecting on the judgement, because he was financially a totally irresponsible person. As to the illegal and improper threats, they admitted that he could be held accountable for writing such letters, but then, to my amazement, became very sentimental about it and said, after all, I was not out for vengeance and how would it look for somebody in my position to take action against a little unknown boy in New Jersey and what satisfaction would it be to me if I do, and couldn't I just give him $500 and settle the whole thing up. I thought it was one of the most astounding proposals I had ever heard, particularly when it was made by people who had been engaged as my own representatives and for whose services I must pay my own money, and I told them there was no question of vengeance involved but a question of right, of my own future, and of my own protection.

I told them that it was a little strange to hear vengeance connected with my name in such a case, where I have myself been outraged, wronged and threatened by such a person, and when I went to the most extreme lengths at first to persuade his family to get him to behave in the proper manner. Since talking to these lawyers and Mr. Mitchell, I have talked to Mr. Perkins, who agrees with me that I should not make this settlement, that even if I recovered nothing, if all is gone, in view of what has now happened I must proceed against him, and this seems the only right course left open to me, even though it will cost me a good deal of additional money, involve me in more publicity—which of course is one of the threats they make use of—and put me to much extra expense and time and worry.

Finally, the worst disappointment of all has been the human disappointment in people whom I trusted and who I thought were my friends. I knew all these people in the beginning as friends of mine and even after all that has happened they still have the gall to call me up and ask me out to dinner, and why I haven't been to see them lately. They even sent me a Christmas card. I think the greatest disappointment—I have had time to get used to the other one—has been the conduct of John Terry.[1] I suppose in his own concept of the thing he has done nothing wrong, or thinks he has not. Well, perhaps he has not. All I can say is now, without anger, with heart full of sorrow, it seems to me he has sold me out for an occasional dinner. John was my friend, or said he was. I introduced him to these people. When

[1] John S. Terry was in an anomalous position in regard to this case, for he was also a warm friend by now of the Dooher family. Tom introduced him to the Doohers, and he and Tom visited the family many times together. The Doohers were unaware of Tom's changed feelings toward them, and still regard him in memory as a dear friend. Tom also never even suggested that Terry give up his friendship with the Doohers nor was there any break in his friendship with Terry.

this thing happened about a year ago John was outspokenly indignant about it. He assured me there was no doubt in his mind what the family would do, that they were too fine to allow a thing like this to happen, that the boy was simply acting in the heat of passion and anger and Irish temper, and when he cooled down he would himself see the proper course. John was with me when I went out, at the mother's own suggestion, to see her and other members of the family, and when the mother suggested that if I would get the boy a job at Scribners then I would be sure to get all of my manuscripts back—it was John himself who told me that this was not proper—that even if I could get the boy a job at Scribners, which I couldn't, it was not proper to have to bribe a person to be honest. John acted then as I expected him to act. Since then he continues to call me up, to ask me what I've been doing and if we could not get together to have dinner, but I know he also continues to visit these people, his friendly relations with them have not altered a bit. In fact, he wrote me the other day and told me that they were very eager to have me come out with him. Well, I may be wrong, but I can't see how I can go out there or, in fact, how I can continue to see John. And in this, other people who know about this matter agree with me. I am not prejudiced enough or narrow enough to say to any one, love me, love my dog, but it is no longer a question of that. If this were some trivial quarrel or temporary falling-out between friends to which John was an innocent bystander, I could perhaps understand the position he has taken. But it seems to me it is something more than that, it seems to me that it is a matter in which his old friend—or at least he has always told people for the past three years that he was an old friend and had known me since Chapel Hill days—has been not only wronged and outraged but has had his property taken from him and his character threatened and defamed by a member of a family with whom John still maintains friendly and cordial relations. I suppose John's attitude would be that it was only one member of this group who did this thing, that the others, in his estimation, are innocent, and that he himself is doing nothing wrong in continuing to accept their invitations and in frequently seeing them. If this is his view, I shall certainly make no attempt to change it. But I do feel now that just as it has been highly improper for these people to continue to invite me to their home and to send me Christmas cards of affectionate greeting, so would it be highly improper for me to respond in any way or to see them. And I not only feel this from the point of view of right and justice but also from the point of view of my own rightful self-protection. My work, my reputation, my future have been threatened and menaced and my property has been unlawfully withheld. My lawyer, Mr. Perkins and other friends of mine, whose judgement I respect, believe that it would be impossible for me now to have any further connection with these people, whose position, whatever else it may be, is certainly friendly to the member of their own group who has done these things. So far as I can see, that is John Terry's position too, and I therefore do not see how, under these circumstances, I can continue my friendship with him.

I am sorry to have to tell you these things because I know you were fond of John, as I was too. I have, however here given you a straight and accurate account of what has happened, and I want to ask you hereafter, if he writes you or you write him, not to say anything about me or what I plan to do that might be in any way useful to any member of this group with which he is intimate. As to the Merediths, I do not know them as well as I know John, although I have known Lacey off and on for many years. I do not believe he would do anything to injure me but inasmuch as he is very intimate with John and roomed with him

for years and writes him frequently, I should like to ask you not
to say anything in his presence either about my affairs or what
I propose to do.

This is all a very sad business. It seems to belong to the experience of life so I suppose sooner or later I would have to find
out about these things. I shall come through it all, of course, at
the cost of a great deal of money, worry and disillusionment. But
maybe I'll be the better for it in the end. I hope so. At least, I
have not lost my faith in life in spite of all these sad and painful
experiences. I can still remember all the good ones I've had and
all the decent, fine and honorable people I have known, and still
know, who would not sell you out for a few dollars and who
would be loyal to the end.

I'm going on with my work and in spite of everything will
push forward until I complete a new job. Fred spoke to me in
his letter of trouble which the Wachovia Bank is now making for
you concerning the house in Spruce street. I suppose this too all
goes to make up the sum of those bad [sic] and bitter experiences
we have in life, but I believe we may yet get through them somehow. Fred didn't tell me much about the Wachovia trouble, but
I wish when you get time, some of you would write and tell me
more about it. The one advantage that I've yet had in all my
own legal difficulties thus far has been that there was never any
question of the right. The only mistake I made in these three
affairs was possibly my own carelessness and unbusiness-like
method in allowing an irresponsible and unscrupulous person
to take my property and to see if he could sell it on an agent's
basis. But of course at the time that this happened I did not
know the person was either unscrupulous or irresponsible. On
the contrary, I should have sworn he was just the opposite, a
member of a poor but upright family, whose integrity I would
have sworn to and moreover, devoutly religious in the Catholic

faith. Well, I don't know what it proves unless it proves that one cannot be too careful, but I hope that all of us will come through to a better time.

Write me when you can and give me the news and let me know if you need anything. Meanwhile, with love and best wishes to you all,

Your son,

Tom

865 FIRST AVENUE
New York City
April 6, 1936

Dear Mama—

It has been a good time since I heard from you. You were on your way back from Florida when you last wrote and I presume you are back in Asheville now, and I hope that the winter is over and that you have been getting some good spring weather.

We have had a very long and severe winter here as I suppose you know, but during the last week or two there have been definite signs of spring and I think it really ought to come soon.

I have put in a pretty busy winter, what with lawyers, law suits, and trying to get my property back from people who have walked off with it. I can't tell you all the details now, but there has been one thing after another. I hope the worst of it is over and that I may have learned something from the experience— namely that there are a great many people in this big city who never expect to do an honest stroke of work provided they can find someone they can make an easy living out of. I try not to take these things too hard, because I met, in addition, a great many very fine and honorable people and, as I say, I just hope that from the unpleasant and disappointing experiences I shall learn to be a little more cautious in the future.

I have made a good many notes and done a good deal of thinking about my next book and recently I have begun to get some of the preliminary typing done. I hoped that I might get away for awhile and possibly go south this spring for a visit but now that I am definitely started on the book I hate to break into it and I feel, furthermore, that I ought to get back to steady day to day work again.

I hope everyone in the family is all right. I have had no news for some time, not since I heard from you last, I think. I want to thank you, by the way, for your very useful and very much appreciated gift of socks and neck-ties. They came at a time when I really needed both articles very much and they have seen good service.

Things go along about as usual with Scribners. I have seen Mr. Perkins, Mr. Dashiell and Mr. Wheelock very frequently—almost every day in fact. They are all well and ask to be remembered to you.

Please take care of yourself and let me know at once if there is anything you need and I'll send it to you. Meanwhile, until I hear from you again, with much love to you and all.

Your son,

Tom

[Easter Card]

THURSDAY, APRIL 9, 1936

DEAR MAMA: I send you all my love and best wishes for a Happy Easter—and many more to come. Write if you need anything.

With Love

Tom

THOMAS WOLFE
865 FIRST AVENUE
NEW YORK, N. Y.

MAY 28, 1936

Mrs. Julia E. Wolfe
48 Spruce Street
Asheville, N. C.

DEAR MAMA:

I have been meaning to write you for a long time, but have got back to work again and have been keeping pretty busy. I am just going to write you a note this morning, and will write you a long letter later.

I got a letter from Fred this morning, and he tells me that Chester Arthur and a friend of his had paid you a visit. I hope they did not bother you too much and that you were not too tired out. I don't know Arthur very well. I met him and his wife going down in the elevator of this building where I lived last winter and saw him two or three times during the winter. He seems to be a nice enough fellow and, I think, is friendly to me and what I do. I don't know whether he told you, but he is the grandson of Chester Allen Arthur, who was president of the United States when you were a girl. He came by here with another young man—I suppose the same one who visited you— several weeks ago and told me that he was starting off on a trip through the South and would I give him the names of some people I knew. I gave him the names of people in Virginia and a good many in North Carolina—in Raleigh and Chapel Hill, Durham, etc. He said he was going to Asheville, and I told him you were living there, and suggested that he go to see you; but I did not know he was going to stay two or three days, as Fred said he had. However, I hope everything was all right, and that you liked him.

I am back, hard at work again, after a winter in which almost everything has happened. I will write you at greater length and tell you the news later.

My law suit, I guess, is settled. They settled finally for $500.00 and in addition put up a hard luck story and wouldn't I please give her something extra, so I made her a present of $150.00. My lawyer has worked like a dog on the case for the last year, so of course I will have to pay him. All in all, the miserable thing has cost me a flat one thousand dollars. Still, you will agree there is a good deal of difference between $500. or $650. and the ten thousand dollars they were suing for; also. The woman is now compelled to sign an iron-clad agreement, in which she acknowledges that aside from *Look Homeward Angel* she has no claim of any sort upon anything I ever do, and of course so far as we are concerned, that is Scribners and Perkins and myself, 'there has never been any argument about *Look Homeward Angel*. I told her she would continue to get her 10 percent from that book, even after she did the thing about the German edition, which annoyed me. I could have gone to court with it, my lawyer told me he was convinced that if we fought the thing through to the end, we would unquestionably win; but first of all there would have to be a jury trial, and of course a jury trial is a very risky thing, particularly where a woman is involved, because a woman can work upon their sympathies. My lawyer said we could have fought it through and eventually he was sure win the case, but the lawyer pointed out that if we did, this would mean a great deal of additional expense to me, I would have to pay him for his service, and it would also mean a great deal of extra time and worry and trouble when I should be at work. He left the decision up to me: whether I wanted to settle for the $500. or spend that much and perhaps more in money, time and trouble in fighting the thing through the court. I talked it over with Perkins and we decided to give them the money and have done with it.

The $500., by the way, was my own idea. I made the offer. Nothing was forced upon me. Only a day or two before, in fact, her lawyer had been demanding $2,000. and commissions on everything I ever do. Well, I am out of it now, out of this particular piece of trouble, anyway. I suppose I have won out and beaten them, but it has cost me a thousand dollars. There was no way on earth it could have been avoided. I found out in the last year that anyone can sue you. Whether they know you or not, whether they have any claim upon you or not, whether they have an ounce of justice in their suit or none at all, they can sue you, and often they can take advantage of the knowledge that you have to earn your living through your work and that you will probably pay them something rather than lose everything, which is the power to work and earn your living. You can win a suit, of course, except that you never really win—you have to go to the expense of hiring a lawyer, of fighting the thing, paying your lawyer's fees, losing sleep and time and work through worry, so of course you never really win. The other day I found grey hairs in my head and after the events of this past year, it is no wonder. However, I am delighted to be back at work again. As long as I can work, I think everything will come out all right.

I got pretty tired and took a three or four day trip down to Pennsylvania a week or two ago. A friend of mine who has a car drove me. We kept off main highways as much as possible, took back-country roads and saw some of the most beautiful farming country in the world. We got as far as York Springs, went out and visited the graveyard where Papa's folks were buried, stopped off in York Springs and saw Jim and Dorothy and Aunt Mary, and came on back through Pennsylvania, up the Delaware, into New York State, across the Hudson through beautiful scenery, over the Bear Mountain Bridge and back to New York. It was a good trip. I saw some wonderful country, and came back feeling a lot better.

Mr. Roberts and Mrs. Roberts are in town, by the way, visiting Margaret. Mrs. Roberts wrote me the other day, after all these years. Her letter, I am afraid, still showed resentment about what she thinks I said about members of her family in *Look Homeward Angel*; nevertheless, she said they still cared for me and wanted to see me while they were here. I wrote back and told her that I would like to see them, that I was glad to know they wanted to see me; but that as far as the matters she discussed in her letter were concerned, I would rather not talk about them if it was going to cause pain and confusion and misunderstanding to anyone. She wrote me another letter in reply to this one and asked me to let her know when I could come and have dinner with them. I suppose I will go and hope that everything turns out for the best.

This is all for the present. I hope this finds you well and taking care of yourself. The way it now looks, I may stay here the greater part of the summer and keep on working. Write me if you need anything. Meanwhile, with love and best wishes,

Your son,

Tom

Mabel has written me from Wash:—Wants me to come down —if I can get away for a day or two some week end I'll try to do it— Don't say anything to anyone, one way or another, about my lawsuit: I want to have done with it now and have no more complications— Mr. Perkins is well and sends his best: he and his family are moving to the country for the summer in a few days!

[*Post Card*]

ALPBACH, TIROL
Aug. 2, 1936

DEAR MAMA: I have been living in this house—400 years old—an old one—for a week. To-day I start back for Munich and Berlin, and will sail next week if I can get a place on a ship—all ships crowded—This is Austrian Tirol—some of the most beautiful mountains and valleys in the world.

Love,
TOM

[*Post Card*]

MUNICH,
August 28, 1936

DEAR MAMA: This is a beautiful city—I stayed here one time for several months; it seems very familiar to me now— Am on way back to Berlin and hope to be home soon.
TOM

[*Post Card*] View of Potsdamer Platz

BERLIN,
Sept 3, 1936

DEAR MAMA: This is one of the busy squares of Berlin. I am here for a few days before sailing for home.
TOM

[*Post Card*]

PARIS,

Sept. 13, 1936

DEAR MAMA: I had to come here to get a ship—all German boats were filled— Am leaving Thursday and will probably be back in N. Y. when you get this card—

Love,

TOM

THOMAS WOLFE

865 FIRST AVENUE

NEW YORK, N. Y.

OCTOBER 14, 1936

DEAR MAMA:

I've been meaning to write you for the last week or so but there has been so much to do since I got back that I've not had much opportunity before. Fred tells me you are driving up to Washington with him and, according to his schedule, you are due to leave Asheville this morning. Accordingly, I am sending this letter to Mabel's address in Washington. I am expecting Fred here Friday night. I am sorry that his visit has got to be so short, but I am looking forward to seeing him and talking to him and hearing the news.

I have a lot to tell you about my trip this summer. So much, in fact, that I'll have to wait until I see you to do it. I am glad I got to make the trip. I felt all summer that it might be the last time I saw Europe before another great war breaks out. It is hard to see how they are going to keep out of one. They are building up tremendous armies everywhere. The munition fac-

tories are running night and day. The air is full of bitterness
and hatred towards each other. Germany is a wonderful country
and the Germans are great people, but it looks as if, under this
present regime, they are heading for war. And during the week
or two I was in France it was evident that that country was also
in a dangerous political condition. Two street fights broke out
between opposing political factions on the streets of Paris right
around me. I saw these two episodes, and I suppose you could
multiply them by the thousands. I saw a great deal this summer.
It was exciting and interesting, but I was finally glad to get
back home. We have serious troubles of our own but we are
not yet menaced by over-population—by this tremendous pressure
of constricted space and of peoples crowded together without
room to expand which I believe accounts for so much of the
trouble over there.

I am back at work again. I am very eager now to get on with it.
I hope and believe that most of the troubles and distractions of
last year, the law suits, people walking away with my manuscript,
people pestering and bothering me with every kind of scheme—I
hope all this is practically over now and that I may have some
peace. I still have the young Irish boy in New Jersey to deal
with, but the lawyers have taken such action that he cannot sell
the manuscripts he still has in his possession. He and his lawyer,
I am informed, are now fiddling around for a compromise settlement, but it seems to me, there ought to be no compromise at all.
He should be compelled to return my property to me, and whatever money from the sale of manuscripts he may have in his
possession. I think we will get the manuscripts back all right. As
to the money, that's a different matter. He is, of course, financially irresponsible, and if he has spent the money, I suppose
that's all there is to it.

It was a pretty hard and bitter year, full of disillusioning experiences, and I found out the hard fact that there are people who call themselves your devoted friends who will sell you out for a little cash. But I found some good people too. It is not all bad. Anyway, I got through the year with only a few gray hairs. I've had the experience. I'm at work again, and that's that.

This is all for the present. I'll give Fred all the news when I see him Friday. I hope you have a good trip up from Asheville and that you find Mabel and Ralph, and all, well when you get to Washington. Have a good time and let me know if you need anything. I want to see you but I am at work here every day now and very anxious to get on with it. Perhaps, if you stay there with Mabel a week or so, I could get a train Saturday afternoon or night and spend Sunday there. But let's not decide this yet. I'll talk to Fred about it.

Meanwhile, with love and best wishes to all,

TOM

THOMAS WOLFE
865 FIRST AVENUE
NEW YORK, N. Y.

DECEMBER 24, 1936

Mrs. Julia E. Wolfe
48 Spruce Street
Asheville, N. C.
DEAR MAMA:
Just a short note before Christmas. I'll send you a telegram tonight which should reach you Christmas morning, but I'm writing this brief note to wish all of you a happy Christmas and a prosperous and happy New Year.

I'm dog-tired—so tired, in fact, I'm afraid I won't be able to enjoy Christmas. The Perkinses invited me for Christmas dinner and of course I like to see them. They are a nice family.

The day after Christmas I'm coming South for a week or ten days. I may stop off overnight in Washington and see Virginia and Fredericka, and Olin Dows, if he is still there, then to Richmond perhaps for a day, then the whole way to New Orleans where I have friends and where I plan to be for New Year's. Then back for a day or two in North Carolina to see some friends at Chapel Hill and Raleigh. I had thought that I might come home, but am so wretchedly tired at the present moment that I want to try to get away and forget about my work for a few days anyway. I think a few days away from here will fix me up, and of course I don't want to come home unless I feel well and look presentable. I've done over a quarter of a million words in less than three months' time. I'm pretty tired but I'll be all right.

This is just to send my love to all of you—you, Mabel and Fred and Ralph—and to wish you all a happy Christmas all together. I wish I could be with you but the main thing now is to get some rest. If my head would only stop working—the more tired it gets, the faster it goes. I sleep at night but a thousand things keep going through my head when I'm asleep. I just need to get away a little while.

This is all for the present. Merry Christmas and love to all of you.

Your son,

Том

ROANOKE, VIRGINIA,
April 28th, 1937.

Mrs. Julia E. Wolfe,
48 Spruce Street,
Asheville, North Carolina.

DEAR MAMA:

I am on my way home and expect to arrive there in a few days. I am going to Bristol, Virginia, tomorrow and from there I shall probably go over to Burnsville and stay a few days. While there I hope to look up some of our relatives whom I have never seen, visit Grandpa's birthplace and get a little more sleep.

Don't worry about me. I am all right again and feeling 100% better than when I left New York ten days ago. I was desperately tired—more than I have ever been. I have written over a half a million words since October and in addition, as you know, I have been fighting all along the line for the past year or so with crooks, parasites and lawyers. The lawyers now assure me that "we" have come out splendidly on all fronts and in fact won a glorious victory. I don't know who "we" means but as nearly as I can figure it, it means principally the lawyers. At any rate, there is not a great deal left except my power to work and my faith in human nature, which, in spite of everything, is stronger than it ever was. I am going to be all right. I am doing the best piece of work I have ever done and after a few more days of rest, I will be ready to go back and start in again.

I want to come down to see you and talk to you and find out what this Wachovia Bank business is all about. If there is any way I can help, I want to do so.

It will be a very strange experience, I think, coming back to Asheville after all this time. It is my home town and certainly I have no feeling for it or for any one there except the kindest and best. I don't know what their feeling is but I hope it is the same. At any rate, I am coming down to see my family. I should like to see some of my friends but I am still too tired to be pawed over and asked ten thousand questions. I know you all understand how I feel.

I am enclosing with this letter a copy of a will I made the other day in New York. Don't get alarmed. I intend to go on living for a long time; but inasmuch as the will I made a few years ago no longer seemed to me to be a good one, I thought I had better make a new one now. It was drawn up by a good lawyer, who assured me that everything was taken care of and that he had made it as simple as possible and had covered everything. You can either keep it or give it back to me when I see you in Asheville; but I thought it best for you to become acquainted with its terms and provisions as concerning you and the family. Accordingly I am sending it on to you.

I am afraid as regards this will I am a little bit in the position of the man who said: "If we had some ham, we would have some ham and eggs if we had some eggs." If anything happened to me right now, I don't know just how much any one would be able to realize out of my so-called estate; but of course with a writer there is always the chance that the continued sale of his books or manuscripts or other royalties may amount to something after his death. At any rate, I put the whole thing in the hands of two of the ablest and very best people I know, Mr. Perkins, who is the first executor, and Nat Mobley, who was a classmate of mine at college and who is now vice-president of an insurance company in New York.

This is all for the present. I will call you up in a day or two and hope to see you all soon.

With love and best wishes to all,   Your son,

TOM

865 FIRST AVENUE,
New York, N. Y.
June 3, 1937

DEAR MAMA:

I got your letter and was glad to hear from you and interested to read what you said about the cabin. Yes, I suppose there are more modern and up-to-date places around Asheville with electric lights, new beds, etc. but I did not have time to look for them and I honestly thought that the Whitson cabin [1] was, for my own purpose and for the peace and seclusion I am looking for and which I have got to have, the best place that I saw. I suppose oil lamps are somewhat of a handicap but, after all, I was born in a house where we all used oil lamps, and surely I ought to be able to endure a minor inconvenience of this sort now. As to your own fears of loneliness—and not liking to be alone out in the country at night—I know of no way in which you can get peace and seclusion, and not get it, at the same time. What I need desperately at the present time is to get away from the noise and tumult of New York, to get away from towns and cities and, for a few weeks at least, to get away from too many people. I need it for myself and I need it for my work, and that is why I have taken a chance on Whitson's cabin in the hope that I will find it there.

Meanwhile, I would appreciate it very much if you would write me, sending me a few practical suggestions as to what you think I will need out there, and what I ought to bring down with me. I am going to bring a few books, my manuscript, and aside from that I hope to bring as little as possible. It does not pay to move furniture unless one is moving permanently and I do not think I shall need much furniture at the cabin. Please

[1] Tom rented this cabin in the mountains near Asheville for the summer of 1937.

write and let me know about these things and whether I shall bring my bed linen and towels, etc. and if so, how much.

This is all for the present. I am hard at work and have just finished another story. I will write you later on when I have more time. Please let me know about these things when you can. Meanwhile, love and best wishes to you all.

Your son

Tom

865 FIRST AVENUE,
New York, N. Y.
June 26, 1937

Mrs. Julia Wolfe,
Spruce Street,
Asheville, N.C.

DEAR MAMA:

I got your letter but have been so busy this is my first opportunity to answer you. I have been working all the time since I came back but plan to finish tomorrow, Sunday, when Miss Nowell[1] is coming here to work with me in an effort to get one more story ready. I have written five stories since I came back and have sold two of them. Miss Nowell is sure she will be able to sell the other three. Of course, this is good news as I need money to go on working.

My plan is to leave here some time next week for Asheville. I intend to go to my cabin immediately. I have had no rest or quiet since the publication of *Look Homeward Angel* almost eight years ago and now I have to have it. Max Whitson writes that everything is ready at the cabin and that he has waxed the

---

[1] Elizabeth Nowell, now Mrs. Charles Perkins, had become Tom's literary agent several years before this. She was also one of his most trusted friends. She gave him very valuable assistance in editing his stories.

floors and bought some new furniture. I shall bring my sheets and bedding and move right in. I have never been so tired in my life and now must have rest. I hope that I can get it in the cabin. If not, I shall have to go where I can get it. I am bringing a great amount of manuscript with me and shall work on it this summer.

I hope this finds you all well and of course I am looking forward to talking to you when I have had some rest. Meanwhile, with all love and good wishes,

Your son

TOM

December 21, 1937

DEAR MAMA:

I am just hustling this letter off tonight so that it will be sure to get to you in time for Christmas, and I wish you love and good health and happiness, for Christmas and for many years to come.

I am going to send you a little present in a day or so but just want to get this letter off tonight. There is a lot to tell you but I will not try to tell you here——except that my troubles, I hope and pray, are beginning to resolve themselves. I think you know about the Scribner matter now because Fred told me he was giving you the letter I sent Perkins so that you could read it. A great deal has happened since then; several publishers have been after me, the decision has been hard to make, but I have finally decided to go with the firm of Harper & Brothers. It is an old house, the oldest in the country and it has always had a fine name. They offered me very fine terms, but what was more important, they all seemed to want me very much, and I hope and believe now that I will prosper and be happy with them and do my best work. I intend to try with all my might. I will write you details later.

I want to know all about the trial and what is happening, of course, but I also wish you would stay down there in Florida long enough to get a little rest. If you need anything at all or lack money to keep you there, I will get it for you at once, and expect you to let me know right away if you need anything. I am feeling much better now and much more settled now that I have made this great decision—I am still a little sad about leaving my old friends with whom I was associated for so long a time, but I am sure they are still my friends and wish me well as I do them.

I have been invited out to the country by one of my new editors[1] for Christmas. He is a young man, just my own age, married and with a child just a year old. I think he is a very fine fellow and I believe I am going to have a good time. I want you to enjoy yourself too, so let us all try to put care and worry out of our heads and enjoy Christmas with a good heart. I send you my love, and shall write you more news later on. Meanwhile with all best wishes for Christmas and New Year's—

Your son,   Том

December 27, 1937

DEAR MAMMA:

Here is a little Christmas present.[2] Please forgive me for the delay as I was out in the country with my new editor and his family for Christmas. I intended to telegraph it to you Friday

---

[1] This was Edward Aswell, of Harper & Brothers, New York. He and Tom became close friends, and it was he who performed the tremendous task of editing The Web and the Rock, You Can't Go Home Again, and The Hills Beyond.

[2] A check for $15.00.

night before leaving the City, but the last moments here were so filled up with seeing people and doing things that it slipped my mind. Please rest up and enjoy yourself while down there; stay as long as you can, and if you need anything, let me know right away.

I am beginning to feel happier and better. However, have been deeply grieved this Christmas because I have thought so much about my friends and associations at Scribners. Really I believe I am at the beginning of one of the happiest and best times of my life. These new people are fine people, they are young people, and they believe in me so utterly that it makes me want to do everything in my power to try and deserve and justify their belief.

With all love and good wishes for your happiness for this Christmas and during the coming year,

Your son,

TOM

114 EAST 56TH STREET
New York, New York
c/o Miss Elizabeth Nowell
February 15, 1938

DEAR MAMA:

I intended to write you a day or two ago so that my letter would get to you on your birthday. However, I shall send this special with the hope that it will arrive in time anyway. I have been involved with lawyers and in court myself: there has not been much time to think of anything else, so that accounts for the delay.

I had my day in court in Jersey City one week ago when my case was tried: as you perhaps know I was suing the fellow in

New Jersey who took my manuscripts a couple of years ago and never returned them, and he was replying with a counter-suit for about two thousand dollars, claiming that this sum was due him as his commission for acting as agent for my manuscript.

I won the suit completely and overwhelmingly: there was nothing left of him when we got through. In fact, he made such damaging confessions on the stand that he would be in very serious trouble now if I pushed it. He testified that he had burned some of my manuscript, and when the court asked why he replied that it had contained bad language and obscene material. He could of course be prosecuted for this, but I think we shall wait to see if he obeys the court's instructions—if he should attempt to withhold any of the manuscript still in his possession, or destroy any of it, I could of course then take steps against him.

He further testified that he had sold at least four items or batches of manuscript after I got out an injunction against him in 1936 restraining him from further sale and, according to his testimony, he had received between four and five hundred dollars from the sale of this manuscript, none of which he ever turned over to me. The Judge ordered him to repay this money in full, without commission. Of course, it is very doubtful that I shall receive any of it: he is not a responsible person—it quickly became evident to the court that if he was not positively unbalanced, he was certainly not a normal type.

I hate to think of what it has cost, and of what it will cost before I get through paying the lawyer. It has taken two years and a terrible amount of time, money, worry, energy and delay: probably what manuscript I get back will not begin to pay for the cost of the whole thing, but I had to defend myself not only to recover my own property, but to protect myself against his own counter-claims for two thousand dollars, and his claim that I had appointed him as my agent, with unlimited authority, forever.

It has been a sad experience, for he was a member of a family in whose honesty I had the most absolute confidence—people who had had me to their home on many occasions, and who were always assuring me of their affection and friendship. I know now how careless I was in intrusting manuscript to a boy of this sort, but the whole thing came up so casually when I was a guest in his home I allowed him to take the manuscript because he had nothing to do and his family was poor—I could not have been more surprised at what happened if a member of my own family had done it.

At any rate, I hope it is all over now for good: this is the first time in almost three years that I have not been threatened and harassed by one suit or another, sometimes I had two on my hands at the same time—it all comes down to the same thing in the end, people and crooked lawyers trying to extort money from someone who has received some public notice. My experience with the law and with courts has been a pretty costly and a bitter one: I hope I have learned something from it, and that I shall never have any other experience of this sort—although that, of course, is too much to hope for.

I have received no further news about your own case with the bank, or whether anything further has been done. The last information I got from Fred was that the lawyers had taken your deposition at Miami and that you had come through very well. But there is going to be some kind of trial at home, isn't there? I understand that the children are suing the bank and that I am included in the suit as one of the heirs. I have never understood clearly just what all the issues were, but I know no one in the family would misrepresent me or would do anything that involved me without informing me beforehand. At any rate, I would like to know all about it, to be told what is happening. Naturally where your interests are concerned, mine are too: I want you to win your case and keep possession of your house and your remaining property. So please let me hear all about it.

I hope now that I have settled all my own troubles in such a way that I will be left alone in peace to do my work without further interruption. It has been a trying ordeal, but maybe I will be the better for it: you cannot do a concentrated piece of work with people firing pistols in your face and with bullets whistling around your ears—it is like trying to fasten your mind on something with a raging toothache.

This is all for the present: I hope you will have good news to tell me when you write and that I shall have the pleasure of hearing the bank has been thwarted in its attempt to take your property from you.

Meanwhile, I send you all my best wishes for a happy birthday, and for many more years of good health. With love to all,

Your son,

TOM

114 EAST 56TH STREET
New York, New York
c/o Miss Elizabeth Nowell
April 11, 1938

DEAR MAMA:

Just a few lines to acknowledge your long letter, which I shall try to answer more fully later.

Virginia and Fredericka were here for two days. They arrived

Friday night and went back yesterday afternoon. They said they had had a wonderful time, and I hope they had. I tried to do all I could to make their stay a pleasant one, and a friend of mine, Mrs. Saunders,[1] who is editor of the *Junior League Magazine*, very generously gave up a large part of her time to entertaining them and took them around when I was busy and couldn't be along. I took them to a night club and to Broadway and to dinner, lunch, etc., and Mrs. Saunders took them to Radio City, to the Music Hall, to the Waldorf, and to the place where she lives over on the East River. They managed to get around and see some of the big stores for themselves; so all in all I think they saw about as much in their two days as they could be expected to see.

I noted the contents of your letter, and was very sorry to hear that there was sickness in the family. But I hope that now with good care and medical attention everyone will feel better.

I am also glad to know that your own testimony in the bank suit is finished, and I hope that now your lawyers will be able to present your case in such a way that the family will win.

There is no use in going over the mistakes that were made in the past and in regretting what might have been if people had only acted differently. For my own part, I can assure you that I have no feeling of bitterness and do not propose to pass judgment on what is over and done. I only hope that in the future everyone will profit from the experience of the past, and try to manage things better.

This is all for the present. I am glad to know you are so well, and hope you continue so. Don't try to overdo housework, climbing up stairs, and jobs of that sort. You are apparently in re-

[1] Mrs. Sally Faxon Saunders, a native of Kansas City, Mo., now of New York.

markable health for a person of your years, but at your age you should not attempt to do the work you did twenty or thirty years ago.

I am sorry if I don't seem to write more often. My impression is that I have written you all a good deal, a great deal more than I used to. I only ask you to remember that people do make a lot of demands on me and on my time now, and the greatest demand is the obligation of getting my work done.

Please let me hear from you when you can. Meanwhile, with love and best wishes,

Your son,

Tom

114 EAST 56TH STREET
New York, New York
c/o Miss Elizabeth Nowell
April 21, 1938

DEAR MAMA:

Your Easter package arrived in good shape, except for the Easter egg which got somewhat crushed in transit. The package seems to be stuffed with good things, and I assure you it could not have arrived at a better time, because now that I am living in a place that has no kitchen and no ice box, I must go out whenever I want something to eat; so it is mighty good to have something on hand now. Thank you very, very much. I appreciate it.

I think I told you that Fredericka and Virginia Gambrell were here and stayed two days. I was pretty tired but I did all I could to entertain them, and enlisted the help of one of my friends, who also took them around. I have not heard from them yet, but they told me they had a good time.

Also, Doris Westall was here last week and got in touch with me through Miss Nowell. I took her and a young friend of hers, a nurse, out to dinner. They seemed to be very nice girls, and I had a very sweet postcard from Doris yesterday, thanking me, and a very nice necktie which she sent me as an Easter present.

There is not much other news, except that I am keeping at work here and hope to be left to finish my job without further interruptions and worries from lawyers, etc.

I want to go away somewhere out of the city this summer, but cannot spend too much time in looking for a place, because I want to keep on working. A friend of mine at Harpers is going to take the week-end off next week and drive me around, so that I can see some places for myself.

I will not come home this summer. I must keep at work, and I must also try to get some rest. Last summer was a calamity from both angles: I had not had any let-up for years, and I was desperately in need of one. I cannot take the chance again, because I have too much work to do and must get finished. It is all very well to talk about regular hours to eat and sleep, and so on, and leading regular lives—but the most regular life a man can lead is to get his work done, and not to be tormented and harassed by every kind of worry; and if this part of it goes well, he will probably enjoy good health, even though he drinks a gallon of coffee a day and stays up until four in the morning.

I am getting away from here next month for a short trip out to Purdue University in Indiana—but please do not tell anyone. They are paying me well to come out and talk to a student gathering about writing, and I am accepting because I think it will give me some diversion and relaxation before I start in on a summer's work.

If you know anyone who has kept a record or has a file of the bank trials in Asheville, or any other material of this sort touching on the period of the boom and after the boom, I wish you would put him in touch with me. If it is reasonably complete I will either buy it outright or borrow it, or if someone will lend it to me I will take good care of it and send it back when I am through with it. I have written both Jack Westall and Mrs. Roberts several times, but although they have promised to send me the material I want within a few days, nothing has come of it yet. I suppose a good many of us are inclined to be longer on promises than on performances, but since what I ask for probably will cost someone a little time and trouble, I have no right to complain.

This is all for the present. I hope this finds you well, and all going well with everyone. Easter was cold and gray here, but it has turned off into beautiful weather since then, and Spring is coming with a rush. I know it must be very pretty at Asheville now, and I hope you are getting lots of good weather so that you can get out as much as possible.

With love and all good wishes,

Your son,

Tom

114 EAST 56TH STREET
New York, New York
c/o Miss Elizabeth Nowell
May 7, 1938

DEAR MAMA:

I have been so busy here that I had forgotten that tomorrow is Mother's Day, but I want to get this off to you now and to wish you health, happiness, and an active life for many years to come.

I got a long letter from Mabel yesterday which I am going to try to answer in the next few days. There is not much time left before I go West— I believe I told you I had accepted a speaking engagement at Purdue University, and I am going out there in another week or ten days. I am going to use that also as the opportunity to take a holiday and to get some rest—for every effort I have made, including the trip home last summer, has been spoiled. As I have got at least a year of very hard work before me, it is pretty important that I get it now, and I hope nothing comes up to interfere with it this time.

I read what Mabel had to say about the lawyers, and I am glad you have tried to have a definite understanding with Frank Carter and the others about how much they expect to take as their fee. Mabel spoke of a compromise with the bank and this might perhaps be the best solution. I have observed, however, that lawyers themselves often propose a compromise: they are looking out for their end of it, they have found it profitable to get the thing over and done with in the easiest manner, collect their fees, and then go on to something else. It is a familiar part of their technique: I have had it happen to me—they alarm you with gloomy predictions of the possible outcome if you go ahead and carry the case to court, but after you have consented to the compromise and it is all over, they become very belligerent and tell you that they would have liked nothing better than to fight the whole thing through, and have no doubt they would have been successful. I suppose, however, with lawyers working on a contingency basis, a compromise is almost inevitable. The lawyers are going to look out for themselves and would rather take the certainty of getting something than the chance of getting a good deal more or nothing. However it all works out, I hope it all works out to your advantage.

Mabel referred in her letter to "the scandal" but did not tell me what it is. What is it? I was not aware that there was one, but should like to know. I am glad to know that otherwise everyone feels better. Mabel spoke of leaving Asheville again, and I suppose it is very hard to make a go of things there with conditions as they are.

I at last heard from Mrs. Roberts about the result of her efforts to get a record of the bank trials for me, and it didn't pan out to very much. The man they were going to get them from—I think his name is Toms, and he has or had something to do with *The Advocate*—was willing to let me have them for ten days or two weeks if I would post a bond of $1,000! This seems to me to be one of the most fantastic and outrageous proposals I have ever heard—to demand that anyone involve himself for such a sum of money all for the privilege of looking over the files of an obscure little newspaper in ten days' time. Of course, I wrote Mrs. Roberts and thanked her for her trouble, but told her that any such arrangement was out of the question.

Jack Westall promised, in a letter, to get me anything I wanted if I would tell him what it was. I wrote and tried to tell him as clearly as I could, but have never heard from him again. Mrs. Roberts also told me at the beginning that she had "everything," but it was packed away in such a way that it would take a few days to get it out. I don't know what happened to this, but I have never heard anything more about it.

Mabel suggests that Wallace Davis would be able to provide me with a great deal of interesting information. I have no doubt that he would, and I certainly have no personal feeling against Wallace Davis, but I don't think that he is himself in a position to give impartial judgment, and I think it would be very hard for him not to give a one-sided view of things. All I want is just the record of what happened. I understand that the best record appeared in the little labor paper— I understand it was called *The Advocate*. I understand that *The Citizen* and *Times* gave a very evasive and sketchy account of the whole proceedings. If you know of any way I could get this information, I wish you would let me know. People are very easy in their promises, but I find it is very difficult to get them to fulfill them even in such a simple matter as this one, which I am willing to pay for.

I am very grateful to the people I have written to who have tried to help me, but I am afraid some of them have tried to make a very mysterious business of the whole thing, pussy-footing about with an air of great mystery, and whispering and hinting that I have such and such a project in mind. Of course, if you really want to publish anything in Asheville so that it is known from Beaucatcher Mountain to West Asheville in five minute's time, this is the way to do it—just whisper it and swear someone to secrecy, and the whole town will know it, and a lot of other things you didn't know yourself, before you've had time to get around the corner. There is nothing at all mysterious or secretive about what I want. I simply want a record of what was public news and that everybody in town knew about. Now surely there must be some way of getting this without any further delay and foolishness.

Mabel tells me you spoke over the radio for the fiftieth anniversary celebration of the Bon Marche. I have never myself had the experience of talking into the microphone and don't know how I should do. One of the Lipinsky boys wrote me and asked me to contribute an article for the anniversary, but I had to write back and decline, because I didn't have the time for it. However, I wished them luck and continued success.

I am sure everything is very pretty at home now. The weather has been fine here and last week-end I went out into the country with some friends, driving as far as Hamilton College in central New York state, and seeing some very beautiful country.

I am hanging on here more or less, trying to do what I can before I go away, but I am tired and have to push myself to get anything done. I know that a few days and a complete breakaway will make all the difference in the world. I will be back here by early June, and I suppose I will try to find some place out of town to spend the summer and to keep on with my work. Anyway, I will let you know.

I heard from Effie and from Fredericka and Virginia, and all are well.

This is all now. With best wishes for health and happiness and good fortune to you all,

Your son   TOM

Mrs. Julia E. Wolfe
48 Spruce Street
Asheville, North Carolina

[Card]

CHEYENNE, WYO.,
June 5, 1938

DEAR MAMA: I'm getting some rest and seeing some new country and should be ready for work again when I come back to N.Y. in a week or two— Have been in Denver seeing friends and am now in Cheyenne over 6000 feet up, but so flat you wouldn't know it— Am going further West today—

Love,   TOM

[*Card*]

SEATTLE, WASH.,
June 16, 1938

DEAR MAMA: This is wonderful country out here— I believe we have some relatives in Oregon but have not been able to locate them—

TOM

[*Post Card*] View of Crater Lake

PORT KLAMATH, OREG.
June 21, 1938

DEAR MAMA: No post-card can ever do justice or give the color of this marvellous volcanic lake over 7000 feet up—surrounded by mtns.—and today—June 20—with snow ten and twelve feet on ground— I am travelling with two newspaper men from Portland who have invited me to go on this wonderful trip under auspices of A.A.A. We left Portland this morning, will make California tonight and in next two weeks will cover the West, 4500 miles, and every National Park—

TOM

[*Post Card*] View of Mariposa Grove, Yosemite

CAMP CURRY, CALIF.
June 21, 1938

DEAR MAMA: Another lovely spot and thousands of people— cheap enough for stenographers, school-teachers, bookkeepers, etc— They come here from all over—but mostly from California (We drove about 600 miles yesterday)

[*Card*]

PORT KLAMATH, OREGON
June 21st 1938

Forgot to tell you I ran into our Westall kin in Seattle Washington— Albert and his sister Marjorie (children of John)—they are nice people and gave me family tree of all of them out here— Also Mr. Harris—whose mother was a Penland—*your* mother's sister—he is your *first* and my second cousin— All send love—

TOM

GRAND CANYON, NORTH RIVER
June 25 1938

We've been travelling so fast I haven't had time to send you this—but this is one of the big trees in California 700 miles back— Tomorrow, Utah, Zion & Byer Canyon.

[*Post Card*] View of Old Faithful Geyser

YELLOWSTONE PARK, WYO.
June 30, 1938

We got here at 6:30 in time to see this spout at 7:05— It is a wonderful sight and the whole park is full of wonderful things— In one week we have come the whole way down California from Oregon, over the desert and up—3100 miles.

[*Post Card*]

GLACIER NATIONAL PARK

June 30, 1938

DEAR MAMA: I am finishing up a wonderful trip in a day or two in which I have covered the entire West and all of its National Parks— I really feel as if I knew something about the country now—

TOM

GLEN RIDGE LODGE WASH.

July 2nd 1938

This mountain is 14,500 feet—more than twice the height of Mt Mitchell— I am looking at it as I write and there are six feet of snow outside my cabin on the 2nd of July— Winding up wonderful trip today and in Seattle tonight.

[*Card*]

SEATTLE, WASH.

July 4, 1938

DEAR MAMA: This is a wonderful city in a wonderful part of the country.

TOM

[*Postcard from Vancouver, B.C., July 6, 1938*]

Wed. July 6.

DEAR MAMA: This is a beautiful little city, and the capital of British Columbia. Like its name it is Victorian and seems very slow and quaint after U.S.

TOM

["This is the last-written message to me—sent the day he took desperately sick. He told Mabel he went to bed, and next day took train back to Seattle. He called a taxi and asked the driver to drive him around and show him some of city—he hated to leave without seeing some of its interesting places. The taxi driver tried to show and explain different places but he said he was very sick, fever high, and when they got to station he felt so chilled— asked the porter to give him a warm seat on the train—said he must have looked sick—sensed every body looked at him. He went to New Washington Hotel, Seattle, tried to use remedies to break up his cold and fever—but failed: and on Monday called up a friend, James Stevens[1]—said he would have to have help. And he took him to his doctor.—(Ruge)." *Julia E. Wolfe.*]

[1] James Stevens, author of *Paul Bunyan.*

Index

Index

A

Adams, Mr., 95
"Adding Machine, The," 48, 54
Advocate, The, c.f. Asheville, N. C.,
    Advocate, The
Albert Ballin, S.S., 162
Albert Hotel, c.f. New York City,
    Hotel Albert
Alsace-Lorraine, 174
Alpbach, Tirol, 332
America, 11, 36, 63, 86, 89, 95, 99,
    103, 105, 117, 136, 138, 140, 142,
    197, 201, 293, 308
American Mercury, The, c.f. *Mercury,*
    American, The
Amiens, France, 165
Amsterdam, 309, 310
Anderson, S. C., 40, 206, 209
Andover, Mass., 236
"*Angel on the Porch, The,*" 178
Antwerp, 133, 135, 169
Arizona, 314
Arlington, Va., 219
Arnold, Professor, 105, 109
Arthur, Chester, 328
Arthur, Chester Allen, 328
Asheville, N. C., 1, 6, 20, 28, 38, 39,
    43, 44, 50, 51, 64, 67, 69, 70, 72,
    76, 82, 91, 92, 95, 98, 109, 116, 139,
    154, 163, 176, 178, 181, 182, 186,
    194, 197, 203, 218, 222, 225, 231,
    232, 238, 240, 242, 249, 254, 257,
    258, 266, 268, 274, 284–288, 301,
    307, 313, 317, 318, 326, 328, 333,
    335, 337, 340, 350; *Advocate, The,*
    352, 353; bank-trials in, 206, 349,
    352, 353; *Citizen, The,* 95, 108, 109,
    188, 189, 213, 353; economic de-
    pression in, 203, 206, 207, 240, 253,
    271, 285; *Look Homeward Angel*
    and, 188–190, 193, 195, 213, 252;
    people of, 71, 72, 76, 77, 213, 214,
    252, 260, 261, 285; rental of cabin
    near, 261–339–341; The Old Ken-
    tucky Home in, 38, 43, 180, 269;
    Times, 188–190, 213, 353, Wacho-
    via bank in, 13, 36, 37, 94, 325, 337,
    345, 346
Asquith, Lady, 95
Astors, the, 77, 82
Aswell, Edward, 342
Atlanta, Ga., 22, 317
Atlantic City, N. J., 194, 197
Austria, 170
Avignon, 110
Aycock, John, 39

B

Baker, George Pierce, 10, 25, 30, 36,
    38, 39, 41, 45, 48, 49, 54, 56, 57,
    60–63, 65–67, 72, 77, 78, 103
Balsam, N. C., 257, 259, 261
Baltimore, 133, 135, 168, 241
Barry, Philip, 45
Bascome Hawke, A Portrait of, 232,
    280, 285
Bath, England, 97, 129, 130
Beggar's Opera, The, 39
Belgium, 131, 133, 135, 168–170
Belleau Wood, 104
Benge, Mrs. Jessie, 180
Berengaria, R.M.S., 128
Berlin, 49, 308–311, 332
Bermuda, 68, 236
Bernstein, Aline, 123, 151, 199
Big Short Trip, The, 232
Biloxi, Miss., 317
Biltmore, N. C., 76
Bingham, Colonel Robert, 6
Bingham School, The, 6
Bonn, Germany, 171
Bookman, The, 193
Boom Town, 206, 283, 285
Boothbay Harbor, Me., 180, 181
Boston, Mass., 9, 22, 23, 33, 37, 39,